OZZIE

OZZIE

by

OZZIE NELSON

Prentice-Hall, Inc., Englewood Cliffs, N.J.

Printed in the United States of America
Prentice-Hall International, Inc., London
Prentice-Hall of Australia, Pty. Ltd., North Sydney
Prentice-Hall of Canada, Ltd., Toronto
Prentice-Hall of India Private Ltd., New Delhi
Prentice-Hall of Japan, Inc., Tokyo
10   9   8   7   6   5   4   3   2   1

Library of Congress Cataloging in Publication Data
Nelson, Ozzie.
    Ozzie.
    Autobiography.
    1. Nelson, Ozzie.
PN2287.N36A32   790.2′092′4 [B]   73–11063
ISBN   0–13–647768–2

To Harriet

PREFACE

If you were sitting with me now in the upstairs den of our Hollywood house, you'd see a large, comfortable, wood-paneled room with a big desk, a huge sofa, a couple of leather chairs, and lots of tables with lamps on them, all conveniently placed.

I've spent a lot of time up here since I started writing this book about eight or nine months ago, and I must say, it would be difficult to imagine a more pleasant place to work.

The whole gang is coming over to dinner tonight: David and June; Rick and Kris; my brother Don and his wife Connie; and all the grandchildren—Danny, Tracy, Jamie, Matthew, and Gunnar.

I know the family will be happy to learn that I've finally finished writing the book. It's a bit longer than I thought it was going to be, but then again I've been around for quite a while.

I'm sure you've often heard the old bromide that when someone has fallen off a high building, or realizes that he is about to be involved in some terrible catastrophe, his whole life passes before his eyes. After looking over thousands of clippings, countless magazine articles, old letters, and radio and television scripts, and pestering old friends and relatives to check on names, dates, places, and anecdotes, I am convinced that there just aren't any buildings tall enough for me to fall off and cover half of the things that happened. Regardless of what my birth certificate says, I must be over a hundred years old.

Harriet and I received a letter a few months ago from a lady who lives just outside of Philadelphia. She said that she had been meaning to write to us for several years to tell us about an incident that happened when she was teaching a Sunday School class. Her class consisted of little boys of kindergarten age. One day she asked them if they knew who were the first man and woman on earth and one little fellow raised his hand and said, "Ozzie and Harriet."

She said, "No, I think you'll find it was Adam and Eve," and the little boy said, "Oh, yeah, I always get them mixed up." Thumbing through the pages I have written here and reflecting on the many years they represent, I can understand his confusion.

Writing the book has really been a bittersweet experience. My whole life has indeed passed before my eyes and I have relived the many pleasant times and the fortunately very few unhappy times.

I heard Norman Mailer being interviewed on radio one day and he said that one of the dangers inherent in writing an autobiography is that of falling into one of two traps—of being too self-effacing or too arrogant. I hope I have managed to steer a course between the two.

CONTENTS

PART ONE

Growing Up

1

The date was March 20, 1927. It was my twenty-first birthday. It was a cold dismal day, and as the late afternoon shadows took over it became even more dismal.

I looked down at the sleeping face of the man on the bed. He was breathing quietly now. Several days before, they had moved hin onto an air-filled mattress to ease some of the pressure on his pain-wracked body. It was just a question of time, they told us. All they could do was make him as comfortable as possible. I looked out the window. It had suddenly gotten quite dark. I remember thinking, "The day is fading away and taking a human life with it."

I looked at his face again. He seemed to have stopped breathing. Then I looked down at his neck and I could see a faint pulse beat. I watched it as it gradually got fainter and fainter until it finally stopped. I looked back at his face. It was a wax face—no longer living, cold and still. I pressed the little buzzer by the side of the bed. A nurse appeared at the door.

"I thought I'd better tell someone," I said. "My father is dead."

Our family at that time consisted of my mother and father, my two brothers, and myself. My brother Alfred was a year-and-a-half older than I, and my brother Donald was an infant of two months.

My father had been in the hospital (New York Hospital, which was then located at Fifteenth Street and Fifth Avenue) for about a month. As they checked him in, he had said to my mother, "I have a feeling they're going to carry me out of here."

It was about a year before this that the doctors had diagnosed his ailment as a rare condition known as osteitis deformans or Paget's disease. Its cause and treatment were then, and probably still are, unknown. The cause of death on the death certificate was listed as "sarcoma." Technically, you cannot die from Paget's disease.

I was a senior at Rutgers when he died. The week before, I had taken the train up from New Brunswick to visit him. My mother, my brother Alfred, and I went into the hospital room together.

"Pretty soft life you're leading here," kidded my mother. "I think you're fooling us."

"I'll be out of here in no time," said Pop.

They both laughed. I thought to myself, "How can they be so lighthearted about this?"

After a few minutes, my mother said she wanted to step outside for some coffee or something. My brother said, "I'll go with you."

The door closed and my father and I were alone. Suddenly the tears started streaming down his face. He turned his head away so I wouldn't see him crying. Men weren't supposed to cry in those days.

"I'll be back later, Pop," I said. I didn't want to embarrass him.

I went out in the hallway. My mother was at the end of the corridor. Alfred had his arm around her. She was sobbing uncontrollably.

"Your poor father. He's dying."

I hugged and kissed her, and she cried and cried. It was okay for women to cry, even in those days.

I spent that night at home and came back to the hospital the next morning. It was Monday. Surprisingly enough, my father seemed much better.

"Why aren't you back at school?" he asked.

"I have a couple of easy classes today, so I thought I'd stop by and see you."

4

"You stop worrying about me and get back to school. I'll be fine."

I guess you might say it was a little game we were playing. I took the train back to New Brunswick. There really wasn't much else I could do.

I talked to my mother on the phone each night and was surprised and delighted to learn that my father was improving steadily. The news was especially good on Friday night. He asked my mother to bake a cake and bring it over to the hospital on Sunday so we could have a little party to celebrate my birthday.

I was called to the telephone at about seven o'clock Sunday morning. It was my brother Alfred with the news that my father had lapsed into a coma shortly after midnight. It was almost noon by the time I arrived at the hospital. My mother and Alfred had been up all night.

When my father died, a whole town went into mourning. We had lived in Ridgefield Park for sixteen years and he had many friends. He was a man whose life had been one of devotion and dedication—not only to his family but to the community in which he lived. His activities were many and varied. He had been a deputy commander of the Boy Scouts of America and a member of the Court of Honor. He had held the post of president of the Board of Education, the Chamber of Commerce, the Free Public Library Association, and the Men's Club of the Presbyterian Church.

An editorial in the *Ridgefield Park Bulletin* commented that his life was applied religion and that Ridgefield Park was a better place to live in because George Nelson had lived there.

Throughout the twenty-one years I knew him I never heard him say an unkind word to or about anyone. To the best of my ability I have tried to pattern my life after his. I haven't always succeeded, but I know that I am a better person for having known him and had him for a father.

A few days after the funeral, I met a high school friend of mine whose father had died a few years before. "How long does it take you to get over it?" I asked.

"You never get over it," she replied.

She was right.

My father was only forty-eight years old when he died. My mother was then only forty-three. She never remarried. She never even went out with another man. I don't think it ever occurred to her. If it did she never mentioned it to us.

2

"I met a peach of a little girl tonight, Mother."

Grandma Nelson never tired of telling me the story of how my father first met my mother and of how he woke up grandma to tell her about the "peach of a little girl" he had just met.

Jersey City was a lively place in 1902. Besides being only a short ferryboat ride away from New York City and the bright lights of Broadway, it had quite a social life of its own. How do I know? Because, first of all, I was a nosey little kid who asked a lot of questions, and second, because I fortunately fell heir to the Orr family scrapbook, which was started before the Civil War by my mother's grandmother.

The old book is filled with items such as the "enjoyable entertainment and reception given at Crescent Hall" where the "hit of the evening" was "Miss Ethel Orr and her renditions of 'Cakewalk In The Sky' and 'Louisiana Lize.'"

It was on just such an occasion that my father, standing in the wings waiting to do a song-and-dance act, asked a mutual friend to introduce him to the "peach of a little girl" who was playing ragtime piano and captivating the audience with "Look Out For The Hoodoo-Doo-Doo Man" and "Stay In Your Own Backyard."

Minstrel shows were immensely popular in those days, and one of the greatest minstrel men of all was a star of tremendous magnitude named "Honey Boy" Evans. My father, who had become quite a popular entertainer in the community, was billed as "Jersey City's Honey Boy" and sang songs like "That Yaller Gal By Side" and "Oh Mr. Moon."

It wasn't long however, before "Jersey City's Honey Boy" and "Miss Ethel Orr" merged with one act—"Nelson and Orr"—and started singing intimate boy-girl duets like "I Would Still Love You:"

> *If your hair were not so curly and your teeth so*
> *pearly, girlie,*
> *I Would Still Love You.*
> *If each morning I'd awaken to the same old eggs*
> *and bacon,*
> *I Would Still Love You.*
> *If you cried until your tiny little nose was red and*
> *shiny,*
> *I Would Still Love You. . . .*

My mother and father were not professionals but they were very, very good. I know this, not only from clippings in the scrapbook, but because not too many years later the act became "The Four Nelsons" with the addition of two little boys—my brother Alfred and myself. But more about that later.

My father during those years was a busy young fellow. Besides his theatrical activities and his steady job as a clerk at the Chase National Bank in New York City, he also found time to play football with a good semiprofessional team, do some amateur boxing (he once knocked out three opponents in one night), bowl on a championship bowling team (he missed 300 once by one wobbly pin that didn't fall), and do some painting. (We still have some of his excellent watercolors.)

The Nelson-Orr merger worked out so well on stage that it wasn't long before my father and mother decided to make it a lifetime arrangement. And so on March 4, 1903, they were married at the home of Grandpa and Grandma Orr and moved into a little house at 255 Clerk Street, where Alfred was born in September of 1904. I came along on March 20, 1906, when my folks were living at 16 Virginia Avenue, just a few houses from the Hudson County Boulevard.

We later moved to Atlantic Street, near Bergen Avenue, and it is of this little house and its surroundings that I have my earliest memories.

I remember a parade where the leader of a group of Scottish bagpipers asked if he could have a glass of water—I remember how impressed I was with his Scottish regalia and the fact that he was so tall that he had to stoop to get through the doorway. I remember I saluted him and he saluted back—just as General Lafayette had saluted Great-Grandfather Bennett when the general rode past the little farmhouse in Stratford, Connecticut, where my great-grandfather was fixing his roof.

I remember insisting that Grandpa Nelson change into his "soldier pants" to march through the house with me while I beat out the tempo on my little drum. (Actually, the "soldier pants" were black dress pants with a velvet stripe down the side.)

I remember the afternoon my brother and I were making believe we were race-car drivers. He had his cap on backwards and was seated on a chair, turning the top of the piano stool as if it were a steering wheel. My mother came home from shopping and gave Alfred a pair of gauntlet-type gloves she had bought him. He let out a whoop of joy—they looked just like the kind the racing drivers wore.

"Where are mine, Mama?" I yelled expectantly.

She looked surprised. "I bought you a pair of mittens," she said.

Of course, they were exchanged for a pair of gauntlets the next day. And of course I forgave her. After all, how was a four-year-old boy's mother supposed to know that Barney Oldfield didn't wear mittens.

The first really exciting event in my young life occurred a few weeks before my fifth birthday. It was on the occasion of Grandpa and Grandma Orr's golden wedding anniversary. It was held at 132 Gifford Avenue where my Uncle Harry and Aunt Lida lived. There were gold rings with little white doves for the ladies and tiny gold airplanes for the men. There was singing and dancing to a string orchestra and Alfred and I were each given a ten-dollar gold piece. It was gay and glamorous and I enjoyed every minute of it—at least until I fell asleep on Mama's lap.

It was just a few months later that we moved to Ridgefield Park, a friendly little town of seven or eight thousand people. This was in 1911, and we lived in the same house at 370 (later changed to 378) Teaneck Road until the fall of 1927.

Ridgefield Park is located in Bergen County, New Jersey, just seven miles away, across the Hudson River, from New York City. In those days, before the George Washington Bridge or the Lincoln and Holland Tunnels were built, most of the male population commuted daily via the Susquehanna or West Shore Railroad and the Weehauken Ferry.

It was a charming little community, the kind that, unfortunately, seems to have passed from the American scene. It was bordered on the west by the Hackensack River, with its shoreline dotted by boat clubs and swimming holes, and on the east by the Overpeck Creek, which obligingly froze over in winter to provide ice for small boys to skate on. There were churches of every denomination and a Boy Scout troop in every church. There was a movie theater, the Opera House, which was packed every Saturday afternoon by noisy kids cheering Bronco Billy and William S. Hart or laughing hysterically at Charlie Chaplin or Buster Keaton.

In the winter we went sleigh riding on Stromeyer's Hill, and in the summer we rode the trolley to Palisades Amusement Park, where we swam in the huge salt-water pool and then rode on "The Racer" (five cents), or, if we were especially affluent that day, "The Big Scenic" (ten cents) with its world-renowned one-hundred-foot drop. After that, there was always a mad dash to get front seats for the free outdoor entertainment climaxed by Professor Holden's one-hundred-and-ten-foot dive into a six-foot tank.

"Are you ready, Mr. Holden?" the announcer would shout to the man standing way up there on the top of that little ladder which swayed dangerously in the breeze.

10

We held our breath while the Professor carefully assessed the wind velocity. Is the wind blowing too strong? Will this be the day when he'll miss the tank and smash himself to smithereens on the sidewalk?

He starts back down the ladder. We groan in disappointment. But wait a second! He has changed his mind! He climbs back up and once again is perched atop that tiny platform. We cheer wildly.

Once again: "Are you ready, Mr. Holden?"

Majestically he waves his hand to indicate that he is about to risk his life for us.

There is a moment of silence, then slowly he lifts his hands from the tiny rail he has been holding on to and falls backwards, turning a complete somersault, and lands feet first in the tank. He springs quickly out, waves to the crowd; a big robe is wrapped around him and he is whisked away by uniformed attendants.

We learned to swim at The Mulberrys, which, in spite of its romantic sounding name, was actually a muddy cove on the bank of the Hackensack River. You had to be very careful crossing all the railroad tracks, and you had to promise your mother that you wouldn't hitch rides on the freight trains and that you would look both ways to make sure the West Shore express train wasn't coming down the track at sixty miles an hour.

By the time I got to high school, however, the river was already starting to get polluted by the refuse from the Bogota and Little Ferry paper mills—not to mention the garbage and raw sewage that poured in from Hackensack and Ridgefield Park. And by the time I left for college the boat clubs and canoe clubs were all gone, along with the boat regattas and the swimming meets.

I don't remember specifically the first time I ever entertained in public, but I would guess it was when I was about five or six years old.

Minstrel shows were still the easiest and most popular format for amateur entertainment, so my brother and I were continuously pressed into service, usually to work in the 'Olio," which meant performing in front of the curtain while the stagehands

11

were changing scenery between acts. The songs we sang were usually taken from popular recordings of the day by name performers such as Van and Schenck, Ada Jones and Bill Murray, Bert Williams and Al Jolson. I recall having the good fortune of meeting Gus Van years later and remembering lyrics to songs of his that he had long since forgotten.

The one performance I'll never forget was my appearance as a female impersonator. I was just eight years old at the time. My brother was dressed up as a little "dude" and I, against my better judgment, was somehow conned into appearing as a little girl. We sang a song from the English music halls called "Out on the Old Front Porch." I remember my opening lines: "There's a fellow following me, I'm as nervous as I can be."

Near the end of the chorus we sang:

> *Everything is lovely and you're cuddled up so near,*
> *When suddenly a voice you know rings out so loud*
> *and clear.*

And from the wings my father sang out:

> *Will that young man go home tonight or have his*
> *breakfast here?*

And we concluded with:

> *Out on the old front porch—Oh Charlie, on the old*
> *front porch.*

The audience seemed to like it and we took several bows. I remember my mother saying to my brother and me, "There, you see what a big hit you were? And you didn't want to put on the costumes!" (My brother hadn't been any happier about his wearing his "little dude" outfit, with the high hat and spats, than I had been about putting on the pink dress.) The following day, our local paper, the *Ridgefield Park Bulletin,* carried a review

12

of the show. I have it in front of me. It is dated March 25, 1914, and reads as follows:

> The Woodmen's "Big Comedy Show" was all that the title implied, only it was bigger. It was original, full of clever acting, wit and funny lines. It couldn't have been otherwise because it was written and managed by George W. Nelson, the town's greatest artist. . . . The vocal solos, chorus and instrumental solos were right up to the minute and were masterfully rendered.

Now here comes the crusher:

> Little Master and *Miss* Nelson are born artists and displayed remarkable ability. [The italics are mine.]

Needless to say, that was the last time anybody ever talked me into appearing in drag.

Except for the "really big shows," where an orchestra was hired for the occasion, my mother usually accompanied Alfred and me on the piano. Although she could read notes after a fashion, Mom always preferred improvising her own chords, and the results were often unusual and occasionally rather startling. We learned very early in life, however, that regardless of how many clinkers the piano player hits, you never never glance over in her direction—especially if she's your mother.

Right up until she died a few years ago at the age of eighty-three, Mom still could be counted on to liven up a party with a few piano solos in her own inimitable ragtime style.

In one of Ricky's recent albums, *Rudy the Fifth*, he has a terrific cut of "Honky Tonk Woman" which includes a great piano interlude by Rick. I asked him where he picked up that style and he said, "It's half Ray Charles and half Grandma Nelson."

One phenomenon of the stage, professional as well as amateur, that seems to occur at some time during the run of every play (and which, of course, is the nightmare of every actor) is that

13

someone invariably walks on stage with his fly open. This unfortunate incident occurred during one of the shows my father directed. It was a courtroom sketch and intended as a comedy, but it was not supposed to be quite as hilarious as it turned out to be.

My father was playing the part of the Judge, and Walter Hubbell, one of our local scoutmasters, was playing the part of the District Attorney. Seated in the first row of the audience were my Grandmother Orr and my Aunt Mame. My Aunt Mame was fat and jolly with a ribald sense of humor and a raucous laugh to match. I should mention here that my father, during rehearsals, had warned the atmosphere people to position themselves so as not to block the principal players from the audience's view.

"In case any of the principal characters should accidently get behind you," he cautioned, "step aside so that the audience has a clear view of them at all times."

The sketch was just getting underway when the District Attorney, in accordance with the script, asked if he might approach the bench. As he walked forward, my Aunt Mame let out a whoop that shook the rafters. It didn't take the rest of the audience long to follow suit as one by one they discovered that poor Walter Hubbell had neglected to button up his pants.

Out of the corner of his mouth, my father whispered, "Walter, your fly is open." Poor Walter, covered with embarrassment, made several attempts to ease in back of the atmosphere players, but they, not realizing his predicament and following my father's directions, moved aside. Finally, while shielding himself with a sheaf of legal papers held in one hand, Walter managed to get himself buttoned up with his other hand as the audience burst into applause.

In thinking about it later, I'm convinced that the manual dexterity he had acquired in the Boy Scouts, while learning to tie difficult knots, had undoubtedly saved the day for him—or at least what was left of it.

I was most fortunate that I grew up in a happy household. Ours was a hugging and kissing family with a great feeling of closeness and genuine affection. I can remember, as a little boy, sitting on my mother's lap and hugging and kissing her—she smelled feminine and gently fragrant, like lilacs. Then I would sit on my father's lap and hug and kiss him. He smelled very masculine, like fresh linen and cigars.

My father was five feet ten and only weighed about one hundred and fifty pounds, not a big man—at least not by today's standards—but he was always in superb physical condition. Many times I saw him tear a deck of playing cards in half—and if you don't think that's tough, try it sometime. Unfortunately for the nonbelievers who furnished the cards, he never learned to put them back together again.

He also had another parlor trick that never failed to amaze us. He'd hold his derby hat in front of his chest, and we'd tie a string around him (and the hat). Then we'd remove the hat, and he would expand his chest, filling out the void left by the hat until the string was so tight you couldn't even slide your finger under it. This was not only a difficult trick to do but, as I've just discovered, it's also pretty difficult to describe.

Like most kids in small towns in those days, we grew up playing whatever sport happened to be in season. We played baseball in the spring, swam and played tennis in the summer, and skated and played basketball in the winter. There were two tennis courts on our block, which gave me such a headstart that I won my first high school athletic letter for playing on the tennis team while I was still in the eighth grade.

I am told there is a picture hanging in the Ridgefield Park Public Library of the first football team my brother and I played on. We called ourselves the Pugeot A.C. and we were undefeated. This was in 1916, when I was ten years old. In the picture, I am the one holding the football. Not that I was the captain—in fact, I was the youngest and, at seventy pounds, the smallest member of the team. It's just that it was my football.

There was always plenty of music around our house. It seems that all our relatives either played or sang. My mother, as I mentioned before, played piano, as did my Grandma Orr, my Uncle

Harry Brooks, and my cousins Sis Brooks and Mary Emma Moore. Whether it was my Uncle Jackson Orr singing "Walkin' For the Cake," or my Aunt Mae singing "My Hero" from *The Chocolate Soldier*, or Grandma Orr singing "Polly-Wolly Doodle," there was always music when the relatives came to visit.

Although the only professional was Aunt Mae, who was with the Boston Opera Company and later headlined in vaudeville, they were all good, or at least sounded good to my brother and me. Naturally, on these occasions Alfred and I always sang a few songs (without too much coaxing), as did my mother and father.

Most of the music rehearsals for the local shows my father directed were held in our house, so many a night my brother and I fell asleep to the accompaniment of singing and piano playing. Of course, later on when I started playing banjo, violin, and saxophone, the place really began to swing.

A few years ago, while visiting back east, I stopped by to take a look at the old house on Teaneck Road. A lady named Ella Marshall, who lived in the neighborhood, heard that I was there and came over to say hello. She had been born in the house on the corner and still lived there.

"I remember when you moved here in 1911," she told me, "and I remember when you left in 1927. In fact, we were all kinda glad when you moved out—you know, all that loud music."

She might have had a good point at that. After all, a saxophone or a banjo in the hands of a fourteen-year-old boy can be a lethal weapon.

There were very few unhappy moments in my childhood, and as a result the few that there were left lasting impressions. During the summer of 1913 we went down to Asbury Park for two weeks' vacation at a little boarding house on Sunset Lake. I remember one Sunday afternoon my Cousin Herbert's coming over to tell us that Grandpa Orr had had a stroke and was not expected to live. I remember my mother and father hurriedly packing and our taking the train to Jersey City. There had been whisperings around the family that Grandpa had given up attending church and instead had been greatly influenced by the

16

writings and lectures of Robert Ingersoll, the famous agnostic. This was confusing to a seven-year-old boy who attended Sunday school regularly, because Grandpa Orr was a kind, gentle person who certainly deserved to go to heaven if anyone did. And so I prayed and explained this to God.

After Grandpa Orr died, Grandma Orr lived with us most of the time. One night we were awakened by her crying out in terrible pain. My father phoned for Dr. Knox, who came over and gave her an injection that let her sleep. The pain had been caused by a stone passing through her kidney. She had had eleven children, but she said that this had been worse by far than the pains of childbrith.

Unfortunately she had these attacks several times after that, and on one of these occasions, when I was about ten years old, I did one of the few noble acts I have ever done in my life. On this particular night (the attacks always seemed to occur in the middle of the night) there was a severe snowstorm, and Dr. Knox took a long time getting to our house. Grandma was suffering terribly and unable to keep from crying out. I prayed to God and asked him to take whatever sins Grandma had committed in her seventy-three years and charge them to my account and to make me suffer instead of her.

I didn't tell my folks about it because I figured this was a confidential arrangement between God and me, but I remember I fully expected all sorts of misfortunes to descend upon me. Evidently, however, Grandma Orr's sins were few and far between, because God and everyone else have been awfully good to me throughout the years. And strangely enough, Grandma never suffered another attack.

3

"Darn it, Mom, why didn't you grow!" I used to say to my mother.

"Look how tall Alfred's getting," people would say, referring, of course, to my brother (who, although only a year-and-a-half older than I was, could literally "eat apples off my head"). And then they would add: "But it looks like Ozzie's going to be short like his mother."

I finally reached a slightly taller than average height of five feet ten (actually I'm only five nine and three-quarters, but then everybody lies about his height), although I thought I'd never get there.

To give you an idea of how slowly I grew, though Mom was barely five feet tall I was almost fourteen before I reached her. To make matters worse, I skipped from the second grade to the fourth, so every time the boys lined up I was sure to be at or near the end of the line.

Being small had few advantages. In fact, the only one I can think of is that when playing baseball I was hard to pitch to and, as a consequence, I got a lot of bases on balls. The disadvantage of being small, however, was not only athletic (I was constantly having to tackle guys twice my size), it also had a discouraging effect on my social life. I kept getting crushes on the best-looking girls in the class, like Eleanor Blair, Bibs Emerson, and Maude Adams, and they kept growing away from me.

People were always guessing that I was two or three years younger than my actual age, which is okay when you're in your

18

sixties or even when you're in your thirties, but devastating when you're twelve.

Most little boys grow in sections—one year it's the nose, then maybe gigantic ears or teeth appear. But usually by the time they're about eighteen or nineteen, the various parts catch up to each other, and the ensemble sort of falls into place. I was no exception. During the years from about seven to nine, while my brother Alfred was growing an inch taller every week (or so it seemed), the only increase in my measurements was in the size of my head. That wouldn't have been so bad if it had been the top of my head—at least then I could have marked it on our wall height chart. But it was the back of my head which was elongated, or to put it more bluntly, my head stuck out in back.

I probably never would have learned about that if it hadn't been for Felix Fischel. Mr. Fischel owned the town haberdashery shop, and one day my mother took me down there to buy me a hat. Mr. Fischel tried on several, but they were all too small—then several more, with the same result. Finally my mother exploded: "For goodness sakes, don't you have a hat to fit a seven-year-old boy!"

"I'm sorry lady," said Mr. Fischel "but this little boy has a very large head. Look how it sticks out in the back." (I've often wondered why people talk about kids as if they weren't there. Casting directors do it too—only with actors, regardless of their age: "Well, if she took about ten pounds off and had her nose fixed. . . .")

I don't remember if we ever found a hat to fit me, but I do remember that I suddenly became very self-conscious about the size of the back of my head. Up until then, having only viewed myself full-face in the mirror, I had assumed that my appearance was quite normal. But now I began to have my doubts.

I expressed my concern confidentially to a couple of my close friends. Dodie Bellinger suggested that I sleep on my back with a board under my head, and Billy Marsh suggested that I keep a rubber band around it so that it would expand upward. I didn't have much confidence in Billy's suggestion, however, because he also claimed that he had read someplace that you would grow faster if you stood in fertilizer for an hour every day, occasionally sprinkling water on yourself.

Actually, the protruding-head situation didn't bother me too much, but the fact that I wasn't getting any taller was a constant worry. We had a "chinning bar" that my father had put up in the doorway of our bedroom, so every morning and every night I would hang there for as long as my arms would hold me, hoping to stretch myself a little.

Fortunately, nature seems to have worked out certain compensations for little guys, and so as the years went by I began to realize that I was a bit quicker and better coordinated than most of the boys my age who were taller and heavier than I was.

There were no gang fights in those days, at least in our town. Although we all carried pocket knives, they were never used as weapons. There were, however, fist fights almost every afternoon after school, at least while I was in the lower grades. I was involved in very few of them, thanks mainly to the fact that word had gotten around the school that my father had taught me how to box. This suited me just fine, because at Washington Irving Grammar School there were some very tough little kids.

My strategy for avoiding the schoolyard brawls was simple. Every time I sensed that I was being sized up and that a challenge was imminent, I would invite the other kid over to my house for some cookies or doughnuts. After we were there for a while I'd suggest that it might be fun to put on the gloves and box a little—just taking it easy, of course. Now, there is a great deal of difference between punching and warding off punches with your bare fists and doing the same thing while you're wearing big boxing gloves—especially if you're ten or eleven years old and have never had them on before. Thanks to my father's guidance I was pretty well schooled in blocking and slipping punches, so these encounters almost always wound up with the other kid and myself doing very little damage to each other.

The one kid I was afraid of, however, was a tough little guy named Jack Fitzpatrick. Jack was only six months older than I, and maybe an inch or two taller, but he was the scourge of the sixth grade. He loved to fight and could completely demolish kids a head taller than he was. He had already taken on practically all the other kids in the class, so I knew it was only a question of time until he got around to me.

I remember one day he said to me, "You know my real name is John but if anybody ever calls me that I'll knock his teeth out."

I realized then and there that it was time for me to make my move. "Would you like to come over to my house some afternoon, Jack?" I said. (You notice I didn't call him John.) "I've got some boxing gloves and we could box a few rounds."

"Yeah, I heard about that," he said, "but I don't like boxing gloves. I like to fight with my bare fists."

The next day was Saturday, and Alfred, Billy Marsh, and I went to the matinee at the Opera House. The movie was almost over when Jack's cousin, Bert Stallwood, came down the aisle and tapped me on the shoulder. "Jack said to tell you he's waiting out in the lobby for you."

"What for?" I said.

"He said you and he were supposed to fight this afternoon." This was not exactly the greatest news in the world. It would be bad enough to have Jack beat me up in a vacant lot someplace, but in front of the movie theater on a Saturday afternoon with practically every kid in town to witness my humiliation?

"It's the first I heard of it," I said, trying my best to hide the quaver in my voice.

"Well, he'll be waiting for you," said Bert, and went back up the aisle.

Now, there were two ways to get out of the Opera House. You could go out through the main lobby, which on this particular day meant coming face to face with Jack Fitzpatrick, or you could slip out the side door. I decided to slip out the side door. Moving carefully in and out of the crowd, I made my way past the corner and was soon a block away from the theater. My brother and Billy, not having heard my conversation with Bert, were com-

21

pletely unaware of the frightening encounter I had so narrowly averted.

"I'm not really afraid to fight him, it's just that my mother wouldn't want me to be fighting in the street. She'd say it was a disgrace to the family." This is what I tried to tell myself, but I knew it wasn't true. The truth was I was afraid I'd get licked.

Suddenly I heard a shout from way down the block. I turned around and my heart sank. It was Jack and Bert. They were shouting and running toward me.

One of the greatest fighters, pound for pound, who ever lived was "Terrible Terry" McGovern, who was the bantamweight champion of the world around the turn of the century. He had written a book, and since he was one of my boyhood idols I had memorized practically every word of it. Terry had said, "Try to avoid a fight at all costs but if you find that you have to fight make sure you get in the first punch and make it a good one."

There was no doubt about it. This was Jack Fitzpatrick coming up the hill and I had to fight him or run.

Now, from Main Street to Bergen Avenue is a long block, and it's all uphill, and here was Jack running all the way. By the time he got to me he was puffing like a steam engine. He tried to say something but he was all out of breath.

I leaned back and hit him as hard as I could. He spun around and I hit him again and he stumbled against a hedge and fell down.

Suddenly a lady came rushing out of the house brandishing an umbrella. "You kids stop this or I'll call the police!" she shouted. We all ran.

When I got home I told my mother proudly, "I had a fight with Jack Fitzpatrick and I knocked him down."

"You ought to be ashamed of yourself," she said. "What are you trying to do, disgrace the family?"

Jack didn't come to school on Monday or Tuesday or Wednesday or Thursday. On Friday morning, I went down to the boys basement (as it was delicately referred to) and there was Jack waiting for me. Nobody else was there. Just Jack. We stood there for an instant just staring at each other, and then he said: "I just wanted you to know the reason I couldn't come to school was because I had an abscessed ear. It had nothing to do with the fight."

"I'm sorry, Jack," I said, "let's not fight anymore." And then we shook hands. That was the scene: two little ten-year-old boys shaking hands in front of the urinals in the boys' basement of Washington Irving Grammar School.

We never did fight again. Not with bare fists, that is. But two years later we both joined Troop 3 of the Boy Scouts and we must have boxed each other at least ten or fifteen times in the bouts that followed the scout meetings. It was always a draw.

I wish this had a happy ending but this was not to be. I was called home from college one week-end to be a pallbearer at Jack's funeral. He had been killed when the car he was riding in skidded off the road and crashed into a tree. He was eighteen years old.

The year 1918 was one of tremendous excitement. America's entry into World War I had turned the tide and victory was in sight—victory that was supposed to make the world "safe for democracy."

Scarcely a week went by that we didn't perform at some sort of local function, either a fund-raising banquet, or a musical show, or some other form of entertainment connected with the war effort. Sometimes it was Pop, Alfred, and I, with Mom at the piano, and sometimes, when there was an orchestra in the pit, it would be just the three of us.

Camp Merritt, an army embarkation camp, was located about seven miles north of Ridgefield Park, so we occasionally went up there to entertain the troops. This was especially exciting because servicemen, then as now, are among the world's most appreciative audiences.

I remember we used to do a little sketch we called "The Frontline Trench" that never missed. It started with Alfred, dressed up in a beat-up army uniform, holding up two empty beer bot-

23

tles and looking up at the sky through them as though they were binoculars. After a moment, my father, dressed as an officer, would enter:

POP: What's up?

ALFRED: The observation balloon. They are signaling. Aid is needed in the front-line trench at once!

POP: Aid is needed in the front-line trench at once? But who will take the message??
WHO WILL TAKE THE MESSAGE??
(*I would then come bouncing on, wearing an outrageously ill-fitting uniform, give a hokey salute, and say:*)

ME: I sir, I will take the message.

POP: (*Putting his arm around my shoulder.*) My brave young man, your father must have been a soldier.

ME: (*Hanging my head.*) No, my father was a coward—but my mother—my mother's blood tells me to go to the front-line trench at once.

ALFRED: (*Still gazing through the "binoculars."*) They are signaling again!

ME: Yes, it's my mother's blood calling me to go to the front-line trench.

ALFRED: (*Slowly and deliberately.*) FIVE THOUSAND MEN HAVE JUST BEEN KILLED IN THE FRONT-LINE TRENCH.
(*Upon hearing this, I would turn slowly toward the audience with a sickly look on my face.*)

POP: (*To me.*) My brave young man—you must take the message at once!

ME: I cannot.

POP: You cannot? Why not?

ME: FATHER'S BLOOD IS BUTTING IN!!

I remember I drew a cartoon that was published in the *Ridgefield Park Bulletin*. It depicted Kaiser Wilhelm being hit on the head with a brick labeled "USA—Fourth Liberty Loan." I sent it to my cousin, Gus Nelson, who was "somewhere in France" with the 105th Machine Gun Battalion. He wrote back: "Every time WE hit them they think they get hit with a whole LOAD

24

of bricks." Such was the spirit of the times. After all, this was the war that was to end all wars.

I remember the cheering and shouting that went on in the seventh grade the day they announced that the Armistice had been signed. Not only was the war over but all classes were dismissed for the day. I went home and wrote a little poem to commemorate the occasion. It started out smoothly enough:

> *The whistles started blowing*
> *And the church bells rang*
> *The school boys shouted*
> *And the girls all sang. . . .*

By the time I got to the last stanza, however, the meter had undergone a dramatic change and my lofty phrasing of the opening lines had succumbed to a more down-to-earth approach—as witness:

> *Old Kaiser Bill shall rule no more*
> *For he's wheezy in the dome.*
> *So now let's pray for the glorious day*
> *When the Yanks Come Marching Home.*

Actually, Armistice Day couldn't have come at a better time for me, because it took the attention away from a highly embarrassing moment that had befallen me the day before and which was being giggled at around the classrooms. What had happened was this: Miss Sullivan, my homeroom teacher, had given me a large glass beaker and asked me to return it to Mr. Davis at the chemistry laboratory in the high school building, which was across the schoolyard.

Somehow I managed to get confused in the strange hallways and accidently walked in on a class in progress. Judging from the writing on the blackboard it was a chemistry class, but definitely not the chemistry laboratory.

The lady teacher smiled pleasantly and said, "May I help you?"

"Yes," I said. "I'm looking for the. . . ." Suddenly a horrible thought struck me. Is it "laboratory" or "lavatory"? I knew what both words meant, but I had suddenly drawn a blank as to which was which.

It was very quiet and everyone was looking at me. I had to take a chance. Holding up the beaker, I said, "I'm looking for the lavatory."

"I believe you mean the laboratory" she whispered to me. "It's down the hall, second door to your right."

I got out of there fast.

While we're on the subject of bathroom humor, I hope you'll hold still for a bit of crudity I indulged in one afternoon a few months ago. I was going in for my annual check-up with our family physician, and Harriet, who had been at the doctor's office that morning, handed me a little vial and said, "Dr. Calmenson's nurse, Joan, said she wants you to bring in a specimen this afternoon."

Being a dutiful patient I followed instructions, and when I went into the office I handed the vial to Joan and said, "Harriet said you wanted this."

"Oh, thank you," she said.

I said, "It's okay with me. Actually I was a little surprised, though. Most people just want my autograph." Fortunately, Joan has a good sense of humor.

I thought my twelfth birthday would never get there. What was so wonderful about becoming twelve years old? I could then become a Boy Scout. (The age limit has since been lowered to eleven years, but then it was twelve.)

Scouting was very big in Ridgefield Park in those days, and besides, Alfred and all his friends were Scouts.

Months before, I had memorized the Scout Oath and the Scout Law and had learned to tie a square knot, a bowline, two half hitches, and all the rest, so I passed my Tenderfoot tests at the first meeting I attended.

For the benefit of those few who are not familiar with such things, there are prescribed tests listed in the Boy Scout *Handbook*. By passing these tests a boy advances from Tenderfoot to

26

Second Class and then to First Class, with the tests becoming progressively more difficult. When he becomes a First Class Scout, he is eligible to try for merit badges and qualify as a Star Scout, then a Life Scout, and finally, after accumulating twenty-one merit badges, he reaches the rank of Eagle Scout, which is as high as he can go.

My immediate objective, of course, was to knock off the Second Class and First Class tests as quickly as possible so I could get started on the merit badges.

I had no trouble making the fourteen-mile hike or demonstrating the proper first-aid procedures or cooking a fairly edible hunter's stew, but the toughest of all for me was a comparatively easy one—and one of the Second Class tests, at that. It was called "Scout's pace."

Scout's pace consisted of alternately running and walking—fifty steps each. For the test, you had to cover one mile in exactly twelve minutes give or take ten seconds. In other words, your time for the course had to fall between eleven minutes, fifty seconds, and twelve minutes, ten seconds.

There was a measured mile on Euclid Avenue, one of the few paved streets in town in those days, and one Saturday afternoon Scoutmaster Hubbell (remember him?) stood there, stopwatch in hand, as two other kids and I waited for the "go" signal.

I covered my first mile in eleven minutes and thirty seconds—much too fast. One of the other boys made it the first trip. Me? I was too fast, then too slow, then too fast. . . . After I had covered six miles, Alfred went home to tell my mother not to hold up supper for me.

Finally, after pulling my skinny little body up and down that asphalt street for nine miles, I managed to come in within the prescribed time. I slept very well that night.

Out of curiosity, I recently bought a 1972 Boy Scout *Handbook,* and thumbing through it I noticed, among the many changes in the requirements, that Scout's pace is no longer listed anywhere. I guess too many mothers complained about their little kids missing supper while Scout's-pacing mile after mile up and down Euclid Avenue.

27

4

In the *New York Herald Tribune* of Sunday, July 4, 1920, the following article appeared on page 1:

300 BOY SCOUTS TO SEE EUROPE

Pick of Organization in America Will Sail
Tuesday on Transport Pocahontas

Three hundred happy eager-eyed Boy Scouts assembled at Fort Hamilton yesterday to be mobilized for their trip to Europe as representatives of America at the International Convention of Boy Scouts, which will begin July 30 in the stadium at Olympia near London, England.

This group represents the pick of the nation's boyhood, for its members have been chosen by rigid competition from 400,-000 Scouts in every State and Territory.

Among the "happy eager-eyed Boy Scouts" were Alfred Nelson and Oswald Nelson of Troop 3, Ridgefield Park, New Jersey. My brother and I had become Eagle Scouts just a few months before and had been fortunate enough to be selected, along with four other boys, to represent the North Bergen Council.

There had been no record of anyone ever having become an Eagle Scout while he was still thirteen years old, so I had wanted desperately to be the first one. With a little bit of help from my friends and a great deal of help from my brother, I had just managed to squeeze it in with a month to spare.

I kept a day-by-day diary of the Jamboree trip, and even now when I read it, more than fifty years later, certain memories come back vividly:

Tuesday, July 6

We laid all our issue equipment out on our bunks for inspection and cleaned up the place around us so as to leave the camp as clean as it was when we came to it. We loaded up our packs and marched to the dock. We were taken to Hoboken by a tug. At Pier 5 we met Mom, Pop, Grandma Orr and many others from the town. At half past twelve we kissed them goodbye and boarded the U.S.A.T. Pocahontas. We went out on the deck and waved goodbye to our relatives. At one o'clock the ship sailed. As the pier with its mob of crying mothers and other friends and relatives faded away, I turned around and looked over the long expanse of water ahead of me and wondered if I would enjoy the trip.

A pretty funny incident occurred our first day out. To set the scene we have to go back to Fort Hamilton, where we camped for several days before embarking:

In all latrine barracks during World War I, there were separate toilets set aside for those unlucky doughboys who were being treated for a venereal disease. I remember walking into the latrine one day at Fort Hamilton and there down at the very end of the huge room was a rosy-cheeked little Boy Scout seated on a toilet above which was a huge sign that read "Venereal." There must have been at least a hundred toilets there, but he had selected one of the three marked "Venereal." I guess he thought it was something special—who knows.

Now, getting back to the first day on the Pocahontas. . . . They had separate latrines for separate purposes—one with long troughs and another with seats. I was in the one that just had the long troughs when another Scout came in, looked around and looked around, and finally said to me, "I see all these urinals here, but I can't seem to find the venereals."

For the most part, the trip across was fairly uneventful. I worked out as often as I could with the boxing team, but my activity was considerably limited; the smallpox vacination I had received in my left arm had become infected, and during the trip they had given me three typhoid shots in the right arm. I attended all the workouts, but since I could hardly lift either arm, I spent a lot of time bobbing and weaving.

Alfred and I also did a lot of singing accompanied by me on a ukulele that I had gotten as a birthday present that year. George Alberque, another of the Ridgefield Park boys, had done some entertaining at home, so we taught him a lot of our songs as well as some of the sketches we had done with my father. We sang for the Scouts, we sang in the salon for the regular passengers, we sang for the soldiers, we sang for the officers and for the crew. We sang and sang and sang.

We docked at Southhampton, England, July 16 and were taken to an encampment a few miles outside London where boys from over thirty nations were gathered for the world's first International Boy Scout Jamboree.

My most vivid recollection of the next few weeks was of being perpetually tired. We would no sooner get to bed than the bugle would be blowing first call and we'd have to drag ourselves out of our cots. I slept everywhere—on busses, in subways, at the services in St. Paul's Cathedral, in a secluded corner of Westminster Abbey, in the aisle of the balcony of the Empire Theatre during the third act of *Irene* (I was awakened by people stepping over me on the way out), and during most of the performance of *Chu Chin Chow*. (This last was no small accomplishment, because the singing was very loud.)

When we weren't being reviewed by Sir Baden Powell, founder of the Boy Scout movement, or Lloyd George, British minister of war, or the duke of Connaught or some visiting American senator, we would be practicing for one of the many pageants we later presented at Olympia, a huge stadium in London.

Among the pageants I took part in was a miniature Wild West show which featured the famous Black Horse Cavalry troop from

Culver Military Academy and a group of "Indians" presenting "authentic" tribal songs and dances. It wasn't until after I had learned the songs and dances that I discovered we "Indians" were also supposed to ride horses bareback at a full gallop around the arena for the exciting finale. It was exciting for me, all right. The nearest thing to horseback riding I had ever experienced was at the ten-cent pony rides in Asbury Park. I can recall the sheer terror I felt, hanging on for dear life while those damn horses sprinted for the exits.

One night they held a dinner dance in our honor at the Washington Club in St. James Square and invited a group of very nice English girls to be our dinner partners and to dance with us. Lady Nancy Astor was our official hostess and Alfred and I sang for her. She was a great audience. She laughed in all the right places and applauded enthusiastically at the end of each number. I had heard of her, of course—she was American by birth and the only female member of Parliament.

As we were leaving, we all lined up to shake hands good night and I thought to myself, "Wait till I tell the guys back home that I shook hands with Lady Astor!" She shook hands with Alfred, with George Alberque, then Milton Emerson—now it was my turn! To my utter chagrin, she gave me a little hug and then a pat on the fanny. How do you tell a thing like *that* to your friends at home, for gosh sakes?

The big disappointment of the trip, however, was the fact that I was eliminated in the first round of the boxing tournament. I was selected to represent the American delegation in the 6 stone 6 (under-ninety-pounds) division, which was listed under the rather unglamorous classification of "Chicken Class—Division Three." My opponent was the ninety-pound champion of London, but actually he didn't look too ferocious to me.

To make sure that my memory doesn't play tricks on me, I'd like to refer to my diary once again:

The first round had just started when he was warned about holding. We continued fighting until the end of the round.

31

I had found that a straight left was my most effective blow. In the middle of the second round I caught him on the chin and he went down but was up like a flash. In the third round my lack of sleep was beginning to tell on me. My arms felt like lead but I was encouraged when a straight left caught him on the nose and the claret started to flow. At the end of the bout we were mixing it fast. I then went to my corner and awaited the decision of the judges. They decided he had beaten me by a few points. I congratulated my opponent, whose nose was still bleeding and went up to the dressing room.

I remember how surprised and disappointed I was at the decision. They had explained to us before the fight that points would be given for good defensive work, but I felt that I had landed the most effective punches and should have gotten the verdict.

I was concerned that my father would be disappointed at my not winning, but one night after we got home he read aloud to us something that Alfred had written in a letter to him. After some comments about the questionable decision, Alfred had written: "But Ozzie was a game loser. He ran over and shook his opponent's hand and congratulated him."

Pop said he was just as proud of me for my good sportsmanship as he would have been about my winning. I was not sure I understood his feelings at the time, but years later I did. It was when our son David was eleven years old and he and I were playing in the annual Labor Day Paddle Tennis Tournament at the Bel-Air Bay Club. Now, lest this sound like some slightly effete social event, I hasten to add that it was so grimly competitive that entire families were known not to speak to each other for years following some clash of tempers on the courts.

David and I had reached the finals. We were in the third set of an extremely close match when one of our opponents hit a low, hard shot that was just about impossible to call. It could have just knicked the base line or it could have just missed it. Unless you were standing right over it there was no way to tell.

The umpire, not being quite sure how to call it, hesitated

32

just an instant and David immediately settled the issue by calling out, "Good shot!"

It was a crucial point, and I knew how eager he was to win and how disappointed he was when we finally lost, but I was really proud of him for his integrity and good sportsmanship and I told him so.

The sting of my defeat in the London Jamboree boxing competition was eased somewhat by my victory in the ice cream eating contest. Actually it wasn't a contest—it was more like an exhibition. What happened was this. One afternoon another scout and I attended a local carnival not far from our camp. I went up to the ice cream booth and ordered an ice cream cone and was served one that seemed to me to be rather meager—at least by Wrede and Koop standards (Wrede and Koop being the Ridgefield Park ice cream parlor.)

"This is pretty small, isn't it?" I said.

"Well now, if you don't think it's big enough for you, Yank," the man across the counter said, "why don't you order a double?"

There was something about the way he said "Yank"—in fact, something about his attitude in general—that made me feel that he was issuing some sort of challenge. It was Great Britain against America—John Bull vs. Uncle Sam.

"I'll have one dozen double vanilla cones," I said. "Put them in a box and I'll eat them right here at the counter."

"Okay, Yank," said the man. "One dozen double cones coming up."

I don't know how the word got spread around the carnival grounds so fast, but I couldn't have eaten more than four or five of the cones before a sizable crowd had gathered to watch this amazing little boy who was undoubtedly the ice cream eating champion of America and possibly of the whole world.

Six, seven, and eight went down without too much trouble, but by the time I got to nine I was beginning to feel a little queasy. And about halfway through the tenth I was beginning to feel like I might explode any minute.

"You don't look so good, Yank," said the man across the counter.

33

He had a big grin on his face and the fact that his teeth were yellow didn't help my condition any.

"I'm fine," I said. "I'd like a glass of water, please."

I don't know how I did it but somehow I managed to down the entire dozen and was rewarded with a cheer and a round of applause from the crowd. I acknowledged it with a courteous little bow, making sure I didn't bend over too far. At this point I wasn't too sure what might happen or from what direction.

I must say my opponent, Mr. Yellowteeth, rose to the occasion. "Good for you, Yank!" he yelled out and then flashing me a toothy smile he added: "And just for that, here's a double on the house—absolutely free."

I'm not sure that thirteen double ice cream cones is a world record, but I do know that I felt very, very heavy as I sloshed my way out of there.

It's a lucky thing that this happened *after* the boxing competition or I never would have made the weight for the Chicken Class. I would have had to enter the Rooster Class or maybe even the Turkey Division.

I don't recall exactly how many performances of our Scout pageant we gave in London, and my diary isn't too specific on that point (I would guess it was at least four or five). But I do have notes on all the points of historical interest that we visited, and we didn't miss many. St. Paul's Cathedral, the British Art Museum, the Tower of London, the Wax Museum, Warwick Castle, Stratford-on-Avon, and, to quote my diary: "many other famous places too numerous to mention."

At Shakespeare's home we saw his desk and his chair. The chair had a felt rope across it, and there was a little sign that said that no one was allowed to sit in it. So the Ridgefield Park boys took turns engaging the guard in conversation while we each quickly sat in the chair. A Scout is trustworthy, loyal, helpful, friendly, courteous, kind, and sneaky. Incidentally, this also applies to Girl Scouts: some thirty years later Harriet served as the decoy while Ricky climbed under the ropes and stretched out on Napoleon's bed while David took his picture—or maybe it was me!

34

Before we leave England, I feel that I must call your attention to one more notation in my diary that demonstrates the crisp, precise literary style I was employing back in 1920. I was describing our visit to Windsor Castle at Eaton:

It was a wonderful place with famous paintings, rooms, furniture, armor, etc., all over. We climbed up to the top of the highest tower. The view was fine. We stayed up there awhile and then came down.

We left London early in the morning of August 9, crossed the Channel, and after landing at Boulogne boarded a train for Paris.

An unusual incident occurred during the train ride. (*Note:* I think a word of warning is in order here. If you happen to be eating while reading this or if you have a sensitive stomach, perhaps you'd better read this page later on, or better yet skip it entirely.)

At any rate, on the train to Paris the Ridgefield Park delegation was seated in one small compartment, with Harry Fisher and Milton Emerson seated opposite Alfred and me. Suddenly Harry said, "Pardon me fellahs, but I've gotta go to the bathroom." He left the compartment and headed down the aisle, but returned almost immediately with a pained look on his face. "This is awful," he said, "there's only one terlit (don't forget we were from New Jersey) and about twenty-five guys waiting in line—and I gotta go awful bad." In order to clarify the situation and still phrase the explanation as delicately as possible, let's give Harry's problem a number and say he was referring to number two.

Someone—I forgot who—suggested he might try going out the window, so Harry pulled down his pants, my brother pulled down the window, and Harry stuck his fanny out into the cold air. Somehow, however, it just didn't seem to work out.

Suddenly Milt got a brilliant idea. Picking up Harry's hat, he said, "Here—why not use this?" So, believe it or not, Harry relieved himself of his discomfort, as they say in the laxative com-

35

mercials, using his Boy Scout hat as a receptacle—and then threw it out the window.

Needless to say, we were all hysterical with laughter. The first one to recover was my brother. "I've often heard the expression 'in your hat,' " he said, "but this is the first time I've ever seen it demonstrated."

For years later I speculated on a scene of a Frenchman walking down a railroad track. Suddenly he spies something. "Mon Dieu," he says, "un chapeau!" Let's hope he looked it over carefully before trying it on.

Our headquarters for the next five days was at the Lycée Michelet, a boarding school just outside Paris that had been vacated to accomodate us during our stay. I still have fond recollections of the huge soft beds—or maybe they just seemed huge and soft after the army cots we had slept on during our encampment in England. Come to think of it, they were the first real beds we had slept on since we had left home.

Once again we hit all the tourist spots: the Louvre, Notre Dame Cathedral, Versailles, Napoleon's Tomb, the Luxembourg Gardens, and of course the Eiffel Tower. I say "*all* the tourist spots" —we did miss a few, like Maximes, the Moulin Rouge, and the famous Folies Bergères (although I seem to remember making a little detour in order to view the interesting photographic display in the lobby).

We sang songs, listened to speeches, were reviewed by notables, sang more songs, listened to more speeches, and were reviewed by more notables. On our final day in Paris we assembled at the Arc de Triomphe and marched down the Champs-Elysées to the Grand Palais, where we put on another pageant. The Paris edition of the *Herald Tribune* of August 12 carried a large picture and a story covering the event:

Swinging briskly under the Stars and Stripes to the tune of a Sousa March, three hundred American Boy Scouts marched in Paris yesterday afternoon. Down the long line of the Champs-Elysees from the Etoile, they came, bare-kneed and khaki-clad, carrying their flags high and marching as only youth can march, the quick-step in their ears and pride in their hearts.

"Comme ils sont chics, les gosses," said Parisians who lined the way and "chic" they were. Lithe, vigorous, clean and young, they were good to look at. Americans watching were glad to acknowledge them as they went by.

I cut the article out of the paper and mailed it home to Mom. And why not? It isn't often than an eighty-five-pound fourteen-year-old boy is described as "chic, lithe, and vigorous"—and there I was right in the foreground of the picture.

Further down in the article they described the scene at the Grand Palais:

> The floor of the Grand Palais was roped off to leave a large clear space in the center in which the Scouts could give their performances. . . . A group of Scouts dressed in superb Indian costumes pitched their tepees to the delight of the French youth in the balconies, probably as much imbued with the romance of "Le Far-West" as their American comrades. . . . Thirty of the Scouts dressed as Indians mounted on pie-colored pintos and broncos gave a clever and daring exhibition of bareback Indian riding and stunts. The scene took the observers back to Buffalo Bill.

As you have probably guessed, I was, as usual, one of the "Indians." I don't remember whether my horse was a pie-colored pinto or a spotted mustang, but I know he was the meanest-looking animal I've ever laid eyes on. I knew I was in trouble the minute I saw him—or rather he saw me. You've heard the expression "horse laugh"? This isn't a myth. Horses do laugh— or at least this one did—and at me. I got the feeling he was wait-ing for me. Perhaps the English horses had sent word to him about me or something. At any rate, as soon as I walked over to him he turned his head around and laughed right in my face. I thought at first he was going to bite me, but it was just a sneaky ploy to get me to move to the rear, whereupon he quickly

37

lifted his tail and let go with what I could only interpret as a derogatory comment.

"Okay, Indians, mount your horses and trot them slowly into the arena!" called out the pageant director.

"Easy boy," I said as I climbed gingerly onto the monster's back, hoping he understood at least a little English. I was expecting the worst, but to my pleasant surprise he stayed with the group and trotted along most amiably. Little did I know that he was just biding his time.

The "clever and daring exhibition of bareback Indian riding and stunts" mentioned in the article referred, of course, to the earlies-mentioned elite Black Horse Cavalry troop from Culver—that is, it was supposed to. My participation was supposedly limited to taking part in the Omaha war chant and dance and then to remounting my horse, circling the arena at a full gallop, and exiting amid Indian yells and gunshots.

There was no question about the full gallop. The only question was, would I be able to hang on? As we made the final turn, it was quite obvious that I wasn't the only "Indian" having difficulties. It seems that the exits were much narrower than those in London and the horses were beginning to bunch up. The Culver boys were supposed to lead the pack, but nobody had told my horse and there was nothing I could do about it. Whether I wanted to or not, I was riding a winner. To him it was a race, and since he was carrying about twenty-five pounds less than the other horses we were soon right up there among the leaders.

I like to think it was unintentional—that he really didn't try to mash me up against the wall. All I remember is that there was a mad pile-up and that I started to fall off but fortunately managed to grab onto one of the big Culver guys and slide off the back of his horse. Somehow I landed on my hands and feet and then scrambled out of the way as one by one the horses were pulled to a stop.

"What the hell are you trying to do, Nelson?" the big guy yelled.

What the hell was I trying to do? I was trying to keep from

breaking my goddam neck, that's what the hell I was trying to do.

We gave one more exhibition before we left Europe. That was in Brussels, Belgium. We had only twenty-nine "Indians" this time, however. One of the "Indians," one of the smaller ones from New Jersey, wasn't feeling well that day. After all, you can push your luck just so far.

We sailed for home about a week later on another army transport, the *Princess Matoika*. Our port of embarkation was St. Nazaire, France. The afternoon before we left, all those who wanted to go into the town to do some last-minute shopping were permitted to do so. We were given a couple of hours and were then to meet at a specified time and march back to the docks.

Whether the scoutmaster in charge of our little group didn't know the town very well or simply got lost, I'll never know. But all of a sudden we found ourselves marching through the red-light district. On both sides of the cobblestone street there were girls of all ages, sizes, and shapes. They were standing in the doorways and hanging out of the windows. They had all come rushing out to see the "American Boy Scoots." Since it was a warm summer afternoon they were, let us say, rather scantily clad.

"Hup, two, three, four! Eyes front!" called out the scoutmaster. "Keep up the pace, boys!"

"Hey, American Boy Scoots! We want American Boy Scoots!" called out the girls.

"Hup, two, three, four! Eyes straight ahead!" called out the scoutmaster.

Actually, he had very little to worry about anyway. Ever since our first day in Paris when the chief of the Medical Staff gave us that terrifying lecture, complete with slides, most of us were thoroughly convinced that all we had to do was drink out of the wrong glass or touch the wrong doorknob and a finger would drop off.

The trip home was about as uneventful as the trip over. There were a couple of army units on board with us, and among them was a divisional heavyweight boxing champion, an Indian named Chief Halpren, who took me under his wing and boxed with me every afternoon. Once again Alfred and I did a lot of singing and entertaining, but this time without any musical accompaniment. One of the kids in our troop (unfortunately one with a fat behind) had accidentally sat on my ukulele our first day out at sea.

The *Princess Matoika* arrived in New York on the evening of September 4, and after a farewell banquet at the Commodore Hotel, the First International Boy Scout Jamboree was officially brought to a close. Speaking for the youngest member of the delegation, I can assure you it was sheer heaven to get back home once again to clean white sheets and good home cooking.

One more short note before we close the book on the Jamboree. Some of the Scouts from out of town stayed overnight as guests of the hotel management, and I read in the paper that the chambermaids were surprised to discover the next morning that the boys had not only cleaned up their rooms but had made their beds. Evidently the ladies weren't familiar with the third Scout Law: "A scout is helpful."

5

My sophomore year at Ridgefield Park High School was memorable mainly because it marked the beginning of what proved to be a long-time involvement with dance music—first as a musician and then as an orchestra leader—and also because during the fall of 1920 I played in my first game of varsity high school football.

You might well ask why any coach in his right mind would allow a fourteen-year-old boy of my size to play on the team. Well, first of all, I no longer weighed only eighty-five pounds. By virtue of eating lots of protein food and working out with pulley weights that my brother and I had installed in our bedroom, I had ballooned up to ninety-two pounds and was to reach ninety-five by the time the season was over.

Secondly, our football coach, Mr. Erickson, about whom I'll go into detail later, believed in giving everybody a chance to play as soon as the first team had run up a safe lead.

My first playing experience was against one of Ridgefield Park's traditional rivals, East Rutherford. In the closing seconds of the game, with "the Park" leading by a couple of touchdowns, Coach Erickson decided to clean off the bench, and I was sent in on defense along with the rest of the scrubs.

Unfortunately, the guy with the ball broke through our line and ran right at me. Another kid and I managed to throw him to the ground and the game ended right there. I must say, however, that I learned two valuable lessons on that one play. First, to get down real low when tackling a big guy with high knee

41

action, and second, to get myself a much better athletic supporter, preferably one with a heavy metal cup like baseball catchers wear.

Ridgefield Park High at that time had quite a good orchestra consisting of eight or ten enthusiastic young students who played at the daily assemblies in the auditorium. Among them was a fourteen-year-old pianist named Frank Leithner who was an exceptionally fine musician.

When my father succumbed to my urgings to buy me a banjo to take the place of my deceased ukulele, Frank and I teamed up to form a small orchestra—that is, if you can consider two musicians an orchestra.

Since I already knew quite a few chords on the ukulele, I tuned my banjo the same way, but for some reason, possibly just by chance, I tuned it F, B-flat, D, G instead of C, F, A, D.

My musical education having been limited to about six months of violin lessons, I had to learn new songs by picking them out by ear or having Frank teach them to me. Fortunately he could sight-read with the greatest of ease, so he would call out the chords to me as he read them off a piano copy.

Once again, however, for some unknown reason we used our own special technique. Instead of using the technical names for the chords, we made up our own names for them—for example, an F 7th was "triangle," a C 7th was "thumb," a B-flat 7th was "first," and a D major was "lighthouse." Frank would sit at the piano reading off a new song and yelling out "bambolina," "tulips," "sunset," and so on.

(We later went to Rutgers together, but when Frank dropped out at the end of our freshman year and moved to New York to join Vincent Lopez's orchestra, I was in big trouble until I learned the right names for the chords.)

As soon as the football season was over, Frank and I spent practically every afternoon at either his house or mine practicing little special musical effects and working out our own arrangements for the piano and banjo. As a result we soon developed

42

quite an extensive repertoire consisting of "April Showers," "Margie," "Say It With Music," "Dardanella," and all the other popular songs of the period. Except for a couple of appearances at the high school assemblies, however, we didn't really get a chance to demonstrate our skills, such as they were, until several months later.

The opportunity came from old Mother Nature herself. The local Women's Club had scheduled a dance to be held at the auditorium of the Overpeck Fire House on a Saturday night in February. However, as often happened at that time of year in New Jersey, what started out as a mild flurry of snow soon developed into a first-class blizzard.

The ladies had hired a union orchestra from New York City, but transportation being what it was in those days the only one to show up was the drummer. Someone—probably my mother, or maybe it was Frank's mother—suggested that he and I be pressed into service. I don't remember where they caught up with Frank, but they located me at the local hangout, Wrede and Koop's Ice Cream Parlor.

I don't know whether it was because, like the U.S. Marines who always used to arrive just in time to save the day, we arrived just in time to save the dance, or whether they were clapping loudly to warm their hands, but with all due modesty I must admit we were a smash that night. We not only furnished the music for the dancing, but we also entertained during the intermissions: Frank played some classical selections and I sang some songs and presented some original sketches with Frank's piano accompaniment. At the end of the night we received five dollars each and could now consider ourselves bona fide professionals.

It wasn't long before we were receiving offers to play not only in Ridgefield Park, but also in Hackensack, Englewood, and occasionally even in New York City. If it was a private party held in someone's home, it was usually just Frank and I on banjo and piano, but for the bigger dances in auditoriums and gymnasiums we added a violinist (Frank's brother) and a drummer and called ourselves the Syncopation Four.

43

The standard price for musicians in those days was four or five dollars per night. However, finding ourselves in the fortunate position of being in demand, we soon discovered that people were willing to pay ten dollars apiece for our service—and in 1920 that added up to a lot of money, especially when we were averaging two and sometimes three jobs a week.

Since Frank was also only fourteen and no bigger than I, it was not uncommon for the hostess to look a bit startled when two little boys in kneepants showed up at the front door and announced that they were the musicians that had been engaged for the evening.

I recall one night in Hackensack when we were booked to play for a private party at the home of a Mrs. Hart, whose husband was the county prosecutor. When she saw Frank and me she was ready to cry. She had invited about fifty guests, all very important to her husband's career, and thought that someone had played a very unfunny joke on her. I remember saying to her, "Just let us come in and play one number for you, and if you don't like us we'll go home."

She not only let us stay but became one of our biggest boosters and recommended us to so many of her friends that we soon had the Hackensack territory practically sewed up.

I'm not sure whether the passing of the years has mellowed my memories or if a small New Jersey town in the early 1920s really was that pleasant a place to be growing up in, but in retrospect my junior and senior years in high school were most happy times.

I had spent the summer of 1921 at Camp Ripawam, a Boy Scout camp on the Kanawakee Lakes at Bear Mountain State Park, New York, so I returned to school in the fall in really fine physical condition and ready to make a bid for the quarterback spot on the football team. Alfred had enrolled at Rutgers College in New Brunswick, so I was now the sole occupant of our bedroom and the proud possessor of my first pair of long pants. Also, to my horror, an occasional sprinkling of "unsightly blem-

44

ishes" had started to pop out on my face, so I sent away for all the various remedies that the magazine ads offered to alleviate the embarrassment caused by acne vulgaris (which, we were informed in the booklets, is the medical term for pimples). I finally settled on a smooth grey salve called Poslam's Ointment, which when carefully applied was barely noticeable—to the eye that is. To the nose it smelled like a dead salmon that had been lying in the sun for two or three days.

Our football coach, Carl Erickson, was a fine man—a brilliant strategist far, far ahead of his time. He put together a bunch of hard-nosed kids who loved to hit and loved to win. We had a few close games and even lost one in my junior year—although we later beat the same team in the league playoffs when a kid named Marty Cottrell kicked a thirty-yard field goal in the mud. But mostly we "emerged victorious," as the Madison Square Garden fight announcers used to say, by lopsided scores.

Playing quarterback on a team like that was a dream come true. We won our league championship in both 1921 and 1922 (my junior and senior years). In 1922 we were undefeated, and I was fortunate enough to be selected as first-team quarterback on the All-Northern New Jersey–Bergen County All-Star Team along with two of my teammates, Gordon Adams and Le Baron Bracht.

Fortunately our games were played on Friday afternoons, so Frank and I and the Syncopation Four were still able to roll along in high gear. By this time I had saved up enough money to buy myself a saxophone and had learned to play it fairly well, thus adding a bit more versatility to our little group. Also, since my father had bought our first family automobile, a 1920 Chandler, Frank and I were now able to extend our territory and drive to jobs that had previously been too far away for us to accept.

It's difficult to realize, living in our present society where automobiles are an accepted part of practically everyone's life, that my generation was the first to grow up driving automobiles. Learning to drive came naturally to us, as it does nowadays to millions of kids every year, but it was a totally different story with the fathers on our block, most of whom were in their mid-forties. The big problem seemed to be a tendency to push down on the gas pedal instead of the brake when trying to stop the car. Mr. Starr, who lived next door to us to the south, crashed into the side of his house; Mr. Peterson, who lived on the north side of us, went out of control coming into his driveway and swept away half our front porch; and Mr. Venator, who lived across the street, went through the back of his garage twice—until his kids finally painted "STOP" in big letters on the back wall. This seemed to do the trick.

Self-starters in cars were not too reliable in those days, and as a result broken arms from crank handles kicking back were as common as today's broken legs at ski resorts. Fortunately, however, our family managed to escape any personal injuries, although we did manage to pick up a couple of dented fenders.

My personal contribution to the dented-fender department came on a cold winter night when the car slid backwards on the ice while Frank and I were on our way to play a date in Jersey City. Fortunately the other car wasn't damaged, but I noticed that the man who was driving it seemed to look me over rather strangely when I got out. It didn't occur to me until later that he was probably wondering what a sixteen-year-old boy was doing wearing a tuxedo. I'm sure he thought I was some kind of fancy little dude instead of a working musician.

David had a similar experience when he was seventeen and bumped fenders with a man on the corner of Wilshire Boulevard and La Brea Street in Hollywood. Unfortunately, however, he was on his way to a Hawaiian costume party. David said he drew quite a crowd, standing there in his grass skirt and bare feet, explaining to the police officers that it really wasn't his fault and that he didn't cross against the light. (Does this incident sound familiar to you? We used it later on one of our television shows.)

Early in the spring of 1923 I drove over to Englewood and took the Rutgers scholarship examinations. Rutgers did not have

46

state university status at that time, but a full-tuition scholarship was offered to any graduate of an accredited high school who passed the examinations. I had visited my brother at New Brunswick a few times and had been tremendously impressed, not only with the members of his fraternity but also with the members of the football coaching staff with whom I had talked.

Another factor that made me partial to Rutgers was their famous Glee and Musical Clubs. Since my first year in high school I had attended their annual concerts at the Oritani Field Club in Hackensack and had dreamed of the day when I too would be a member of this talented group. (As it turned out, this took me a lot longer to achieve than I had expected.) And so, when word came through that I had passed the examinations, I decided to spend my next four years at Rutgers.

"And so I settled down," as the famous old song goes, "in that noisy college town 'On the Banks of the Old Raritan.'"

6

"You must be kidding. What did you say your name was?"

"Nelson—from Ridgefield Park."

It was the first week in September of 1923, and I was in the field house at Rutgers getting a bad time from the equipment manager, who didn't want to issue me a uniform.

"Isn't my name on the list there?"

"Nelson, Oswald G.?"

"That's right."

"I don't know if I've got anything small enough for you— Here, try these on." He piled the stuff on the counter. "And don't say I didn't warn you. You go out there and they'll squash you like a bug!"

I put the stuff on and went out on the field. There were about sixty guys out there. There were a lot of big old guys, a few small old guys, and some big young guys, but it was quite obvious, as I looked around, that I was the only small young guy. (I was seventeen years old and had just weighed in at a disappointing 131 pounds.)

I recognized some of the players. There was Homer Hazel, all 240 pounds of him, who would be selected for Walter Camp's All-America team for the next two years; Heinie Benkert, who would later play with the New York Giants; Howie Raub, a giant 260-pound tackle; Dave Bender, Bus Terrill, Carl Waite. I had seen them all play against Notre Dame and West Virginia and Lehigh and Lafayette, and now here I was on the same field

48

with them—Neilson Field, where the great Paul Robeson and Bob Nash (the only man Jim Thorpe had ever backed away from) had won All-America honors. And there, high upon a portable tower, was the dynamic old man who had coached them all: George Foster Sanford, teammate of the Yale immortals, Hinkey and Heffelfinger. He had never played in a football game in which his side had been scored upon. He had wanted to coach at his alma mater, and when they turned him down he offered his services to Columbia. And in 1902, in a viciously fought game at the old Polo Grounds, his team had beaten the favored Elis 5 to 0. It was his boast that no Sanford-coached team had ever taken a physical beating. He was a tough old man and he taught hard, rough football, specializing in the use of elbows and knees. Some of the scrimmages were sheer mayhem. "Bloody Thursday" was a tradition.

I remember one scrimmage during my senior year when things had gotten especially rough and tempers were beginning to flair. Jack Carney, older brother of Jackie Gleason's sidekick, Art Carney, was playing defensive end, and it was my job to block him, one-on-one. He had been coming in high, so I decided to come up under him with both elbows. Unfortunately, Jack decided to change his tactics at the same time, and instead of hitting him on the chest I accidently caught him across the face and broke his nose.

Old "Sandy" came charging across the field bellowing like a bull. "Get off the field, you little mucker!" he yelled at me. I headed toward the field house on the double. "If there's one thing I can't stand it's a mucker!" he shouted after me, "and you're the dirtiest I've ever coached!"

A minute later Jake Besas, our roly-poly little trainer, came in. Jake had been with Sandy since his days at Yale. He was chuckling and shaking his head. "The old man sure likes you," he said.

There were only about five or six of us freshman who had been invited down to early practice. It was easy to spot us. We were the only ones wearing black jerseys and we were huddled

49

together in a little group. Among them were Frenchy Hanf, an All-City linebacker from Brooklyn; Cupe Goldschmidt, a six-foot–four-inch All-State tackle from Montclair, New Jersey; and Al Brown from Flushing, Long Island—Al Brown, who was to be my roommate for four years and close friend for life.

Out on the playing field, Homer Hazel was kicking booming spirals of seventy and seventy-five yards. Quarterbacks and halfbacks were catching the punts and trying to run the ball back against big fast ends who were coming down the field like tornadoes.

By this time Sandy had come down from his tower and was pacing up and down the sidelines. "What we need this year, gentlemen," he announced, "is a few more big guards and tackles." Suddenly he spotted me. "Are you a tackle?" he asked.

I felt reasonably sure he was kidding, but I wasn't taking any chances. "No sir, Mr. Sanford," I said, "I'm a quarterback."

"Okay," said Sandy. "Let's see you go out there and catch some punts."

One of the lonesomest feelings in the world is to stand back there all by yourself, waiting to catch a spinning football that seems like it's never coming down and knowing full well that those feet you hear coming closer and closer belong to guys whose job it is to annihilate you the moment you catch the ball.

Hazel kicked one a mile high, and just as I caught the ball two of the annihilators hit me. One guy hit me high and the other guy hit me low. The ball bounced out of my arms and dribbled along the ground. Welcome to Rutgers!

"If you're afraid to catch that ball, kid, turn in your suit and go home!" He was up on the tower again and bellowing through a megaphone. I caught every ball after that—and held on to them. In fact, I ran a couple of them all the way back. I was afraid of those guys who were tackling me, all right, but I was more afraid of that tough old man up there on the tower—the tough old man who was to become such a tremendous influence on my life, whom I learned to regard with great respect and admiration and who paid me the compliment of making it obvious that he regarded me the same way.

50

Freshmen weren't eligible to play on the varsity in those days, but we scrimmaged against them almost every day and played a short schedule of our own. We ran up a rather strange record: of the four games we played, we won one and tied three. It was fun, though. I played sixty minutes every game, and Mom, Pop, and Alfred came down and watched them all.

Being a freshman at Rutgers in 1923 was an ego-deflating experience. All freshmen were required to wear little black beanies and green neckties throughout the year. On cold winter mornings you were expected to get up early and sit on the toilet seats to warm them for the upperclassmen. For the first two weeks you had to carry your books in a market basket, wear a big sign around your neck that said "FRESHMAN," and, most embarrassing of all, break into a trot whenever an upperclassman whistled at you while you were crossing the campus. (In case you're wondering how they could possibly enforce rules like that, the answer is that they had large wooden paddles.)

Probably the most rigidly enforced rule of all was the Monday-through-Friday curfew. No freshman was allowed off campus after eight o'clock at night without special permission from a designated upperclassman. This was, of course, bitterly resented, because it seriously interfered with one's social life. Fortunately, however, I quickly figured out a way to get around the rule. First, I'd get permission to go off campus to play a dance job, then all I had to do was find a girl who didn't mind going to the movies with a banjo, a saxophone, and a guy in a tuxedo.

The year 1923 was a good one for dating girls—in New Brunswick, anyway. New Jersey College for Women was just across town, the Johnson & Johnson factory was right next to the campus, and then there was this secretary who worked in the athletic office. I think, however, I'd better save that story for the next book. We're trying for a "G" rating on this one.

There was the sign in the lobby of the Rivoli Theatre. It was more than I could resist, so I went up to the box office, asked for an application blank, and signed up. (I had a lot of guts in those days.) The sign read:

51

AMATEUR NIGHT!
NEXT MONDAY
TWO BIG SHOWS

1st Prize $10

2nd Prize $5

3rd Prize $3

The act I decided on consisted of singing a song while accompanying myself on the banjo, then quickly segueing into a saxophone solo. This was followed by one chorus of the Charleston to the tune of "Sweet Georgia Brown" played by the pit orchestra.

I don't remember what all the other people did—there were about five or six acts on the bill—but I remember that there was one guy who recited "The Kid's Last Fight." And then there was the little old man who did the waltz clog. Him, I'll never forget.

I went on next to last and, judging by the applause (heavily augumented by a lot of my friends), there was no doubt that I would walk off with the first prize—ten dollars per show—two shows—twenty dollars—not bad!

The old man and his wife congratulated me as I came off stage. They were a nice little couple, very friendly and obviously devoted to each other. Just as he went on she gave him a kiss on the top of his bald head: "For luck!" she said. I watched him from the wings as he went into his dance.

It was just a simple waltz clog to the tune of "Rosie O Grady." That is, I thought it was simple until he got to the last eight bars. Then, without warning (My God, what is he doing!!), he suddenly flung himself into a back flip. Now, as everyone knows, when you do a back flip you're supposed to land on your feet. He didn't. Instead, he landed on his head. . . . Yessir, right on his bald head on that hard stage. His wife screamed and rushed out onto the stage. I rushed out there with her and together we picked up the poor little guy and stood him on his feet. "I'm okay," he said. But I had to hold him to keep him from falling down. The applause was thunderous. He got first prize, of course,

52

but I didn't mind losing to him. I was just happy that he hadn't fractured his skull.

When I came off stage I couldn't find either him or his wife. I saw the guy who did the recitation. I said, "How is he?"

He said, "How is who?"

"The little bald-headed man. Didn't you see him? He landed right on his head."

"Are you kidding? That's the finish of his act."

"You mean he lands on his head every show?"

"Oh no, it just looks that way. He makes that noise by slapping his hands on the stage. . . . Are you playing Bayonne tomorrow night? We're all going up to Bayonne and then we've got Newark for Wednesday night."

I watched the little old man do the next show, but this time I let his wife drag him off by herself. You can fool me once, but enough is enough.

I got second prize each time. Ten dollars for the two shows. That wasn't too bad. I didn't go to Bayonne, though. It was too far, and besides, I had classes the next day.

It was about the third week in September that the *Rutgers Targum* ran the article that I had been eagerly awaiting—the announcement of the tryouts for the Musical Clubs.

The "Combined Rutgers Glee and Musical Clubs" was definitely the glamor organization of the campus. Each Christmas hiatus they made a personal-appearance tour that was invariably sold out in advance and which was climaxed by a final concert at one of New York's leading hotels.

As I mentioned earlier, one of my cherished dreams had been to appear someday with this fine group. The *Targum* article, however, made this thought so exciting that I could scarcely stand it. It wasn't just the announcement of the tryouts—that was exciting enough—it was the accompanying announcement of this year's schedule. The first concert of the year was to be held in—I could hardly believe it—Ridgefield Park!

Headlines in the *Ridgefield Park Bulletin* danced in front of my eyes. "Local Boy Star Of Concert"—and then the article it-self: "The enthusiastic audience that packed the Knights of Columbus Auditorium last night . . ." etc., etc.

The tryouts were held in a room on the second floor of Van Ness Hall. Present were the head of the Music Department and several assistants. As I was ushered in, one of them, noticing that I was carrying a banjo, said, "We really don't need any more banjo players. We have too many now."

"I don't just play the banjo, I do a specialty act," I assured them.

"Go ahead," the man said.

I remember I played and sang two numbers. At the risk of sounding immodest, I recall that I wasn't even nervous. I had performed so many times, before so many different kinds of audiences—and now, singing two Van and Schenck special ar-rangements with sure-fire patter choruses, I felt totally at ease and completely confident.

"Thank you," said Professor McKinney. "The results of the au-ditions will be posted on the bulletin board tomorrow afternoon. Next please!"

When David was about six years old he attended Gardner Street Public School in Hollywood. A friend of his named Anth-ony Loveman also went there. It seems that the children of the first grade were divided into three groups in accordance with their reading skills. The best readers were put in the Blue Group, followed by the Reds, and finally the Greens. The two boys had walked home from school together and were playing in our back yard when I heard Anthony ask David what reading class he was in.

"I'm in the Blues," said David.

"No, you're not," said Anthony.

"Yes, I am!" insisted David.

"No, you're not!" said Anthony. "I went by there this morn-ing and I looked in and there you weren't!"

The day after the auditions I hurried to the bulletin board at Van Ness Hall where they had posted the list of the successful candidates for the Musical Clubs—and "there I wasn't."

54

I never tried out again, but in 1931, when our band was head-lining at Loew's State Theatre in New York City, a representative from Rutgers asked me if I would come over between shows and make a guest appearance with the Musical Clubs, who were giving a Concert at the Waldorf Astoria. And so I finally got to sing my Van and Schenck arrangements after all, three years after I was graduated. When I told the audience that this was a special pleasure for me since I had once been an unsuccessful candidate for the Musical Clubs, I must admit that Professor McKinney laughed and applauded louder than anyone else.

I not only had the distinction of making the Musical Clubs three years after graduation, but I also became an All-America football player about the same time.

Ed Sullivan was a sportswriter for the *New York Daily News* at that time, and since he and his wife Sylvia were frequent visitors at the Glen Island Casino where I was playing, I once said to him, "Ed, would you please do me a favor? I keep reading in various show-business columns and press releases that I was an All-America football player. This simply isn't true. I'm very proud of the fact that I played on the varsity for three years, but I didn't make All-America and it's embarrassing to keep reading this. Would you please set the record straight for me?"

"Are you kidding?" said Ed, "that's what show business is all about. It's all a big build-up. The public knows it and they want it that way. Stop worrying about it."

So if Ed ever comes back on television with his variety show and introduces "the greatest dancing bear in the world," forget it! There are probably five bears in the San Diego Zoo who can dance rings around him.

I recently took a look at my college yearbook, the *Scarlet Letter*, and judging by the imposing lineup of activities listed under the grim-faced picture that represented me in 1927, one's first reaction would be: "How did he ever find time to do all those things?" The answer lies in the fact that, except for football, I didn't enter into any activity with any degree of dedication. I had an unfortunate tendency to lose interest in things once I had achieved a fair degree of proficiency. Like so many young people in college today, I had no idea what I wanted to do with my life and I was terribly disturbed by the feeling that precious time was passing and I was hopeless to do anything about it.

I was taking what we called a "fresh air" course, majoring in English and political science, so my studies presented no problem. As a result I spent most of my time day dreaming, attending trials at the courthouse, and going to vaudeville shows—pretty much in that order. There were two theaters in town that played vaudeville: the RKO House, which played ten acts, and the Opera House, which played eleven acts. Since they each changed their bill twice a week, that made a total of forty-two acts I would see each week. An added inducement was the fact that the members of the football team all got free tickets.

Football, of course, was so much a part of my life that there was no way I could lose interest in that, although it ceased being fun after my sophomore year for the simple reason that playing on a losing team not only is no fun, it's sheer misery—and we had two miserable years.

At the end of my freshman year, Mr. Sanford announced that he was retiring from coaching and was turning the reins over to one of his assistants, Jack Wallace. It was typical of Sandy that he left a wealth of material for the incoming coach, and as a result the 1924 season was one of the most successful in Rutgers history as we compiled a record of eight victories against one defeat.

I say "we," but my chief contribution to the season was being responsible for scoring one touchdown—and unfortunately that was *against* Rutgers. One of the "breathers" on an otherwise tough schedule was a game with St. Bonaventure. Our first-string quarterback had a slight injury, so the coach decided to rest him up for a week and play me at quarterback.

Following the opening kickoff, we quickly drove downfield for a touchdown. We were on our way to a second score when a most unusual exchange took place in the huddle. I called for Homer Hazel, our All-America fullback, to carry the ball off tackle. To

56

my amazement, he glared at me and growled, "For Chrissakes, don't you know anybody's signal except mine?" I could hardly believe my ears—a guy complaining about carrying the ball too much? And with his wife and two children sitting in the stands?

"Shut up!" I snarled back. "I'm calling the signals!"

"Why, you little punk," said Hazel. "I'm old enough to be your father"—which wasn't true—he was only thirty-one and I was eighteen.

There are two schools of thought on fielding low punts that hit the ground before you can get to them. One says to get out of the way and let them roll (which they sometimes do for forty or fifty yards), and the other says to take a chance and grab at the ball, hoping it bounces the right way.

Near the end of the second period, the St. Bonaventure punter booted a low, driving kick that came bouncing along the ground, and I decided to take a chance. Obviously, however, this wasn't my day. The ball suddenly took a crazy bounce sideways and I had to pull away quickly to avoid its hitting me. One of their ends, thinking I had touched the ball, scooped it up and ran the remaining thirty-five yards to our goal line. Unfortunately, the referee shared his opinion and ruled it a touchdown.

The half ended soon after, and as I was heading toward the club house, trying to hold back the tears, I felt a big arm around my shoulder and heard a deep voice say, "I saw that whole thing and there was no question about it. You didn't touch that ball at all." It was Paul Robeson. A moment later he was joined by Heinie Benkert, who was to become the leading scorer in the East that year. "Don't worry about it, kid," Heinie said. "I did the same thing the first game I played in."

I played better the second half. I intercepted two passes, recovered a fumble, and made some pretty good runs and some pretty good tackles. We won, 35 to 7.

I guess I've played over that crucial play in my head at least a thousand times. Funny thing, though, in my mind I never let the ball roll. It always bounces the right way and I grab it off and run for a touchdown—sixty-five yards.

Most of all, though, when I think about the game I remember that, in my moment of misery, two people were kind enough and thoughtful enough to seek me out and try to console me.

Rutgers throughout the years has had some outstanding swimming teams, and the 1925 team was no exception. Since my roommate, Al Brown, had been an outstanding scholastic star (he had once lost a special fifty-yard freestyle match to the great Johnny Weissmuller by only two-fifths of a second), I decided to try out for the team. It was soon apparent, however, that my Hackensack River crawl simply didn't propel me fast enough to keep up with the elite group that represented Rutgers that year, so I decided to concentrate on diving.

Intercollegiate diving in those days was done only from a low board. As I recall, there were four compulsory dives and four optional dives, with scoring, as today, based on performance and degree of difficulty. My optional dives were among the simplest in the book: a backjack somersault, a half-gainer, a one-and-a-half, and a half-twist. Obviously, however, we were a little weak in the diving department that year, so I was selected as the second diver.

Our first meet was at home against Syracuse University. It was held at night and the bleachers were filled to capacity. As we went out to take a few practice dives, I suddenly realized that I had never before done any diving under such strong lights. The springboard, the water, and the bottom of the pool all seemed to blend together.

My first compulsory dive was a plain running front dive, often referred to as a "swan" dive. My approach felt good, but just as I left the board I heard a gasp go up from the crowd.

Al Brown was waiting for me as I got out of the pool.

"What the hell are you trying to do?" he asked. "You missed the board by about a quarter of an inch."

They gasped again as I did my back dive, my front jack, and my back jack. I wasn't scoring very well, but there was no doubt about the fact that I was creating plenty of excitment. The big thrill, however, was yet to come—that is, for those who had the guts to keep watching.

A half-gainer, for the benefit of anyone who may not know, is sort of a reverse back dive. You start out as if you are doing a front dive, but as you spring up you bend back toward the board and enter the water as if you had done a back dive.

The gasps started a little earlier this time—about at the top of my spring as I arched backward. They turned into groans as I crashed into the board with a sickening thud and flopped into the water in an ignominious heap. I don't know what hit first, but I know I ached all over for days.

My father, who had witnessed my blood-curdling performance, had a few words of advice to offer. He said, kindly, "Why don't you forget about this, son, before you knock all your teeth out or break your head or something. Go out for boxing, instead. It's less dangerous."

Rutgers didn't have a boxing team at that time, but about a year later, in the early spring of 1926, they announced an intermural boxing tournament with gold, silver, and bronze medals as prizes. I hadn't done much boxing since my Boy Scout days, but since I had some spare time on my hands I decided to enter. By the end of the previous football season I had weighed close to 160 pounds, but an attack of the flu had brought me down to 153 or 154. So I decided to take off a few more pounds and enter in the 150-pound class.

My first bout was with a boy named Maurice Berger, a nice young guy with a pleasant, smiling face and black curly hair.

The bouts were scheduled for three two-minute rounds with an extra round in the event of a draw. We had fought about a half a minute when I realized, to my horror, that I simply could not lay a glove on my opponent. He was like a phantom. He wasn't hitting me hard but he was hitting me often—and I wasn't hitting him at all.

About the middle of the second round a strange thing happened. I suddenly found myself removed from reality. I had the feeling that this was all a dream. The floor of the ring was no longer

59

level but was sharply slanted. It was as if we were boxing on the side of a hill and I had to lean sideways to keep from falling over. Then I was in the phone booth at the fraternity house. My father was on the other end of the line.

"How did you do, son?"

"I got knocked out in the second round . . . knocked out in the second round . . . knocked out in the second round. . . ." It went on and on like a broken record.

Gradually and painfully I found myself returning to the realization that somebody was punching me and I was punching back —that this wasn't a dream, that this was really happening to me and that if I didn't get myself together I would be knocked out in the second round.

The other guy was moving a little slower now. *Keep your elbows in close. Hit straight from the shoulder. If only my arms weren't so heavy.*

It's the third round now. Oh God, I'm tired! Where did all this blood come from? It's all over everything—Berger, the referee, the gloves, the floor—me too, I guess. We're all covered with it. That's as hard as I can hit. Why doesn't he go down?

I don't know how many guys had crowded into the gym, but the noise was deafening and they were all on their feet, yelling, stomping, applauding.

I was back on my stool in the corner now. Al Brown was pouring water on me, and George Young, another roommate, was wiping my face with a towel.

"It's a draw" said Al, "you've gotta fight one more round. Save your strength and don't try to get up."

This, of course, was needless advice. There was no way I could make it up off that stool.

"When the bell rings, George and I will pick you up and push you out into the ring."

I wound up with two black eyes, a swollen nose, a fat lip, and a very nice gold medal which I gave to Harriet some years later. I hope she still has it. I'd hate to think I went through all that for nothing.

Before moving on to other, less violent activities, I'll quickly summarize the football seasons of my junior and senior years by categorizing them as disasters. Handicapped by a lack of depth (we had a good first string but were weak in reserves) and an outmoded style of play and coaching, we had little of the "thrill of victory" and more than our share of the "agony of defeat." In my junior year we lost three games that we should have won (Holy Cross 0–6, Lehigh 0–7, and Pennsylvania Military College 13–14) and that would have at least given us a 5–4 season. But we did manage to salvage a degree of respectability in our final game of the season against Chick Mehan's powerful NYU team.

Back in those days, locker room pep talks were considered standard procedure, and old Foster Sanford, who had come back to help out with the coaching that last week, laid one on us that would have made William Jennings Bryan's "Cross of Gold" speech sound like an Ed Sullivan introduction.

I don't remember Sandy's speech in its entirety, of course, but I'll never forget the closing lines:

"It's up to you, gentlemen," he said calmly and deliberately. "The decision is yours. You can end this season in a blaze of glory or a shower of manure!"

Of course, that's not exactly what he said, but I think you get the idea. Be that as it may, we went out there and beat NYU 7 to 6 in the roughest game I've every played in. I didn't hurt at all that night, though, or even the next day. You never do when you win.

Mr. Sanford came back for the 1926 season, supposedly as "advisory coach," but such was the power of his personality that he was soon in complete charge and the "Bloody Thursdays" were back with us once again, bloodier than ever.

Our first two games, against Manhattan and Ursinus, were of the "warm-up" variety and were won without too much difficulty. Our next three opponents, however, were really powerful, well-balanced clubs. In successive weeks we ran up against Washington and Jefferson, Holy Cross, and NYU. I played sixty minutes against Washington and Jefferson, fifty-nine minutes against Holy Cross, and about one minute against NYU.

NYU in 1926 had one of the finest teams in the country. In Conners, Briante, and the great Ken Strong they possessed the nucleus of a backfield that could do it all. The game was played in Yankee Stadium on October 23. Their first play from scrimmage was a sweep around end with Lassman and Weiner leading the interference and Strong carrying the ball. I came up from defensive safety and met this awesome group head-on at the line of scrimmage.

The strange thing about injuries, especially serious ones, is that they invariably happen when you least expect them to.

The pain was excruciating—a broken shoulder hurts like hell —but the disappointment was even worse. I couldn't believe it. This was my senior year. The season wasn't even half over, and yet here I was sitting on the sidelines, my college football career ended. This was certainly not the scenario as I had dreamed it— as I had somehow expected it to be. But then, who's to say that all scripts must have a happy ending?

An old vaudeville cliché used to be: "A funny thing happened to me on the way to the theater. . . ." Of course, nothing funny ever really happens to actors on the way to the theater, unless you happen to be working in New York and consider getting mugged "a funny thing."

Nothing funny ever happens on your summer vacation either, which is why so many kids have to sit for hours sucking on their pencils when called upon to write that time honored composition, "What I did on my vacation."

My summer vacations during college were all pretty much alike. I worked as a counselor at various boys' camps—at Sparta, New Jersey; Honesdale, Pennsylvania; and at Fire Place Lodge in East Hampton, Long Island. Nothing funny ever happened to me during those summers—that is, unless you consider almost being washed out to sea a funny thing. This happened during the summer of 1927.

Fire Place Lodge was a private camp for boys and was located a few miles outside East Hampton, on Gardiners Bay. My brother and I were counselors there during the summers of 1926 and 1927.

Directly across the bay was Gardiners Island, reputed to have been plundered by Spanish pirates in the early part of the eighteenth century and which had been leased out as a hunting preserve by the Gardiner family.

On a foggy day the island is barely visible from the mainland, and on a really foggy day it can't be seen at all. But on a nice clear day it looks as if you could throw a rock over there. As a result, it was not unusual for a visiting parent to say, "I suppose you swim across the bay to the island every once in a while." The truth of the matter was that, as nearly as we could ascertain from the natives of the area, no one had ever swum it. It was not so much a question of distance as the fact that the tides were reputed to be so strong that they would drag you out to sea. Also, according to local fishermen, sharks were often encountered in the vicinity of the fishing nets.

August 5, 1927, was a beautiful day. Not only was it clear and sunny but the water was unusually calm and a pleasant 68 to 70 degrees. And so, at about two-thirty in the afternoon, with my brother Al and a junior counselor named Frank Manning alongside me in a rowboat, I started swimming toward Gardiners Island.

You've heard of the calm before the storm? I had, too, of course, but I had never realized the weather could change so quickly and so violently. We were a couple of miles out when the water started to get choppy and the rain began to fall, lightly at first and then harder and harder. Suddenly and unexpectedly, I swam right into a huge jellyfish.

"A shark!" yelled Frank. "He's been bitten by a shark!" Evidently I had jumped half out of the water.

The wind had begun to blow by now, and soon the rain was pouring down and the waves were getting higher and higher.

"Get into the boat or we'll all get drowned!" yelled my brother. It sounded like a good idea to me too but every time they got close to me a big wave would pull them away again, and every

63

time I tried to swim toward the boat the tide would pull me away from them. Fog had started to close in, and soon it became impossible to see more than ten or twenty yards ahead of us. About all I could do was keep swimming and hope that I was still headed in the right direction. Gradually, however, the storm started to slacken off until finally we began to see the lights from the island flickering in the distance.

In case you didn't happen to read about it in the *East Hampton Star,* I'll quote from the August 6, 1927 edition:

> After battling the storm for fully a half hour the weather changed and Nelson was able to reach the Island after a swim totalling two and one half hours. According to records and native history this is the first time this feat has ever been accomplished. Swimmers have always feared the strong tide and swift currents which run along the island side of the bay.

I don't know if anybody else has swum it since then or not. For all I know, the entire seventh grade may swim it every morning before breakfast. If so, I don't want to hear about it.

If you happen to be in East Hampton some time, you might jump into the bay and try it yourself. But if you should get swept out to sea or a shark should bite off a couple of your toes, don't say I didn't warn you.

7

During the fall of 1929, I had a very full schedule. I think the thing that kept me from collapsing under the sheer weight of it was the fact that I was very young at the time and also that I was involved in things that I really enjoyed doing. I was in my senior year at New Jersey Law School, I was coaching football at Lincoln High School in Jersey City, and I was playing and singing nightly with a small dance orchestra at a tavern in City Island, New York.

My daily routine went something like this. At about eight-fifteen in the morning I would catch a bus at Clifton Place in Jersey City, where our family now lived. The bus would take me to Journal Square, and from there I would ride the subway to Newark.

New Jersey Law School (which has since become a part of Rutgers University) was located just a short distance from the subway station, so I usually jogged the few blocks to make sure I was wide awake.

The morning session, which I was then attending, ran from nine until twelve. I usually arrived back at the apartment about one hour later, and after lunch and a couple of hours sleep I'd drive down to the football practice field. After practice, I'd go back to the apartment, take a shower, change clothes, have dinner, and drive over to City Island.

Our starting time at Bracker's Inn, where we played, was eight o'clock, so in order to avoid the New York City theater traffic I would drive up the New Jersey side and take the Dyckman Street Ferry across the Hudson River. It was a fairly long boat ride, so I was usually able to get in some studying or curl up and take a nap, whichever seemed more urgent at the time.

We played at the tavern until 1:00 A.M. The traffic was light by that time, so I would drive through Manhattan and back to Jersey City via the Holland Tunnel, which had just recently been completed. I usually managed to be in bed by two or two-thirty, and needless to say I was asleep the minute my head hit the pillow.

The bandstand of Bracker's Inn was hardly the ideal place to do my homework, but somehow I managed to get most of it done except on those nights when there was a little too much activity going on between dance sets.

Bracker's catered to a family-type clientele, but they served liquor there and this was during Prohibition, so things sometimes got a little rough. The troublemakers were usually given the old heave-ho pretty quickly, but on those few occasions when things got out of hand I managed to find myself a safe spot. I am a firm believer that fighting, like sex, should be confined to two people at a time. When the bottles, chairs, and bodies started to fly haphazardly through the air, I made sure that I was safely crouched behind the bass drum or under the piano. After all, I figured, I was hired as a musician, not as a bouncer.

The job of head football coach of Lincoln High School was a challenge from the start. I say "head coach." I was also "assistant head coach" and "assistant to the assistant."

I had graduated from Rutgers in the spring of 1927, a few months after my father's death, and the following fall we had rented the house in Ridgefield Park and moved back to Jersey City. Alfred had just graduated from New York Dental College, and my younger brother Donald was, of course, still an infant. My cousin, Herbert Brooks, owned the Clifton Apartments on Clifton Place, and he very generously suggested that we move in there, rent-free, until we could get on our feet financially.

66

I enrolled in New Jersey Law School in the fall of 1927 and officiated at high school football games on weekends. I also played "club jobs"—or "casuals," as they were later called—with anybody who happened to need a guy who played banjo, guitar, and saxophone and could sing an occasional vocal chorus.

I really hated the officiating (nobody likes the referee), so in the fall of 1928 when I heard that Lincoln High School was looking for a football coach, I had immediately gone over there and applied.

The principal of the high school (who was to select the coach) was a very pleasant man named Mr. Enterman. I don't remember what the job paid, but it couldn't have been very much, because I recall suggesting that we make a deal that I get paid double if we beat Dickenson High School and nothing if we didn't. (Dickenson was the big school. Dickinson and Lincoln were supposed to be the big rivals, and the Lincoln-Dickenson game was supposed to be the big game.)

Mr. Enterman said that the job was mine but that he couldn't entertain my proposition for several reasons. First of all, it would be grossly unfair to me, because not only had Lincoln never beaten Dickenson in the school's history, but they had never come within thirty points of them—in fact, Lincoln hadn't won a game for the past ten years. But, more importantly, the emphasis at Lincoln was not on winning but on good sportsmanship and the enjoyment of "taking part." (By this time, of course, I had just about figured that out.)

"Here at Lincoln High," said Mr. Enterman, "we subscribe more to the English philosophy as far as athletics is concerned. If we win—well and good. But we don't want our students to feel that winning is all-important. After all, it's only a game."

You might say at this point, why would anyone in his right mind want to take a job like that? Well, for one thing I had always wanted to take a crack at coaching football; I needed the money—meager though it was—and one thing was for certain: there was no place to go but up.

The first day of practice, about fifty boys showed up. They

67

were the nicest, friendliest, most enthusiastic bunch of kids I had ever seen in my life. Unfortunately, except for about four or five of them, they were also the smallest, skinniest, and most uncoordinated bunch I had ever seen.

We had one other problem, a big problem: It's very difficult to hold a football practice with fifty boys when you have only seven uniforms and two footballs. A quick visit to the local sporting goods store brought more bad news—no more credit until somebody paid the $250 that was still owed from last year. The fact that Dickenson, with three fully equipped teams and dozens of footballs, practiced on the same field didn't exactly make our situation any easier to take.

With all due modesty, there is one thing I do pretty well—and that is to talk. (I remember one time when I was seven years old, my father offered me a penny a minute if I would stop talking for twenty-five minutes. I kept quiet for ten and it was the toughest dime I ever earned.) In this particular situation, I figured my only chance was to bring my message to "the people," so I requested permission to address the student body and faculty at assembly the next afternoon.

I received the permission, but I almost didn't make it to the auditorium. I was halfway up the faculty stairway when one of the vice-principals, an iron-jawed, heavily muscled lady who looked like John L. Lewis in drag, grabbed me by the collar and told me to go right back down where I had come from and go up the boys' stairway. At first I was going to give her an argument, but then I figured, why take a chance—it's be just too embarrassing to have the football coach thrown bodily down a whole flight of stairs.

Someone once said that one day he heard George Jessel give a speech at the launching of a battleship in San Diego and later that same afternoon heard him speak at a *bris* in Glendale—and that George had used the same speech for both occasions. Back in 1929 I hadn't met George yet, but I had had some limited experience on the high school banquet circuit and I had developed a sort of personal technique which afforded a general framework

68

—a sort of "do-it-yourself kit" for preparing speeches for any and all occasions.

It went like this. On being introduced, I would pause for a moment to make sure I had everyone's attention, then I would start with, "When asked what is the greatest fault of the American people, Theodore Roosevelt replied, 'It is a lack of thoroughness.' " I would then explain that we were now afforded an opportunity to correct this, "And speaking of 'opportunity' . . ." would remind me of a story about a night watchman who was patrolling the park. He flashed his lantern in the direction of a park bench and surprised a young couple sitting there. He said, testily, "Are you kissing that girl?" and the young guy replied, "Oh, no sir." "Well, here then," said the watchman, "hold my lantern!"

Now, I'll admit that's pretty mild by today's standards, but it always got a good laugh back in those days. In fact, Henny Youngman still has it cross-filed under "Night Watchman" and "Lantern" jokes.

For a finish I would launch into a stirring poem entitled "Opportunity." It was a favorite of Coach Sanford's and was a real rouser. It started:

> *Master of human destinies am I. Fame, love and*
> *fortune at my footsteps wait. . . .*

(I just made the mistake of reading that aloud, and Harriet rushed out of the room. She has heard it a few times before, along with some of my favorite Shakespearean quotes and some assorted poems by Kipling and Robert W. Service.)

High school assembly groups always make great audiences anyway (anything is better than attending classes), and this particular afternoon everything seemed to fall into place. In between Theodore Roosevelt and the night watchman, I managed to convince them that it was about time Lincoln High School had a football team that they could be proud of and that right now what we needed was money for the Athletic Association.

Everyone became enthused. The girls' counselor suggested that they sell chocolate bars, cakes, and cookies in the hallways during recess, the head of the English Department suggested that they put on a school play, and Mr. Enterman, after emphasizing the fact that it was unimportant whether we won or lost, offered to solicit personally local businessmen to raise enough funds to get some uniforms and footballs.

I had already donated three pairs of football pants and two pairs of shoes of mine from Rutgers, so by the end of the week we were at least beginning to look like a football team.

It's not my purpose here to give you a play-by-play, or even a game-by-game, rundown of my two seasons as coach of Lincoln High. Suffice it to say, however, that those wonderful kids gave me some of the greatest thrills of my life. From the very beginning we were beset with injuries and ineligibilities—seven of our first string eleven were declared ineligible the week before our season opened —but regardless of the odds, they gave 100 percent every game.

What a thrill when one of our ends stole the ball on the last play of the game and ran ninety-nine yards to turn defeat into victory and beat West New York by one point! It was especially thrilling to me because he was wearing my old football pants and shoes.

What a thrill when our kids went into the Dickenson game thirty-point underdogs and barely lost a heartbreaker 7 to 6. The entire second half was played in their territory, and twice our kids were within five yards of their goal line.

Dickenson had a really fine, well-coached team. They had the Singer twins, who later starred with Syracuse University and the New York Giants, and a great halfback named Al Barabas who was to be the hero of Columbia's upset victory over Stanford in the Rose Bowl five years later. This particular afternoon, however, our little guys fought like tigers, and Dickenson was lucky to hang on and squeak through by a one-point margin. One of the high points of the game was when my assistant coach was forcibly ejected from the playing field after he had rushed out to berate an official who had made a questionable call in Dickenson's favor. Actually Mr. Enterman wasn't really my assistant, but he liked to be called that, and by his sitting next to me on the bench I could more easily restrain him from shouting derogatory remarks at the officials and our opponents. After all, it's not easy to convince some guys that it's only a game and that winning isn't everything.

It's hard for me to realize that those kids are in their sixties now. I used to see many of them when they'd drop in to dance to our band or when we made personal appearances at various theaters. Lately, however, except for an occasional card at Christmas, we have lost touch. I like to feel, though, that somewhere along the line I made a worthwhile contribution to their lives and to their characters. I know they did to mine.

Attending law school was, of course, a vastly different experience from my four previous years in New Brunswick.

Rutgers, for the benefit of those who may not know, is one of the prerevolutionary colleges, having been founded in 1766. At the time I attended, it had a typical small-college atmosphere—as well it should have with its enrollment of less than eight hundred students. Most of us lived on the campus, and the social life and extracurricular activities were as important to us as our studies.

It was a very friendly place with a well-established tradition that everyone said hello to everyone else on campus. In fact, this became such a part of our daily lives that I'd often find myself, when in New York City for a weekend, walking down the street saying hello to everyone.

At law school, the atmosphere was entirely different. It was totally impersonal and businesslike. The buildings had been part of an old warehouse and were about as friendly as a concrete slab.

It was my good fortune, however, to have as my professor in contracts a really great teacher named Lewis Tyree. He was a southern gentleman of the old school with a brilliant academic mind and a delightful sense of humor.

Many a student, including myself on numerous occasions, would start to wax eloquent on the nuances of some particular case, with Professor Tyree smiling and nodding his head approvingly. On and on you'd go, getting more and more expansive,

71

building up more and more momentum and taking in more and more territory. Along about this time, the good professor, still smiling pleasantly, would interrupt you—very politely, of course —to ask a question about that "last point you had just made." Strangely enough, the question, seemingly quite innocuous, would prove to be a little more difficult to answer than you had at first imagined.

This would be followed by another polite question, and then another and another, each one slightly more probing and more difficult to answer than the previous one. By now you were beginning to realize that you were rapidly going downhill, until by the time he had finished tearing down your arguments point by point you would have arrived at the indisputable conclusion that where you had actually gone astray was at the very beginning.

Like the downfall of man, attributable to the original sin, you realized that your big mistake had been in raising your hand in the first place.

For years after I had graduated, Professor Tyree and his wife would come by to have dinner wherever we happened to be playing, and needless to say, I was always delighted to see him. More times than not I would take the opportunity to get some free legal advice. Since he was a liberal Democrat and I a conservative Republican, we would often get into some spirited discussions.

I remember one evening at the Lexington Hotel, we were talking about President Roosevelt's handling of the Supreme Court. I felt that the president was creating a judicial imbalance by packing the Court with too many liberal justices.

I presented my views rather strongly, but Professor Tyree, whom I knew felt differently about the situation, merely listened and nodded his head approvingly. Finally, his wife said, "Why don't you answer Mr. Nelson, Lewis? Remember last night at the bridge party? I heard you give some wonderful arguments in support of President Roosevelt."

Professor Tyree turned to her and smiled. "What you don't understand, my dear," he said, "is that Mr. Nelson was one of

72

my 'A' students. He's presenting a most convincing case here. Please go ahead, Mr. Nelson."

"Oh no you don't," I said, "I'm five years older and five years smarter. You can't lead me down the garden path any longer." And he never did again . . . well, maybe a couple of times, but I've managed to forget those.

During the Christmas hiatus of my first year in law school, I made my one and only appearance as a clerk in a haberdashery shop. A piano player friend of mine told me that they were taking on some extra salesmen, for a few weeks during the Christmas holiday season, at the Manhattan Shop on Jackson Avenue in Jersey City.

I'll never forget my first customer. He was a nicely dressed man who told me he was going to attend a wedding the following day and wanted a black-and-white-striped tie for the occasion. Together we looked over all the tie racks, but I finally had to tell him that I was sorry, but that we didn't have that particular type of tie in stock. He thanked me for my trouble and left.

The store was very crowded, but not so crowded that the manager didn't see my customer go out empty-handed. He came rushing over.

"What happened?"

I explained that the man wanted a particular kind of tie and that we didn't have it.

I thought the manager was going to have a heart attack right there on the spot. He staggered over to the nearest counter and grabbed hold of it to keep himself from falling. (I should add that, besides being the store manager, he was quite active in the Jersey City Dramatic Society.) With great effort he finally managed to pull himself together.

"You must be kidding!" he said (*Hamlet*, Act II, Scene 4). "How many ties would you say we have here? . . . Four thousand? Five thousand? We have red ties, green ties, yellow ties. . . ."

"I know" I protested, "but he wanted a black-and-white-striped tie and we don't have one."

"You know what's going to happen?" said Mr. Manager. "He's going to walk down the street and he's going to go into the next men's store he sees and they're going to sell him a red tie or a blue one or maybe a yellow one. Let me explain something to you," he went on. "If we just sold our customers what they came in here to buy, we'd be out of business in six months. We have good merchandise here at fair prices. Now, here comes another customer, let's see what you can do."

He didn't exactly say it, but I got the impression that if this customer walked out of the door empty-handed, I might as well walk right out with him and not come back.

It proved to be an interesting and challenging couple of weeks. There were about eight of us temporary salesmen working there, and we devised all sorts of unusual contests among ourselves. The highlight of my brief career was the night I won first prize (a $7.50 tie) for the most unusual "switch sale." A man came in to buy a grey fedora hat, we didn't have one in his size, so I sold him a black silk umbrella.

About five years later, when our band was playing at the Paramount Theatre, I got a nice letter from the owner of the store asking for an autographed picture. I signed it "To the gang at the Manhattan Shop . . . from your worst salesman." Of course I didn't really believe that, but I thought it was a nice, modest thing to say. I understand they kept the picture on display for many years.

If you happen to be in the vicinity of Jackson Avenue in Jersey City, you might take a look in the window. For all I know my picture may still be there. Whatever you do, though, if you're looking for a black-and-white tie, don't go in. They'll sell you a red one or a blue one—or maybe even a silk umbrella.

I had one more interesting experience as a salesman, and it happened quite by accident. It was during Christmas week of 1933 while we were playing at the Park Central Hotel.

I must confess to being something of a health nut, and even during the winter in New York I never wore a hat and rarely wore an overcoat. Instead, I would jog or walk fast to keep warm.

74

As a result, I was constantly being mistaken for a floorwalker or a bank teller or a salesman.

This particular day I went into Saks Fifth Avenue to do some Christmas shopping. The store was very crowded and I was standing by the tie counter, hatless and coatless (or I should say "overcoatless") as usual, when a nice-looking middle-aged lady approached me. She was holding two neckties in her hand.

"Do you think these would be appropriate for a young man?" she asked. "He's my nephew and he's in college."

"I really think they're a bit somber," I said. "Unless he's very conservative, I think he'd like something more like this," and I showed her a red-and-blue-striped tie.

"Oh yes, that's very pretty," she said. "How much is that?" I looked on the back of the tie and told her the price.

"I'll take it," she said, and then it suddenly dawned on me that she thought I was a salesman. I don't know what came over me but I found myself saying, "Wouldn't you like a nice shirt to go with that tie?"

Well, to make a long story short, as the old saying goes, I sold her three ties, two shirts, and three pairs of socks. And why not? After all, Saks has good merchandise and their prices are fair, and if they only sold people what they came in to buy, they'd be out of business in six months.

PART TWO

Big Band

8

Even though I applied myself diligently while at law school, I was continually aware of a grave doubt as to whether this was the best course for me to pursue—whether I could ever be totally happy as a lawyer. I found certain aspects of the law fascinating. I was intrigued by the drama of the courtroom contests I had witnessed so many afternoons in New Brunswick—contests where people's lives or huge chunks of them were at stake—but I was just as fascinated by the challenges and rewards of football coaching. Adding to my personal confusion was the fact that I felt I had a certain amount of talent as a cartoonist, having sold several cartoons to *College Humor* and *Judge*, plus the deep-seated conviction that somewhere in the general area of show business, whether it be as a musician, an entertainer, or an actor, was where I would find the greatest satisfaction.

It's difficult enough for someone of thirty or thirty-five to make an objective appraisal of his own attributes and shortcomings, but for a young man of twenty-one or twenty-two it's just about impossible.

Strangely enough, I think my reluctance about accepting the thought of making any form of show business my life's work was that undercurrent of the Judeo-Christian ethic that says in essence that anything that is that much fun or is that frivolous cannot, by its very nature, be a worthy or respectable way of making a living.

Actually, I really never had to make the decision. It was made for me.

There was a ruling in New Jersey at that time, and for all I know there may still be, that in order to qualify for admission to the bar a student had to serve a legitimate eight-hour-per-day clerkship in a law office for one year. By the time I was graduated from law school I was so firmly established as an orchestra leader that I decided the only sensible thing to do was to wait until things started to slack off and then serve my clerkship and take the bar exam.

That was in 1930, and fortunately things have been going too well for the past forty-three years to warrant my making such a drastic move.

Of course, I haven't been awfully busy the last couple of years, but I'm not sure that a law clerk's salary, even if it were combined with my Social Security check, would be a sufficient inducement to get me reinvolved with Sir William Blackstone at this late date.

There was a factor other than the clerkship situation that caused me to gravitate toward show business—or more specifically, toward the music business—and that was the emergence upon the scene of the first of the singing idols . . . Rudy Vallee. Yes, Virginia: before Elvis, before Sinatra, and even before Bing, there was Rudy.

For anyone under the age of sixty, it's difficult to imagine the tremendous impact that Rudy had on the music business of the late twenties. With the advent of radio, the leading dance bands of the period—such as Paul Whiteman, Vincent Lopez, Phil Spitalny, Jean Goldkette, Fred Waring, and George Olsen, just to mention a few—were all experimenting with technically involved and often musically complex arrangements in an effort to bring a symphonic feeling to popular musical orchestration.

Rudy sang with an untrained but pleasant voice, and his orchestra consisted of eight musicians, with no brass, who played no formal arrangements but merely a succession of medleys consisting of choruses of popular songs of the day.

80

During my last year in law school I suddenly found myself in considerable demand, not only with my own band but as an individual to play and sing with other groups. This was not so much due to my banjo or saxophone playing but mostly because of a general physical resemblance on my part to the above-mentioned Rudy Vallee.

So I got myself a megaphone, learned all of Rudy's songs, and didn't object in the least when someone would call up and ask if I were "the guy who sang like Rudy Vallee."

One Sunday night early in 1930, I was listening to a program coming over WMCA, a local New York radio station. The program, which featured a dance band and a singing orchestra leader, was known as "Roemer's Homers" and was sponsored by the Roemer Furniture Company. Milton Roemer, the president of the company, was the master of ceremonies, and that night he was publicly answering some irate listeners who had written to him complaining that it was sacrilegious to present dance music over the airwaves on Sunday nights. (I was later to discover that the whole thing was a promotion stunt and that Roemer had written the letters himself.) This, however, was not what interested me at the moment. I kept thinking to myself, "Not only is this band pretty bad, but this guy sings even worse than I do!"

Later in the program, Mr. Roemer compounded the felony (remember, I was in law school at the time) by referring to the singing band leader as a former Yale football star. Since I had never heard of the guy, I felt reasonably sure that this was highly questionable.

It so happened that one of the announcers at WMCA was a fellow from my home town of Ridgefield Park named Bill Melia. Although I didn't know him well, I had met him on several occasions, so I decided to go over to the station and see if he had any suggestions as to how I could get to sing on radio.

Bill turned out to be most helpful. He introduced me to the program director, a very nice lady who asked me if I had an organized band. I of course told her yes, since I knew I could organize one on a few hours' notice. She told me to show up with my band at noon the next day and she would put us on the air for a half-hour. Meanwhile, Bill told me he would have Milton Roemer listen to our broadcast, since the general consensus was that the "former Yale football star" wasn't going to make it.

Since radio was still something new and exciting at that time, it wasn't too difficult to round up the boys I had played with at Bracker's, plus a few others, and quickly rehearse some tunes.

The studio mikes in those days (in case you've never seen pictures of them) were huge, fierce-looking things that seemed to stare at you like some ferocious beast. I remember thinking to myself, "Just relax and be casual." Meanwhile, my knees were beating together like castanets.

Rudy used to greet his radio audiences with, "Hi ho, everybody, this is Rudy Vallee." I decided to say, "Hello there, everybody, this is Ozzie Nelson." Pretty clever, huh?

As the wall clock hit twelve noon, the man in the booth gave me the finger—or perhaps I should say, pointed his finger at me —and to my great surprise I heard myself say, "Good evening, ladies and gentlemen, this is Ozzie Nelson." ("Good evening" at noon time?) I remember thinking to myself (I thought to myself a lot in those days), "At least I got my name right."

I don't know what the broadcast sounded like, but I guess it wasn't too bad, because the program director asked if we could come on every day at noon (at no salary, of course) and told me that there was a phone message for me to call Milton Roemer.

Milton Roemer proved to be an extremely bright, aggressive young man in his middle thirties. He was a heavy set man, a little under six feet, with dark curly hair and horn-rimmed glasses. He looked not unlike the late David O. Selznick. He was a brilliant promoter and a supersalesman in every sense of the word. The two of us worked out a deal whereby I would appear with my band on his radio show every Sunday night, for a modest fee, on condition that I would take him on as my personal manager.

The agreement was that after the musicians had been paid,

he and I would split the balance fifty-fifty. Unfortunately for Milton, however, he had one great weakness. He was a born gambler. For instance, at the end of the first week of our engagement at Glen Island Casino (our first "big-time" professional job) it turned out that we would have about four hundred dollars to split—two hundred each. To me, this seemed like a lot of money. Roemer said, "This is chickenfeed. I'll toss you for the four hundred." Before I realized what was happening the coin was in the air, I was yelling "heads," and a moment later I had four hundred dollars in my pocket.

From then on, we'd toss a coin every week, double or nothing, and he lost at least four times out of five. No matter where we played, Milton would work out some sort of deal whereby he'd take a gamble and almost invariably lose. Like all gamblers, he was superstitious and tried every conceivable gimmick to break his losing streak.

I remember one week in 1931 when I was doubling between the Pelham Heath Inn and the Paradise Theatre in the Bronx, we were tossing for over a thousand dollars—eleven or twelve hundred, as I recall. We were in a drugstore next to the theater and Roemer was about to flip the coin when he noticed an Egyptian, wearing a turban, walking up and down the sidewalk. (The man had evidently been hired to do this as a publicity stunt for the motion picture *Daughters of the Nile* or something.)

Don't ask me why Milt figured an Egyptian would bring him luck, but anyway he went out and asked the guy to toss the coin. Fortunately I won again, or we probably would have been booked into Loew's Cairo the following week.

Lest you get the impression from the above that Milton was some kind of dum dum, I must tell you how we got booked into Glen Island Casino, since it was engineered by him and was a fantastic piece of promotional genius.

We had been performing on the "Roemer's Homers Radio Hour" for about six weeks with Roemer giving the band and me a buildup that was downright embarrassing. Our little orchestra, which consisted of eight of us playing choruses from stock ar-

83

rangements, was suddenly the finest musical aggregation in the land. Our musicians, only one of whom had gone further than high school, were suddenly all graduates of Ivy League colleges, and I suddenly was a Phi Beta Kappa—oh, yes, and I was also the greatest singer of popular songs to come along in the last decade.

Nick Kenny was radio editor of the *New York Daily Mirror* at that time and he and Roemer were good friends, so it wasn't surprising that I often found myself mentioned favorably in his column. Then Ben Gross of the *Daily News* started to take notice of me, followed by Louis Sobel of the *Journal*, Paul Yawitz of the *Daily Mirror*, and several other New York columnists. I like to think that the fact that the Roemer Furniture Store often ran big ads in these papers had nothing to do with it, but I'm sure it didn't hurt.

One day Roemer called me up in an unusual state of excitement, even for him. He had just been informed that the *Daily Mirror* was starting a radio popularity contest in which their readers would send in votes for their favorite radio personalities. Milton saw this as a beautiful opportunity to get me a lot of publicity in a hurry. In fact, the way he went into action, I should have suspected that the contest itself was his idea.

As was to be expected, he told his listeners about the contest and suggested that they send in their votes for me as their favorite bandleader. Meanwhile, he discovered from a newspaper dealer in Newark that in order to get credit for unsold papers the dealer merely had to return the first page. So, for a small consideration, he hired a guy to clip all the ballots from the unsold papers (fortunately, the ballots were on the back page), write in my name, and send them over to the *Daily Mirror*.

The really creative maneuvers, however, were yet to come. One Sunday night, after the contest had been running for about three weeks, I was surprised to hear Roemer make an announcement that went something like this: "Please folks, stop sending money to us. You leave us no alternative but to mail it back to you. Just mail in your votes, but *no money!*"

84

"What was that all about?" I asked, after the show. "Are people actually sending in money?"

"Not yet, but they will now," he answered . . . and he was right. Don't ask me to explain what perversity of nature or careless listening habits brings on something like that, but the money started dribbling in—in ones, fives, and even an occasional ten.

After about three weeks of this, Milton pulled his masterstroke. "You've really given me a problem, folks," he announced to his radio audience. "Judging from the thousand of dollars that have poured in [there was probably a total of about fifty], you nice people obviously won't take no for an answer. So here's what we're going to do. We're going to run full-page ads in the *Daily Mirror*, with a beautiful photo spread of Ozzie, announcing that the ads have been paid for by the 'Friends of Ozzie Nelson.' "

And that's exactly what he did. Of course, the ads also suggested that the "nice people" tune in to the "Roemer's Homers Radio Hour" sponsored by the Roemer Furniture Company.

By this time, as can be easily understood, I was running neck and neck with the big names of the orchestra world. It was utterly ridiculous.

I can imagine a breakfast scene where a wife would say, "See who's ahead in the contest today, Walter," and he would open to the radio page and say, "Rudy Vallee is first, then Paul Whiteman, then Ozzie Nelson . . . *Ozzie Nelson*?? Who's Ozzie Nelson?"

This was exactly the question they asked Milton Roemer when he appeared before the board of directors of the Westchester County Park Commission at Glen Island Casino: "Who's Ozzie Nelson?"

If you drove north on the Shore Road in New Rochelle and turned right just before you reached Larchmont, you would cross over a little bridge, and there, overlooking Long Island Sound, was the Glen Island Casino. It had long been a favorite picnic spot for Westchester County people, who would bring their lunches and sit by the water and watch the boats go by or listen to the German band concerts.

For the summer of 1930, however, the Park Commission had decided to inaugurate a new policy. There was to be dining and dancing to the music of a name band—the biggest and best name available. On this particular day the members of the commission were meeting to make their decision, and Milton the old supersalesman was making his pitch.

"Frankly, gentlemen, I'm rather surprised to hear you ask, 'Who's Ozzie Nelson?' " he said pleasantly. "Would it be possible to send someone out for today's *Daily Mirror*? I'd like to see how Ozzie's doing in the popularity contest they're running."

Fortunately, the newspaper was procured without too much delay. I say "fortunately" because this was obviously more effective than it would have been for Milton to have had to get the one he had stashed out in his car, "just in case."

"Well, what do you know, gentlemen," said he, with a straight face. "This even surprises me. Ozzie's in first place! Rudy Vallee is second, Ben Bernie is third, and Paul Whiteman is fourth."

"You know, I think I've heard my daughter talk about this young man," said one member of the board as they passed the newspaper around.

"Now that you mention it. . . ," said another.

And so it came to pass that, on a balmy night in June, I became the first name bandleader to play at the famous Glen Island Casino—the cradle of more name bands than any other dance spot in the world, where, during the years to come, thousands of young people would listen and dance to Glen Gray and his Casa Loma Orchestra, Tommy and Jimmy Dorsey with "Bing's golden-voiced brother Bob on the vocals," Claude Thornhill, Charlie Barnett, and finally the great Glenn Miller band. Yes, they all got their start at the Glen Island Casino.

Our opening night was a dream come true. It seemed as if everyone in town was there: Paul Whiteman, Vincent Lopez, Fred Waring, Will Osborne, Ted Lewis, Morton Downey—yes, and even Rudy himself.

For the first time, we were broadcasting nightly not only over WMCA but from coast to coast on the CBS network. Before the evening was over, recording executive Jack Kapp had offered us a contract to record on the Brunswick label. For a young man with still two more weeks to go for his law school diploma, this was truly a night to remember.

After the guests had left and my brother Al, my mother, and I were having a quiet cup of coffee and trying to relax from all the excitement, my mother said, "What a wonderful night. If only your father could have been here."

"Don't worry, Mom," I said. "I have a feeling he was."

9

Probably the most popular nightclub in New York City during the period of the early '30s was the Hollywood Restaurant. Located on Broadway in the heart of the theater district, it featured the most beautiful showgirls and chorus girls in the world. Nils T. Granlund, better known as "N.T.G.," was the master of ceremonies.

In anticipation of the usual New Year's Eve sellout crowd, the management had rented the Grand Ballroom of the Edison Hotel for December 31, 1931. They had engaged our orchestra to play for dancing and also to accompany the floor show.

I had expected N.T.G. to show up and announce the acts, but in his place he sent over a beautiful young girl who did a specialty dance and introduced the various numbers.

I remember being astounded that this kid, who looked more like a college co-ed than a professional entertainer, should have so much poise and quiet self-assurance. The fact that she had just about the greatest figure I had ever seen didn't escape my notice either.

We really didn't get much chance to talk to each other that night. We were both too busy and too tired, and besides, a New Year's Eve celebration in the ballroom of a New York hotel is not exactly the best setting for striking up an acquaintance.

The early months of 1932 were spent in Miami Beach, Florida, where we played at the Indian Creek Club, a beautiful private beach and golf club whose membership consisted of a lot of very wealthy but very nice people who gave me a lot of very nice tips on some very nice horses of theirs.

We only worked five nights a week, which gave us plenty of time for all sorts of interesting activities. Besides the ocean and the miles and miles of beautiful sandy beach there were lots of nightclubs and lots and lots of beautiful girls. For ten unattached young musicians it was a most pleasant way to spend the winter.

Despite all the activities, however, I still found time to do a little worrying about the future. Thanks to our constant exposure on radio and recordings, we had achieved a "name band" status in a remarkably short time. However, we were still a small band numerically, and I was aware of the fact that we hadn't, as yet, created anything that was uniquely ours—that would set us apart from a dozen other small bands.

Following our first summer at Glen Island Casino (1930) we had played at the Barbizon Plaza Hotel and the Ritz Tower, and following some one-nighters in ballrooms and several weeks of vaudeville in the metropolitan area, we had returned to Glen Island Casino for our second season. We were scheduled to go back for a third season (following our Florida engagement and a few college prom dates), and I had a feeling that this could well be a turning point for us.

Our first step was to give the band a better sound musically. We had been using only one trumpet—Bobby Mayhew, who had come to us from Paul Whiteman's band. We moved Bobby over to second trumpet (he later left and was replaced by Bo Ashford of the Casa Loma band, one of the all-time great jazz cornet men) and brought in Holly Humphreys to play first. Holly, who had played lead trumpet with Hal Kemp and Fred Waring, played with great confidence and authority. It was he who was responsible for the fine phrasing that was later to be characteristic of our ensembles. On third trumpet we had Harry Johnson, a remarkably talented seventeen-year-old who had just graduated from high school in Atlanta, Georgia. Harry got a beautiful sound, especially in the low register, and was such a well-schooled musician that he could sight-read trombone parts, transposing from bass to treble clef and up a full tone as he went along.

Charlie Bubeck had come in on first saxophone the year before, and more and more we began to feature him on baritone as well as on lead alto. Charlie was, and still is, one of the greatest musicians I have ever known. Using a bass reed on his baritone saxophone, he got an absolutely fabulous sound out of the instrument, and his improvisational passages were truly masterpieces.

The rest of the band was composed of the original group who had opened with me at Glen Island two years before: Harry Murphy, piano; Sandy Wolf, guitar; Joe Bohan, drums; Sid Brokaw, violin and vibes (later fourth saxophone) ; and Donald Wright and Bill Nelson on second and third saxophones—really excellent musicians all. Larry Cramer and Willie Fisher, two teenagers from Bergen County, came with us to write the arrangements. We were all young and enthusiastic and loved what we were doing. I felt extremely fortunate to be surrounded by all this great musical talent.

Our most interesting innovation, however, was the addition of a girl singer to our group. She had a beautiful face, a fantastic figure, and a wealth of talent and experience. As you've probably guessed, unless you've been skipping around or reading from back to front, she was the same young lady I had met at the Hotel Edison on New Year's Eve.

Harriet Hilliard was born in Des Moines, Iowa, of theatrical parents. Her father, Roy E. Hilliard, was a well-known dramatic stock actor and director who helped guide the stage careers of Clark Cable, Warner Baxter, Ralph Bellamy, Lyle Talbot, Milburn Stone, Jack Bailey, and many others. His family name was Snyder, but he took the name Hilliard when he went into show business as a young man of twenty.

Harriet's mother was Hazel MacNutt, daughter of the chief of detectives of Des Moines (he had received a special citation from President McKinley for single-handedly transporting a convicted murderer from Canada to Des Moines) . Hazel had started in

90

show business at the age of fourteen and had starred in musical and dramatic stock companies for over thirty years.

Harriet herself had made her first stage appearance at the tender age of six weeks, when she appeared with Harry Minturn, a well-known leading man of the day, in *Heir to the Hoorah*. It was a nonspeaking part, of course. In fact, it was also a nonwalking part. What it was, was a sleeping part, and I have it on good authority that she slept beautifully through every show. Her first speaking part came when she was older—three-and-a-half years old, to be exact. It was in *Mrs. Wiggs of the Cabbage Patch,* and I have it on the same good authority that, in keeping with Alfred Lunt's advice to actors, she spoke in a loud, clear voice and didn't bump into the furniture.

Harriet attended school at St. Agnes Academy in Kansas City (where Joan Crawford had been a student a few years earlier) and toured with her parents during summer vacations, gaining much valuable experience en route. She recalls one embarrassing opening night when, playing the part of a maid, she got the exits confused and instead of ushering the guests into the dining room ushered them into the ocean.

At the age of fifteen, she came to New York with her mother and studied ballet with Chester Hale, meanwhile appearing in the famous Capitol Theatre Corps de Ballet. One year later she appeared in her first Broadway production, playing the title role in *The Blonde Sinner,* which also starred Enid Marky, Margery Gateson, and Howard St. John. This was on the world-renowned Zeigfeld Roof.

Following this came a series of tours with RKO units which played the top "two-a-day" vaudeville theaters from coast to coast. Harriet played the famous Palace Theatre four times: once with Ken Murray, once with Bert Lahr, once with N.T.G., and (shades of things to come) once in a family situation comedy sketch with Danny Duncan.

Harriet had originally been booked into the Hollywood Restaurant, for a limited engagement, as a specialty dancer. Before long, however, she was singing, working in sketches, acting as "mistress of ceremonies," and, as she put it, "doing everything but sweeping out the joint."

The "limited engagement" had stretched out to almost a year, and Harriet's salary, which had started at $75 a week, was now up to $150, which was a lot of money for a girl barely out of her teens, especially during the Depression days of 1932.

One night shortly after we got back to New York, following our Miami Beach engagement, I stopped by the Hollywood with a friend of mine, Ham Fisher, who drew the famous "Joe Palooka" comic strip. I had already decided that I wanted to add a girl vocalist to the band, not only to sing solos but also to work with me, singing boy-girl duets in musical comedy style. Now it was a question of finding the right girl.

The floor show was already in progress when we got there, and Harriet was doing a "Tea for Two"–type dance routine with the ensemble working in back of her. It took me about thirty seconds to decide that she was the girl I was looking for.

Years ago Jimmie Lunceford used to feature a great old song, "T'aint Whatcha Do, It's the Way Howja Do It." It wasn't so much what Harriet did, but "the way how she did it"—the way she has done everything all her life.

Certain very special people are gifted with a very special talent that can only be described as "style." It's an intangible quality that one is born with. It can't be taught or acquired. It's not only a performing talent, it's a way of life. Harriet is one of those very special people.

We had lunch the next day at Sardi's, which was then and still is one of the most prestigious restaurants in New York, catering principally to the elite of the theatrical world. When I had suggested Sardi's the night before, Harriet had given me an assenting smile as if to say, "Where else?"

I arrived about five minutes late. I had never been to Sardi's before, and since a keen sense of direction is not one of my strong points I had had a little difficulty finding the place. Harriet was already there. "I'm terribly sorry," I said, "but I went down the wrong street. I know this sounds ridiculous, but I've never been here before."

92

"That's okay," she said, "neither have I."

The only reason I mention this is because I thought it was a nice, honest way to start a relationship. And don't forget, that was back in 1932, before honesty became so popular with young people.

We opened at Glen Island Casino on June 15 and stayed there through Labor Day. The place was jammed every night. The engagement was a tremendous success. Before the summer was over, at least a thousand guys had fallen in love with Harriet Hilliard —including me.

In the fall of 1932, through December 31, we appeared at the Hotel Paramount Grill on Forty-sixth Street just west of Broadway. We worked there with Sophie Tucker, who headlined a floor show with a line of chorus girls and showgirls. When I say "worked," I really mean "worked." Our band not only played for the entire show (which went on twice nightly and which I emceed), but we also played for dancing and did two radio broadcasts each night. Harriet sang with the band and also did a specialty dance in the show.

The toughest part of the engagement, however, was collecting our money. By December, the management was about three weeks behind us, and we figured our only chance to catch up was to wait for New Year's Eve, which was sure to be a big night. My brother Al was pressed into service, and he literally stood by the cashier and grabbed the money as it came in. By the time the evening was over he had collected quite a bundle. He said he would have gotten more, but he was competing with several other creditors and two of the other guys had guns.

The collecting and handling of money really became a problem when we went on tour playing one-night stands, which we did almost every spring and summer from 1933 to about 1940. This was the most exhausting but by far the most lucrative part of the dance band business, especially since there were more places to play than there were name bands to play them.

We would usually play from eight-thirty until one o'clock and then drive to the next town, stopping en route to eat. By the time we'd get checked into a hotel it was usually daylight, and by the time we got up and had breakfast the banks would be closed, so as a result we were always carrying a lot of cash with us. (It was the custom of the day for ballroom promoters to pay in cash from the night's proceeds.) Most of this we would stuff into a little suitcase, which for some long-forgotten reason we had dubbed "the Nanny-goat" and which we carried on the bandstand with us and kept under Harriet's chair.

About five o'clock one morning, en route from one ballroom to the next, Harriet and I stopped off to get something to eat at a little bean wagon in Indianapolis. As usual, we carried the money bag with us into the restaurant. We had gotten about five miles out of town when Harriet suddenly turned to me with a look of panic on her face and said, "My, God, the Nanny-goat!" We had left it in the bean wagon.

Needless to say, I made the fastest U-turn on record and headed back toward Indianapolis. We had covered about a mile when in the distance we saw another car coming towards us. As we drew closer we saw an arm extended out the car window, waving old Nanny-goat. It was one of our trumpet players, Harry Johnson. By the rarest of good fortune he and the saxophone player riding with him had happened to stop off at the same bean wagon just as the proprietor was asking if anybody knew who the bag belonged to.

When we got to the hotel I counted the money. It came to a little over ten thousand dollars. I'm glad the guy in the bean wagon didn't open the bag, or he probably would have had a heart attack.

I made an exception that morning and stayed up until the bank opened. No use pressing your luck too far.

In the fall of 1933 we signed to do our first weekly radio series, called "The Bakers' Broadcast." It was sponsored by Standard Brands and was produced by the J. Walter Thompson advertising agency. The star of the show was a little comedian named Joe Penner, who featured some silly catch-phrases like "Do you wanna

94

buy a duck?" "Iz zat so?" and "You nasty man." Standing alone on the printed page they don't read too funny, but he had an unusual delivery and an infectious comedy laugh that immediately caught on with the public. As a result, the program quickly soared to number one in the ratings and gave us a great showcase for our band numbers and special-material duets.

Joe was a terribly insecure little man who had an unfortunate knack for placing his trust in the wrong people. As a result, his career was badly mishandled, and his success, though tremendous while it lasted, was of short duration.

He was on the series for two seasons and then was replaced by Robert ("Believe It or Not") Ripley. We used to see Joe and his wife Eleanor a great deal socially a few years later in California, and Harriet did a picture with him at RKO called *New Faces of 1937*. The next few years, however, we were on the road a great deal, so we gradually lost touch with each other.

We last saw him in 1941 when we were playing the Earl Theater in Philadelphia with Humphrey Bogart and Mayo Methot, who was Bogie's wife at that time. The four of us—Bogie, Mayo, Harriet, and I—had stopped off at the supper room of the Ritz Hotel after our last show and had run into Joe and Eleanor. We hadn't seen the Penners for several years, so it was a pleasant surprise.

Joe was trying to put on the traditional "happy face," but under the circumstances it wasn't too easy. He was touring with a road company of *Yokel Boy,* but the public had lost interest in him to the extent that he was establishing records for all-time low grosses in theaters where he had formerly held the record for all-time high grosses.

We all stayed up quite late. There was a lot of telling of funny stories and a lot of laughing, but with it all, there was an undercurrent of sadness. Joe was still in his thirties, but such are the cruelties of show business that the public no longer wanted him. He was washed up. We knew it, and what was even sadder, he knew it. He couldn't admit it, of course, not even to himself, but he knew it.

Eleanor went in to wake him up for breakfast the next morning and discovered that he had died in his sleep. They were announcing it over the radio as Harriet and I came into the theater.

The producer-director for "The Bakers' Broadcast" during the last season with Joe Penner and the subsequent two years with Bob Ripley was a tremendously talented madman named Ed Gardner, who was later to star in his own radio show, "Duffy's Tavern." Ed was married to Shirley Booth at the time, and the four of us shared many good times together. New York City was an exciting place during the mid-'30s anyway, especially in our situation, where we got to know so many interesting and talented people. We played at the Terrace Room of the Hotel New Yorker, then at the Park Central Roof, then back to the New Yorker, after which we moved to Lexington Avenue and Forty-eighth Street for two very happy seasons at the Silver Grill of the Hotel Lexington.

In spite of the Depression, which had not yet run its course, New York City was really swinging. The town was filled with name bands: Paul Whiteman, Eddie Duchin, Guy Lombardo, Tommy Dorsey, Hal Kemp, Ray Noble, Benny Goodman, Artie Shaw, Eddie Lane, Vincent Lopez, George Hall—the list could go on and on. After hours you could go over to Fifty-second Street or up to Harlem to hear the jazz greats, or, for a change of pace, there was the El Morocco, the Stork Club, or the Mayfair dances at the Ritz Carlton.

By 1934 we had added three more musicians to our organization: two excellent trombone players, Elmer Smathers and "Abe" Lincoln, and a fine pianist named Chauncey Gray, composer of "Bye Bye Blues" and "You're the One I Care For." By virtue of playing together night after night (we took only two two-week vacations between 1932 and 1938), our band had developed a distinctive, easy, relaxed style and a fine overall tonal quality. More and more, Harriet and I were featuring our "boy meets girl" duets, and more and more we were unconsciously establish-

96

ing a pattern of integrating our personal lives with our professional lives. Many of the songs we sang were originals that I wrote especially for us ("Shall We Build a Little House in the Country," "I'm Going Hollywood Over You," "Hey, Hey, Harriet," "I've Got Those Oh What an Easy Job You've Got All You Do Is Wave a Stick Blues," and, a few years later, "I'm Looking for a Guy Who Plays Alto and Baritone and Doubles on a Clarinet and Wears a Size 37 Suit"). But mostly they were popular songs of the day like "You Oughta Be in Pictures," "I Guess I'll Have to Change My Plan," "It's Dark on Observatory Hill"—songs for which I could write extra lyrics so that they also could apply especially to us.

During the summers of 1933 and 1934 we played so many theaters, ballrooms, and college proms that now, forty years later, they are all blended together in one beautiful haze. As a result, when somebody comes up to me and says, "You probably don't remember this, but you played at the prom when I was at Emory University" or "I went to see you and your band at the Colonial Gardens in Rochester, Indiana," or "I danced to your band at Crystal Park in Cumberland, Maryland," I always say quickly, "I believe you." It's not that I'm so agreeable by nature. It's just that the guy is probably right.

Of course there are those special occasions that for one reason or another stand out in my memory: Like the first time we played the Earl Theater in Philadelphia. It wasn't anything that happened on stage that was especially memorable, it was a little extracurricular activity that had been arranged for me by the theater's publicity department. The week before our Philadelphia engagement, we had played the Hippodrome Theater in Baltimore, and the press agent there, having heard that I had done some boxing in college, had arranged for me to spar a couple of rounds with Joe Dundee, the former world's welterweight champion. Actually, we just clowned around a little with no real punches being thrown, but the Baltimore papers gave it a lot of space. Evidently, the Earl Theater press agent heard about it, because when we arrived in Philadelphia one of the events on

97

the publicity agenda was a bout that had been arranged between me and Tommy Loughran.

Now, as any fight enthusiast can tell you, Tommy Loughran was one of the finest boxers who ever pulled on a glove. After winning the world's light-heavyweight title he had moved up to the heavyweight division and had won impressive victories over Max Baer, Jack Sharkey, Jimmy Braddock, Harry Greb, Johnny Risko, and many other leading contenders. In his most recent bout he had lost a disputed decision to the then–heavyweight champion Primo Carnera, and was currently training in a downtown gymnasium for an upcoming bout in Madison Square Garden with Walter Neusal.

I had assumed that our little sparring match was to be a repeat of the Baltimore affair, but evidently nobody told Tommy. I won't bore you with the gory details other than to say that he looked very good against me. He hit me three thousand six hundred and forty-two times and I hit him three times—twice on the shoulder and once on the elbow.

I learned two things: it's difficult to sing with a swollen nose, and it's almost impossible to play saxophone with a fat lip.

Just recently I looked through Nat Fleischer's *Official Ring Record Book* and noted that Loughran lost that fight to Walter Neusal. You know, maybe that punch I gave him on the elbow was harder than I thought.

Then there was the time we played a one-nighter in a small city in upper New York State and the promoters, a couple of small-time hoodlums, decided they weren't going to pay us the twelve hundred dollars in percentage money we had coming to us. After arguing with them for two hours in a bowling alley in back of the ballroom, I finally told them to forget about it, that I would make one phone call to New York and they would be on the blacklist by the next day. Of course, I meant the blacklist of the Musicians' Union, but, as I discovered later, they thought I was referring to the *Mafia's* black list. After a short mumbled exchange between them, they paid me off in cash over the bar while about a dozen sinister-looking characters hung around, watching and passing snide remarks about all the money I was taking out of town. It was like a scene from a "B" gangster movie.

Harriet and a guy from the booking agency had pulled my car around to a side door and had the motor running. It wouldn't be exactly accurate to say I walked out of there—it was more like an escape. I backed up to the door, as nonchalantly as possible under the circumstances, then jumped into the car and screeched out of there and up the highway as fast as I could go. I had a feeling somebody might be pulling out after us and I was taking no chances. Not only was I carrying the twelve hundred dollars I had just collected, but we had about seven or eight thousand more in the little "Nanny-goat" bag in the back of the car.

We drove full speed for about two or three miles, then I turned off the highway and onto a dirt road, and then into a cornfield, where I turned out the lights. A moment later another car went speeding past at what must have been close to a hundred miles an hour. Maybe it was one of the hoods from the bar or maybe it was just some crazy kids out for a joyride. I never did find out. We sat there in the cornfield until daylight and then drove on to Buffalo.

Then there is one very special night that stands out in my memory for a very special reason. It was during the summer of 1935 and we were on a tour of one-nighters. Before we leave the year 1934, however, there is a little story I'd like to tell about Joe Bohan, who, you may recall, was one of our original group at Bracker's in City Island and who was with the band until 1939.

Joe was a really fine drummer. He had a strong, steady beat and held the rhythm section together with a firm hand—or, more specifically, with two firm hands and a steady foot. He was a fine Irish Catholic lad who attended church regularly and was good to his folks. Unfortunately, however, he had one small weakness. He liked to take a drink now and then. Now, there's nothing wrong with that, except that in Joe's case it took very little to get him drunk. Fortunately, he didn't get drunk very often, but on the few occasions when he did, he was quite a handful. As one of the other boys put it, "When Joe gets drunk,

99

he gets drunk all over." One of these occasions was a couple of nights before Christmas, when we were playing at the New Yorker.

The dinner session started at 7:00 P.M., and I usually came on the bandstand about the middle of the first set. This particular evening, as I entered the room I noticed that the bass drum beat was very loud. This was unusual because Joe had a firm but light touch with his foot pedal. The other musicians were making a gallant effort to act as if nothing was wrong—in fact, they were playing it so cool as to make it obvious that something, in fact, *was* wrong.

We had a ruling in the band, at that time, that if anyone got drunk on the job he was subject to an automatic fine of fifty dollars. The last thing I wanted to do was to levy a fine on anyone so close to Christmas, so I decided to make believe that I didn't know that Joe was smashed (which wasn't easy, because he was not only having difficulty keeping his eyes open, but he was having difficulty keeping his head from falling off).

Unfortunately, however, Joe, with that unfathomable logic peculiar to drunks, was either unwilling or unable to go along with the subterfuge, and before we'd gone half a chorus I heard his voice boom out with, "Okay, so I'm drunk! What are you going to do about it?"

I don't recall how we got him through the evening—probably poured coffee down him and walked him around outside during the intermissions—but I do remember we had him reasonably sober by the end of the night. I called him aside then and said, "I'm sorry, Joe, but you know the rules. I want you to bring in a check for fifty dollars tomorrow made out to your favorite charity." Joe said, "I'll make it out to the Christmas fund at the Catholic church in Larchmont."

Several nights later Joe called me aside and said, "Hey, that donation really made me a big man up at the church. They posted a list of the donors on the bulletin board and there I was right on top of the list: 'Joseph A. Bohan—$50.'"

Now, we fade out and fade in again, as they say in tinsel land.

100

It's one year later and Joe came to me and said, "You know what happened last Sunday at church? The priest came up to me and said, 'Well, Joe, I imagine we can count on your usual fifty-dollar donation this year'—so I think I'll get drunk again." And he did!

The evening I referred to earlier as having special significance was during the following August when we were en route to California to play at the Cocoanut Grove. We had just finished playing a ballroom date in Henderson, Texas, and were on our way to Dallas. The boys in the band all wanted to have their cars with them when we got to California, so we drove across the country by automobile. Harriet and I usually rode in the back seat of my car while Harold Lane did the driving. Harold was a slim, attractive, dark-haired young guy with a great personality. He had the official title of "chauffeur," but that was hardly an accurate description of his status. He had been a Greyhound bus driver when we had chartered a bus for one of our one-nighter tours the year before, and by the end of the tour he had been helpful in so many ways that I offered him a job. Harold was a "character" in the true sense of the word and had his own unique style of grammatical construction and pronunciation, which was always picked up and carried on by us all. "Lake Champlain" became "Lake Champagne," a "Hershey bar" became a "Hersie bar," and "dilapidated" became "dilapigated."

The only disagreement he and I ever had was about his salary when he first came to work for us. I had said, "I don't know what you're making now, but I'll offer you a year's guarantee, buy your clothes, and pay your traveling expenses and a salary of forty dollars a week to start."

Harold said, "No, I'm making thirty dollars with the bus company. I think I'm worth thirty-five, but I'm not worth forty." Needless to say, he was soon making twice that, but he always insisted that he was being overpaid.

He was with us for seven years and served not only as chauffeur but as band manager, paymaster, stage manager, master mechanic, chief electrician, babysitter, and, most important, good friend and companion. He was also the first to hear about a lot of important events in our lives, starting with the night of August 17—or rather early morning of August 18. We were about halfway to Dallas when Harriet suddenly turned to me and said, "You haven't said anything for the past fifty miles. Are you still with us?"

"Yeah," I said. "I've been thinking about us. I think we've got enough money saved up now so we can get married. What do you think?"

"Sounds good to me," she said. "In fact, I thought you'd never ask." (Actually, I had suggested it several times, but she had always said she didn't think she was quite ready for marriage yet.)

"Hey, Harold," Harriet called out. "I've just been proposed to. Ozzie and I are going to get married."

"I thought he'd never ask," said Harold.

10

During the spring of 1935, Harriet had done a screen test for MGM. The test consisted of a dramatic scene from *The Postman Always Rings Twice*. Everyone who saw it was tremendously impressed by her performance and thought she would be an excellent prospect for films—that is, everyone except the executives of MGM. While we were appearing at the Cocoanut Grove, however, her picture agent, Leo Morrison, showed the test to Joe Nolan, who was in charge of production at RKO, and Joe immediately offered Harriet the female lead in a picture with Walter Abel at a salary of $750 per week. She immediately turned it down, explaining that she wasn't interested in staying in Hollywood while I was in New York—that she just wanted to get married, have a family, and maybe even get out of show business entirely.

There was no way that I could stay in Hollywood, since we were already signed to open at the Hotel Lexington in two weeks and start our Bob Ripley radio series at about the same time. Both of these commitments were to continue to the following June. Harriet's agent, sensing a commission slipping out of his hands, tried to enlist my help in talking Harriet into doing the movie, but I told him that it was a decision she would have to make for herself. Actually, I was in a rather awkward position. The thought of our being separated for the first month-and-a-half of our marriage (the shooting schedule for the picture was six weeks) was hardly a pleasant one, and yet I didn't feel that I had a right to turn the picture down, since she was the one who was being offered the part. I kept thinking of an item that had appeared in Walter Winchell's column to the effect that Jimmy Durante of the comedy team of Clayton, Jackson, and Durante had been offered a part in a movie without Clayton and Jackson, and Clayton and Jackson had turned it down.

Either Leo Morrison was one hell of an agent or RKO wanted Harriet very badly. At any rate, they kept raising the ante, first to a thousand a week, then to twelve-fifty, and finally to fifteen hundred dollars. At this point, I figured it was about time I said my little piece. It went something like this: "About ten years from now when I'm old and fat and will have lost all my hair and all my teeth, you'll look across the breakfast table at me sitting there in my undershirt, slurping down my coffee, and reading the sports page, and you'll say to yourself, 'To think I gave up a moving picture career and all that money for him!' For the sake of our future happiness you've got to do the picture. After all, it's only for a couple of months. Besides, at this very moment Leo Morrison is perched on the ledge of his office building in Beverly Hills, ready to fling himself into the traffic in the event you say no."

"Okay," she said, "but just this one picture. Then I'm going back home and we're going to start raising a family."

We were married at my mother's apartment in Hackensack, New Jersey, October 8, 1935. The Reverend William Russell, minister of the First Episcopal Church of West Englewood, performed the ceremony. My brother Alfred and his beautiful wife Kay, the daughter of Sheriff William O'Driscoll of Hudson County, New Jersey, were the best man and matron of honor. The others in attendance were Harriet's mother, my mother, and Donald, who by now was a handsome boy of eight. Oh, yes— and there were about thirty-five reporters and photographers, but they were thoughtful enough to wait downstairs until after the ceremony.

Dr. Russell gave us some advice that Harriet and I have always treasured. He said, in effect, that he thought it was a mistake for married couples to have to surround themselves with other people in order to have a good time—that they should develop enough mutuality of interests so that they can enjoy things together without the necessity of always having others present to stimulate them. We not only found the advice helpful to us in our personal lives, we also used it as a basis for the story line of one of our better television episodes.

On the subject of personal relationships, I think one of the most valuable assets to any marriage—an absolute essential if the marriage is to be a happy one—is the element of mutual trust. This is especially true in show business, where the two people are of necessity often separated for weeks at a time.

During the period when I was in law school and playing club jobs with various orchestras, I became very friendly with an extremely talented saxophone player named Charlie Vosburgh. He and his attractive young wife lived in a small apartment in the Bronx. Through Charlie's connections, I got to play a lot of country club dances and fraternity parties in Westchester County and the upper New York City area. Although he averaged two or three club jobs a week, Charlie also worked during the daytime as a bank teller. After playing a dance job we'd usually come back to Charlie's apartment and I'd stay overnight there and drive back to Jersey City the next day. I would either sleep on a couch in the living room or occasionally, when another musician would be staying over, Charlie and his wife Ada would crowd into one twin bed and I would sleep in the other one. On those mornings when Charlie had to get up and go to work, he'd be long gone by the time I woke up. In fact, it wasn't unusual for me to wake up and find Ada still asleep in the next bed.

One day I said to Charlie, "Boy, you sure must trust me, going off and leaving me with your wife like that."

"Are you kidding?" said Charlie. "I wouldn't trust you as far as I could throw a piano. But I trust my wife."

Harriet and I had dinner with Charlie and Ada on our last

trip to New York. They're still happily married and still very much in love.

We got to reminiscing, and I asked Charlie if he'd changed his mind about trusting me. "Hell, no," he said, "I didn't trust you when you were a nice clean-cut young law student, and I certainly wouldn't trust you now that you're a dirty old man."

Harriet and I never had a honeymoon in the traditional sense. On the Sunday before we were married, we started our series with Bob Ripley. We opened at the Lexington Hotel the following Friday, and the next Sunday Harriet and Hazel, Harriet's mother, took off by plane for Hollywood. Why they decided to fly I'll never know: don't forget, this was only eight short years after Lindbergh had made the first solo flight across the Atlantic.

The flying time from New York to Los Angeles in those days was twenty-three hours—sometimes even five or six hours longer—and part of the standard equipment was a cardboard container that was placed beside each passenger's seat. I remember I sent Harriet a telegram that was delivered to her at a fuel stop in Denver. It said, "Keep your spirits up and your breakfast down." She told me later that unfortunately she wasn't able to do either.

Being separated from someone you love very much is a terribly difficult situation, as anyone who has experienced it can readily testify. You have two choices: you can walk around in a daze, constantly mooning about the other person (in which case you not only don't get much accomplished but you wind up being awfully dull company for those around you), or you can keep yourself so busy that you don't have time to think about your missing mate. This second choice, of course, carries with it the obvious danger of being so successful in keeping the other person from your thoughts that you forget about her (or him) entirely.

Neither one of us had too much difficulty keeping busy: I played at the hotel every night plus a luncheon session on Saturday afternoons, and also rehearsed Sunday afternoons for the Ripley show and performed on the show early Sunday evenings, after

106

which I came back to the hotel for the late session. Harriet, of course, was immediately taken in tow by the studio publicity department, and the magazine sob sisters had a field day with the "lonesome bride" interviews. We had agreed to write each other a short note at the end of each day, but the short note usually managed to stretch out to ten or twelve pages. And then there were the phone calls! Transcontinental phone calls were much more expensive in those days, and I'm sure we were among the phone company's favorite customers.

In case you're wondering why all this fuss about a six weeks' separation, I'll fill you in on a little scene that changed things around considerably and lengthened the six weeks to thirteen.

The picture that Harriet was originally scheduled to do was a modestly budgeted dramatic film called *Two O'Clock Courage*. In the meantime, Mark Sandrich, RKO's top director, was making preparations to film a Fred Astaire–Ginger Rogers blockbuster called *Follow the Fleet*. Fred and Ginger were number-one at the box office at the time and at the very peak of their popularity. Irving Berlin had written an excellent score which included such songs as "I'm Putting All My Eggs in One Basket," "We Joined the Navy," "Get Thee Behind Me, Satan," "Here Am I, But Where Are You?" and "Let's Face the Music." There were two other starring roles in the film which were to be played by Randolph Scott and Irene Dunne. Actually, Irene's role was a better part dramatically than Ginger's. There was only one thing holding up the start of the picture: for some reason, Miss Dunne suddenly became unavailable.

What followed would have done credit to any of a dozen "B" musicals. The script would have read like this:

FADE IN:

INT. PROJECTION ROOM #1—RKO STUDIOS

Mark Sandrich, bright young film director, is looking at screen tests in the hope of finding a beautiful young actress to star in his latest musical, Follow the Fleet. *Sandrich is obviously displeased with what he is watching.*

SANDRICH: (*Calling to projectionist in booth.*) Okay, I've seen enough!

The film stops and the lights come up.

SANDRICH: (*Continuing.*) Was that the last one?

PROJECTIONIST: (*From the booth.*) Yes, sir. You've seen ten of them this afternoon.

SANDRICH: Don't remind me.

He sits there dejectedly. Others come into the room. Among them is a young assistant director.

ASSISTANT DIRECTOR: Are you finished here, Mr. Sandrich?

SANDRICH: Yeah. Go ahead. What are you running?

ASSISTANT DIRECTOR: It's a dramatic test. A scene from *The Postman Always Rings Twice.* We're running it for wardrobe and make-up.

Sandrich gets up and heads for the exit as the lights go down and the test comes on the screen. We see a lovely young girl. Her voice and manner are warm, appealing. Sandrich hesitates at the door. He likes what he sees and hears. He slides into a seat in the back row and continues to watch, fascinated. The test ends. The lights come up. Sandrich springs to his feet.

Let's let Louella Parsons take it from there as we quote from her syndicated column of October 24, 1935:

"Who's that beautiful blonde?" demanded Sandrich. "I want to know all about her." "She's Harriet Hilliard," he was told, "brought here for a part in 'Two O'Clock Courage,'"

"That's what you think," he retorted. "She's Harriet Hilliard all right, but she's the girl who is going to have the role Irene Dunne won't be able to play in 'Follow the Fleet.'"

As usual Mark was right. Harriet, who had to rush off to Hollywood after her marriage to Ozzie Nelson, won't play the comparatively unimportant role in "Two O'Clock Courage" but will have the romantic lead opposite Randolph Scott in the new Astaire-Rogers musical. Harriet and Ozzie are building grand dividends for telephone stockholders with their daily long distance calls.

I had found out about it when Joe Nolan and Mark Sandrich had phoned me, pleading with me to talk Harriet into taking the role. It seems she had turned them down flatly, repeating that she didn't want to be a movie star—just a wife and mother. They had wanted her to sign a straight five-year deal, but I suggested a compromise arrangement whereby she would do three pictures a year. She warned them that her next project was to have a baby and so she might not be available when they wanted her. Fortunately, Joe and Mark were both family men and could sympathize with her point of view. They not only agreed to the arrangement, but promised to have her back home by Christmas.

So much has been written and said about the seamy side of Hollywood—the heartlessness, the selfishness, and the petty jealousies of the people involved in the moving picture industry—that I'd like to relate here one of the nice stories.

As I mentioned earlier, the part Harriet was now to play was really a better part than Ginger's. It was a warm and sympathetic role in contrast to the light and brittle part that Ginger was playing. Also, she had two fine torch songs to sing: "Here Am I, But Where Are You" and "Get Thee Behind Me, Satan."

Bear in mind that Ginger was the top female star on the RKO lot and one of the biggest names in the industry—and here was this band singer, who had never made a picture, coming in to share the spotlight. Also, like Ginger, the band singer was young, beautiful, and talented.

I suppose it would make for more interesting reading if Ginger had upstaged Harriet, tried to cut her part down, and let her know in no uncertain terms who the real star of the picture was. But, as I said, this is a nice story. From the moment they met, Ginger literally and figuratively threw her arms around Harriet. She helped her in every way possible, and the two of them quickly became the closest of friends. In fact, they were together so constantly that Mark Sandrich dubbed them Topsy and Eva.

The fall of 1935, although a difficult time for us personally, was successful professionally. The Silver Grill of the Hotel Lexington was a warm, intimate room, ideally suited to the college crowd that we attracted. The lighting and acoustics were perfect, and we broadcast from there coast to coast five nights a week. This plus our weekly commercial broadcasts with Bob Ripley and the tremendous newspaper coverage we were getting all added up to capacity business, even on Monday nights. Some of the stories that were written about us were pretty icky—the long-distance honeymoon stuff and Harriet rushing straight from the studio to her lonely hotel room to listen to me sing to her over the radio—squibs like the item that appeared in Sheila Graham's syndicated column: "If Ozzie Nelson's music sounds particularly sad this evening, blame heartless Hollywood. Ozzie's bride of a week has left home at the behest of Hollywod tycoons."

People seemed to love it, though, and as the dancers crowded up to the bandstand I spent most of my time answering questions about Harriet: Did she like Hollywood? When was she coming back? Was she homesick? I remember kidding her about being a bigger attraction three thousand miles away than she was on the bandstand.

The broadcoasts with Ripley were interesting, challenging, often hilarious, and occasionally frightening. Bob in private was a gentle, kind person, but he was painfully shy with strangers, and so facing the studio audience each week was a terrifying ordeal for him. He would usually fortify himself with a couple of drinks before the show, and on those evenings when he misjudged his capacity it was strictly "anything can happen" time.

Besides leading the band and singing, it was my job to play the part of the "doubting Thomas"—or devil's advocate—or whatever you want to call the guy who represents the public and says, "I find that hard to believe, you'll have to prove it to me." Some of the proof was a little less than convincing, since Ed Gardner was the guy who dug up most of the "Believe It or Not" items—or at least most of those we dramatized on the radio show. In fact, I often suspected that when Ed couldn't come up with a bona fide story, he either made one up or did a little embellishing.

I recall one story about a man who during World War I was supposed to have been on a ship that was torpedoed in the Baltic Sea. He had been scrubbing his clothes with a scrubbing brush at the time and was blown into the ocean but subsequently rescued. Fifteen years later the man was swimming at Coney Island when something hit him on the head. Lo and behold, it was his old scrubbing brush with his initials carved on it. I was supposed to say, "In order to believe that, Bob, I'd have to see the scrubbing brush" (whatever that would prove), whereupon Bob was supposed to say, "I thought you'd ask that, Ozzie, so here it is." Unfortunately, however, it was one of those nights when Bob had tossed down a couple too many, so he just started to laugh and said, "I had it here during dress rehearsal but I guess I lost it. I can't seem to find it anyplace."

I recall another night when one of the guests was a guy named "Shipwreck" Kelly, who held the world's record for flagpole sitting. In order to present Shipwreck dramatically to the studio audience, Ed Gardner had arranged to have him interviewed perched atop a twenty-foot flagpole. At the appropriate moment, we played a fanfare, the curtains were pulled open, and there sat Shipwreck. He was on top of the pole all right, but Ed had neglected to give him a script.

Since I was conducting both the interview and the band that night, the first inkling I had that anything was wrong was when I directed a question to Shipwreck at the top of the flagpole and the answer came from under the piano. In a frantic attempt to avert a minor catastrophe (bear in mind that there was no tape in those days—these shows were done "live"), Ed had grabbed a script, jumped under the piano in order to get an "off-mike" perspective and hide himself from the studio audience, and was reading Shipwreck's lines. As if this weren't confusing enough, Shipwreck decided to help things along by making a gallant but unsuccessful attempt to lip-sync to Ed's voice.

The effect was like a badly dubbed Italian film. By now the

studio audience was in hysterics. In spite of the pandemonium, however, I think I would have been able to finish the interview without breaking up if Ben Grauer, our announcer, hadn't stepped in and said, "I notice, Ozzie, that Shipwreck is not only a flagpole sitter but a ventriloquist as well."

Then there was the Sunday that I walked into rehearsal and was surprised to see a horse on the stage. He was standing inside a strange-looking block-and-tackle contraption that looked like a Rube Goldberg cartoon. "What's going on?" I asked Ed.

"Oz," he answered, "you've got to see this to believe it. We've got a grandmothere here who can lift a horse. Come on over here, Granny, and show him."

A nice-looking elderly lady came over. She got down on all fours, and they fastened some straps around her that were hooked to ropes that went around some pulleys and then were cinched to the horse. The old lady then pushed up from the floor and lifted the horse about two feet. It was an amazing performance.

About ten minutes later, Ben Grauer came in, and, at Ed's request, Granny repeated the performance for him. Then, a little later, she repeated it for Harriet, then for the boys in the band, and finally for Bob himself. (He had heard about her but had never seen her do her act.) I couldn't help but notice, however, that, each time she tried it, it seemed to get a little tougher.

I'm sure that by now you've guessed what happened: by the time we got to the dress rehearsal the poor old girl could barely get the horse off the floor, and when we went on the air she huffed and puffed but couldn't budge him an inch.

It was not at all uncommon for Ed to get a sudden inspiration and rewrite the script while we were actually broadcasting. I remember one Sunday when Bob and I were to interview a housewife from Atlanta. I don't recall the subject matter, but I'll never forget what happened. Just as Ben Grauer was finishing reading the middle commercial, Ed rushed out on stage and handed me some typed pages.

"New pages for the next spot," he whispered, and then rushed over to Bob and the lady from Georgia and handed new pages to them. Since I had to conduct a playoff to the commercial, there was no way for me even to glance at the script changes. Whatever Ed had given me I would have to read off cold.

The first line was mine. I read it and then looked up at the housewife, expecting her to read her line, which was next. Instead, however, she just stared at me with a frightened look on her face, so I filled in as best I could. The next line was Ripley's, but he just grinned at me, shook his head, and shrugged his shoulders. Somehow I managed to fumble my way down the whole page with neither Bob nor the housewife reading their lines. When I turned to the next page I saw what had happened. Ed had given me three copies of page 1, the lady three copies of page 2, and Bob three copies of page 3.

I'd like to relate one more Ed Gardner story before moving on. It's about a "Believe It or Not" that never did get on the air.

I went up to the J. Walter Thompson offices one afternoon to talk over some music cues with our arranger. Suddenly Ed came bursting out of his office. "Oz," he said, "I've got positive proof here of the most fantastic 'Believe It or Not' you've ever heard of in your life."

"Great," I said.

"There's only one problem," he went on, "I've gotta figure out a way to get it past the censors. Do you think they'd let us say 'bosoms' on the air?"

"Come on, Ed," I said, "just because a girl has big bosoms— that's not a 'Believe It or Not,' no matter how big they are."

"Who said anything about size," he said, "it's a question of numbers. She's got three of them!"

11

Joe Nolan and Mark Sandrich weren't quite able to keep their promise to have Harriet back home by Christmas, but they didn't miss by much, since she arrived a few days after New Year's.

The *New York Journal* of January 3, 1936, ran a picture of Harriet and me, taken just as she got off the train at Grand Central Station. The caption above the picture read, "Reunion at the Station." The *New York Daily News* ran a similar picture with the caption, "Ozzie Nelson Smiles." The *New York American* showed Harriet glowing radiantly and holding a huge box of roses. (I don't know what happened to the *Daily Mirror* reporter—maybe he went to the wrong station.) The caption above the picture in the *American* read: "Back to Ozzie—Bride Rushes Here From Hollywood."

The interview that followed told the whole story:

LONG DISTANCE MARRIAGE "THE BUNK"
DECLARES HARRIET HILLIARD

Blond Harriet Hilliard came rushing out of sun-drenched California yesterday into a bleak New York morning with this to say about long-distance marriages:

"They're the bunk."

"Nobody shows a profit but the telephone company."

The slim torch singer, who married boss Ozzie Nelson in October, is an old fashioned girl about marriage.

In a smart gray tailleur with a softly ruffled jabot, she sat in

114

her suite of the Lexington Hotel and intoned happily, "If you knew how glad I am to be back in New York. What do I like about it?—Ozzie."

In Miss Hilliard's opinion, this business of having an apartment in California while one's life partner maintains one in New York is strictly overrated.

Said Harriet, "I didn't get married to keep miles of territory between myself and my husband."

Follow the Fleet opened at Radio City Music Hall the second week in February, and the reviews of Harriet's performance were simply sensational. Henry Sutherland of the United Press wrote, "The picture should be memorable if only for the appearance of Harriet Hilliard. She all but steals 'Follow the Fleet' and gets this writer's vote for Hollywood's brightest film prospect." Harriet Parsons, substituting for Mama Louella, wrote, "If you've seen 'Follow the Fleet,' you know there's a new star on the Hollywood horizon—Harriet Hillard. She has everything, a beautiful face, a gorgeous figure, a swell singing voice and as if that weren't enough, the gal can act." William Boehnel of the *World Telegram* called her "one of the real screen finds of the season—intelligent, attractive and possessing an alluring singing voice." "Not only is she an antidote for sore eyes," wrote Mr. Boehnel, "but she can act as well." Richard Watts, Jr., of the *Herald Tribune* wrote: "The torch singing of Harriet Hilliard is so ingratiating that one is likely to wish the story had been omitted altogether." Regina Crewe in the *New York American* found her "as sweet an ingenue as the season has seen." The *New York Times,* the *Post,* the *Sun*—all were generous in their praise of Harriet's performance. The only dissenting vote came from a lady named Kate Cameron of the *Daily News,* and that wasn't exactly a dissenting vote—she merely abstained. She described Fred and Ginger as "brilliant" and "delightful"—which of course they were—and Irving Berlin's songs as "tuneful and witty," and she commented favorably on Mark Sandrich's "expert direction," but somehow she managed to sit through the entire picture and miss Harriet completely. Oh well, you can't win them all.

Incidentally, Harriet wasn't the only talented newcomer in *Follow the Fleet*. Buried in the credits, playing small parts, were a couple of other kids who went on to do pretty well for themselves—Lucille Ball and Betty Grable.

Besides our house in Hollywood, where we have lived since 1941, we have a beach house in Laguna Beach. And since it is only a little over an hour's drive from house to house, we more or less divide our time between the two places, depending to a great extent on the weather. As a result, we spend a lot of time on the freeway.

Every once in a while, when we run out of conversation about the grandchildren, we revert to an old time-killer from our one-nighter days, a question-and-answer game. You really can't call it a game, exactly—I guess a more accurate description would be a "conversation stimulator" or "thought provoker." As an example, you ask, "If you weren't married to me, who among our friends could you imagine yourself happily married to?" or "Who among our friends do you think is the most attractive physically?" Actually, these two are probably not very good examples—in fact, they're downright dangerous, and a wrong answer could result in ten or twelve miles of absolute silence.

One of our favorite questions (and one which is more loaded than it would seem at first blush) is, "At what three periods during your life do you think you were the happiest?" Of course, Harriet and I have had so many blessings that we have actually known very few periods that weren't happy ones, including the present, but among our early happy times we always remember fondly the winter and spring of 1936. Our professional lives were in high gear, we had no financial worries, we were living in the most exciting city in the world, we were young, and we were very much in love.

Along about the middle of March, Harriet found us a beautiful apartment in a new building at Fifty East Seventy-eighth Street, and we immediately became involved in buying furniture, drapes, carpets, and all the rest of the details that make furnishing your first home such an exciting experience.

116

Fifty East Seventh-eighth is on the corner of Madison, so it is only a few short blocks to Central Park. Central Park was really beautiful in those days, and you could walk through there even after dark. It was especially nice on sunny afternoons when all the proud young parents would be strolling along pushing their baby carriages. It wouldn't be too long before we'd be joining them, because we had just gotten the wonderful news that the stork (remember, we were all very naive back in the '30s) would be visiting us some time in October.

We had scarcely gotten settled in our new apartment when we had to take temporary leave of it to go on tour. Our original band manager, Milton Roemer, and I had come to an amicable parting of the ways, and most of our bookings were now being handled by Sonny Werblin of Music Corporation of America—except for our vaudeville dates, which were booked by an agent named Billy Kent, who specialized in that area.

My differences of opinion with Roemer, which were professional and not personal, had started when Harriet joined the band. Milt was very much against the idea of a girl vocalist with the organization and felt even more strongly about it when Harriet and I became romantically involved and then got married. He felt that our following, which consisted mostly of very young people, would not be interested in romantic songs sung by a husband and wife. In fairness to Roemer, I must remind you that this was at a time when motion picture studios were still reluctant to admit it when any of their stars got married or, heaven forbid, had children.

The period between 1935 and 1940 was a transitional one for bands. Due to constant exposure to music on radio and records, the public was becoming more and more knowledgeable, and many of the outstanding musicians and arrangers like Goodman, the Dorseys, Ellington, Shaw, Basie, Miller, Herman, and Teagarden were gradually emerging to challenge the popularity of the more-established bands, which played good music but of a more commercial variety. I include us in this latter category.

A poll of patrons of the New York Paramount Theater taken in July of 1936 and printed in the *New York Journal* showed us in

117

fourth place following Guy Lombardo, Louis Armstrong, and Eddie Duchin, and being followed by Ray Noble, Hal Kemp, Fred Waring, and Glen Gray—all of us "middle of the road" established bands. Anyone with any degree of sensitivity, however, had to be aware that the base of the public's musical appreciation was broadening and a whole new era was on the horizon.

What do you do when faced with a situation like this? To my mind, you continue to do what you've been doing, only try to do it a little better. You "do your thing," to use an overworked expression, in a way that pleases you and makes you happy. Carl Cons of *Downbeat* magazine, the musicians' bible, interviewed me at the Lexington Hotel, and wrote as follows:

"It's impossible to please everybody" says Nelson, "and the band leader who tries, usually loses his band's identity and style in the confusion."

Ricky said it even better in his recent smash-hit recording "Garden Party": "You can't please everyone, you've gotta please yourself." The Lombardos, Louis Armstrong, Fred Waring, Lawrence Welk—they all survived dozens of style changes by the simple process of continuing to do what they believed in and doing it to the best of their ability.

I don't recall ever sitting down and trying to analyze what we were doing back in the spring of 1936, but I do recall that we did the things we enjoyed doing and we did them as well as we could. Harriet and I continued to feature our boy-girl duets, and of course Harriet's singing of "Get Thee Behind Me, Satan" and "Here Am I, But Where Are You" from *Follow the Fleet* were always enthusiastically received. I was also very pleased that our band was finally getting the recognition it deserved as a musical unit when we had two hit instrumental recordings, "Rigamarolle" and "Swampfire."

Quoting again from the *Downbeat* article:

Ozzie's band is definitely a band of musical understatement, but its restraint implies so much both rhythmically and musi-

118

cally that the final effect is better than if they consciously strived for definite beats and effects. It is a band to be felt rather than heard, and it's subtle suggestions of melodic beauty and rhythmic patterns get under your skin.

As I look over old scrapbooks that were compiled at the time, I see that we were very, very busy during April, May, and June of 1936. For a girl who was pregnant, Harriet really did a lot of traveling—by car, by bus, by train, and by plane. We played ballrooms in Wilkes-Barre, Philadelphia, York, Trenton, Buffalo, Scranton, Shamokin, Greensberg (where the brakes on the bus gave way and we all, including Harriet and friend, bailed out in a hurry as it rolled downhill backwards), Dayton, Mt. Carmel, —the list could go on and on.

Interspersed with the ballroom dates were proms played at Yale, Harvard, Dartmouth, Virginia, North Carolina, Temple, and Lafayette and theater engagements at the Stanley in Pittsburgh, the Fox Theater in Washington, D.C., and the Paramount Theater in New York City.

By the time we opened at the Paramount, Harriet's pregnancy was beginning to show, so for the most part she worked in a close spotlight that never cut below her shoulders. We appeared at the Paramount for two weeks and then went to Loew's Fox Theater in Washington, so by the end of that engagement Harriet was pretty well along. Her biggest problem, besides getting into her stage costume, was the fact that the little guy she was carrying had evidently concluded that her singing was a cue for him to start kicking. Harriet said, "If he's got to kick me I wish he'd at least keep time with the music."

About eight o'clock in the morning of October 24, Harriet woke me up and said, "This is it!" We called a taxi and drove over to Doctors' Hospital, from where we phoned our doctor and Harriet's mother. Hazel and I waited out in the "father's pacing area" for a few hours and then were informed that things were progressing nicely but it would probably be quite a while before the baby would be born, so we went down to the coffee shop to kill some time. We were sitting there talking when a nurse came by and said to me, "Well, I'll bet you're feeling happy."

"Me?" I said.

"Yes. You're Ozzie Nelson, aren't you?"

"Yeah, why?" I asked.

"Didn't anyone tell you? Your wife had a little boy about a half-hour ago."

Most new-born babies don't look too good. I remember a guy who played bass with us for a while in the 1940s saw his son the day he was born and said, "I don't want to see him again until he's fourteen."

David, however, was one of those babies who look good right from the start. He was round and fat and bald-headed. Put a cigar in his mouth and you had Winston Churchill.

We had a very happy household. There was good old Harold, of course, who drove for us and carried on a running feud with the taxi drivers whose favorite retort was to yell "Pants presser!" at him. Then there was Geneva Henry, a nice, friendly lady who came in by the day and did the cleaning and cooking. And then there was "Jonesie"—Miss Elizabeth Jones, R.N., very formal and very British on the outside, but very warm and loving on the inside, who came home with Harriet and David from the hospital for "three weeks at the very most," but who managed to stay for six months.

I remember the day Jonesie told me she didn't like Americans. I said, "But we're Americans—don't you like us?"

"Of course," she said, "I just don't think of you as being American."

"What do you think of us as being?" I asked.

"English, of course," she answered.

Me with my New Jersey accent and Harriet right out of Des Moines, Iowa? English, indeed!

It wasn't until years later that I realized that Jonesie had been trying to be very complimentary.

Many beautiful thoughts have been written about mother love, but I have always liked a touching little piece that was written by Katherine Albert in the December 19, 1936, edition of *Radio Guide*. Of course, since she was quoting my wife talking about my son, it was especially appealing to me:

"Honestly," said Harriet, "I'm not really sentimental and I couldn't understand people who gushed over me before David was born, and talked about 'woman's great experience.'

"But then someone put that helpless little thing into my arms and I knew he was mine—mine and Ozzie's and I felt all warm and wonderful and I couldn't even speak. Such a tiny little boy! A screwed-up little face and little fists."

The band and I had started our second season at the Lexington Hotel early in October, and about the same time we had resumed our weekly broadcasts with Bob Ripley. A fine little blues singer named Shirley Lloyd had left Herbie Kay's band to fill in for Harriet both at the hotel and on our commercial broadcasts.

Harriet came back with us about the middle of December, but RKO had already notified her that they wanted her back in Hollywood in January to start filming two musicals, *New Faces of 1937* and *Life of the Party*. As a result, she had a difficult decision to make: should she take David along with her, or leave him with Jonesie, Geneva, Harold, and me?

Let's go back to Katherine Albert and her *Radio Guide* interview:

"No," she said, "I couldn't be that selfish—taking that little thing all the way across the country in January, running the risk of drafts and changes of food on the train.

"Besides, it wouldn't be fair to Ozzie to take him away.

"I know how I'll feel every time I get a new shapshot or Ozzie writes about a new tooth. But David doesn't need me nearly as much as I need him. Physically, he's in much better hands than mine."

So once again Harriet and I were separated by three thousand miles, and once again the nightly letters and long-distance telephone calls were the order of the day. This time, however, snap-shots and home movies were added. Reel after reel of home movies!

Holly Humphreys, besides being the anchorman of our brass section, was an ardent camera buff, so he took not only the still photos, but the home movies as well. As a special surprise for Harriet we filmed a little scenerio and sent it out to her. The script went like this:

Miss Jones and I are terribly concerned about the fact that David is bald-headed. It's especially puzzling in view of the fact that both Harriet and I have a full head of hair. Suddenly Miss Jones gets an idea. She digs into her purse and shows me a business card of a man who, she thinks, can solve the problem. [*This was all done in pantomime, of course, since sound with home movies was not yet available.*] I phone the man and he is, according to the sign on his desk, a "Doctor of Rugs." [*Actually he is Sid Brokaw, our fiddle player, slightly disguised with a very bad false moustache.*] He comes over to the house and after looking David over carefully, assures us he can handle the case with ease. Whereupon he shoos us out and goes to work. We see him preparing a fantastic concoction of shredded wheat, glue, sawdust, talcum powder and other assorted items and presumably applying all this to David's head. He then calls us in to view the result.

As we enter, David is covered by a large cloth towel. With a showmanlike flourish the "Doctor" whips off the towel to reveal a smiling David with a tremendous, luxuriant head of hair. The operation has been a rousing success.

When we saw the final result of our little movie we were all quite happy with it—that is, all except Jonesie. She was in shock for about three days. "I knew I was no beauty," she confided to me, "but I never realized that I look *that* bad."

"It's just a home movie," I protested.

"But everyone else looked perfectly normal," said poor Jonesie, "so that's what I must look like."

Of course, almost everyone has a similar reaction the first time he sees himself on the screen. We get used to seeing ourselves full-face reflected in the mirror, but when we see a side view, or any angle different from what we are accustomed to seeing, it's like looking at a different person.

After many years of seeing myself on television I have learned to live with my facial shortcomings, but still haven't forgotten the first time I saw myself on the screen. It was about 1932 or 1933, and I had made some sort of screen test for, I believe, Twentieth Century Fox. Bob Hope had made a test the same day and we both went into the screening room to see the results. He had never seen himself on the screen either.

They showed my test first. I couldn't believe what I saw. The make-up man had darkened my eyebrows and given me a cupid's-bow mouth, and with my blond wavy hair glistening under the lights I looked like a fugitive from a gay bar. Not only that, but my nose was too big, my eyes were too small, and, from the side, my teeth looked crooked. As I watched, I kept sliding further and further down into my seat. (Ginger Rogers once told me that the first time she saw herself on the screen she kept sliding down into her seat until she finally wound up right on the floor.)

Bob's test came on next, and he looked great. When the lights came up I got out of there as fast as I could. Bob was right behind me. "My God," I said, "did you see me? I looked like a big fag with a broken nose."

"Are you kidding?" he said. "You looked great. And speaking of noses, does my nose really look like that? And what about my chin?

I don't remember what else we said, but I remember I decided to walk back to the hotel, hoping I'd get run over by a bus, and Bob hailed a cab. As the cab pulled away, I heard a loud report like a pistol shot. I thought for a moment he had committed suicide, but the cab continued on, so I figured it was either the car backfiring or Bob had tried to shoot himself and missed. I must ask him about that sometime.

"Meanwhile, back at East 78th St.", as they used to say in the

123

silent flicks, the luxuriant head of hair David was sporting was, as you undoubtedly guessed, a wig. It wasn't just an ordinary wig, however, it was a beautiful auburn-colored job that looked amazingly natural. I had gotten it off a doll I had bought in a little shop on Sixth Avenue. One afternoon when Miss Jones wasn't looking I had tried it on David and it fit him perfectly. Although he was only four months old at the time, he seemed to enjoy wearing it—or, let's say, he didn't complain about it.

We normally had an hour off between the dinner and supper sessions at the Lexington, so I had always taken a cab up to our apartment to see David during the intermissions, Jonesie having arranged his schedule so I could give him his bottle at that time. With the advent of the wig, however, we worked out a nightly routine which added a little extra something to the visits.

Our first victim was Sonny Werblin. He had dropped by the Lexington to have dinner, so I asked him if he'd like to come up with me to see the baby. Meanwhile, I sneaked out and phoned Jonesie (who by this time was reconciled to the fact that she was living in a pretty nutty household) to get the wig ready. When we got up to the apartment I introduced Sonny to Jonesie and then I said, "Miss Jones, Mr. Werblin would love to see the baby." Jonesie said, "Certainly," and went into the nursery to get him. While we were waiting, I said, "Sonny, I hate to brag, but I really think he's the most beautiful baby I've ever seen in my life." Then Jonesie, smiling proudly, brought him in. If you can imagine being suddenly confronted by a four-month-old baby with an absolutely tremendous head of auburn hair, you can understand the look of panic that came over Sonny's face. He literally gasped a few times and then managed to blurt out, "Isn't he cute!" whereupon I broke up completely.

Sonny said later, "I thought to myself, 'What can I say? The kid looks like one of the Three Stooges.' " Then he added, "We've got to get Eddie Wolpin [one of our music publisher friends] up here to see this."

And that's how it started. It was like an endless chain. Over the period of the next few weeks there must have been twenty-five or thirty people lured up to see David's performance, and

124

strangely enough, everyone's reaction was the same: first the look of sheer panic which seemed to say, "Why didn't somebody warn me," and then the invariable "Isn't he cute!" and, of course, when we'd all stopped laughing, the victim or victims for the night would always say, "You've got to let me bring so-and-so up here to see this."

Reference to Eddie Wolpin brings to mind a whole group of guys that all of us bandleaders worked with very closely—the song pluggers. Nowadays every artist owns his own music publishing firm, but back in those days the music publishing business functioned separately. Each firm had its staff of song pluggers—or "contact men," as they liked to call themselves—whose job it was to see that their songs got played on radio. They were an enterprising group, mostly young guys in their late twenties or early thirties, all supersalesmen, and for the most part fun guys to be with. Much of their success depended on their ability to link up the right song with the right artist, and many of the songs that we introduced and that were associated with us through the years—such as "Love Letters in the Sand," "P.S., I Love You," "Winter Wonderland," "Santa Claus Is Coming to Town," "It's Dark on Observatory Hill," and many, many others—were brought to us by song pluggers who felt that these songs were best suited to our particular style.

Like musicians, most of the contact guys were very big in the practical-joke department and their humor often bordered on the gamy side. One night, two of them, whom I knew very well, came into the Lexington Hotel with a very attractive young girl whom one of the guys, Eddie Kelley, introduced as his niece who had just come down from Wellesley. According to Eddie, she had especially wanted to meet me because I was her favorite singer. She smiled at me very sweetly and asked if I took requests. I naturally said yes and asked her what song she wanted me to sing. Still smiling sweetly, she said that it wasn't a musical request but a personal one. It was indeed personal—very personal, very direct, and unprintable (at least in those days). Eddie and his friend practically fell off their chairs laughing. A few minutes later, all three of them, including the "niece from Wellesley," were on their way to the Roosevelt or the Pennsylvania to pull the same gag on one of the Lombardos or Tommy Dorsey.

Then there was the night back in the fall of 1930 just after we had closed at Glen Island Casino when one of the song pluggers invited me to a big party at his apartment on Park Avenue. It was a black-tie affair, and he told me he had invited some very special people. The apartment wasn't difficult to find because I could hear the music and the party noises as soon as I got off the elevator. I rang the bell, and a very attractive young lady opened the door and said, "Good evening, won't you come in?" Okay, what's strange about that? I'll tell you what was strange about it. She was stark, staring au naturel—completely in the buff. I was careful not to step on her feet as I went in because she didn't even have shoes on. I suppose I should have said, "My wife has an outfit just like that," except that I wasn't married and I hadn't heard the joke yet.

New Faces of 1937 and *Life of the Party* took about three-and-a-half months to film. The separation this time was much more difficult for Harriet than for me. Business at the Lexington continued to be good, and there were always interesting people dropping by. I spent a lot of time with David, who was a healthy, happy baby and a lot of fun to be with. Once a week I'd go over to Englewood for a visit with my mother, Al and Kay, and Don. Don was a bright, well-adjusted little fellow, and every Saturday Harold would pick him up in the car and drive him over to the hotel (we played a luncheon session on Saturdays), and he'd get up on the bandstand and sing a couple of numbers with the band. He loved it and so did the patrons. His big number was a scat version of "Between the Devil and the Deep Blue Sea" which he had memorized note for note from a Cab Calloway recording. He also appeared occasionally on the Ripley show. Whenever one of the dramatizations called for a little boy, Don played the part. He seemed to specialize in presidents: he played Washington as a boy, Lincoln as a boy, and FDR as a boy.

I managed to keep in pretty good physical shape. I'd go up to Stillman's gymnasium and box a couple of times a week—being careful, of course, in my choice of sparring partners—and every night after work I'd walk or jog, depending on the weather, from the hotel to the apartment. It was about thirty-five blocks, so it was a good workout.

Meanwhile, poor Harriet out on the coast was lonesome, homesick, and for the most part bored to death. "Here I am," she wrote me, "sitting on a crummy movie set doing nothing while I'm missing three precious months of my baby's life that I can never recapture."

Most people who have never worked in pictures don't realize how really tedious it can be. There are only two jobs on the set that are any fun—the director's and the camera operator's. Directing, of course, is a gigantic ego trip, and if you have a good script and good actors you can get by with little more than a beard, a pipe, and one of those jackets with leather patches at the elbows. Camera operating, however, is a different thing. The operator is strictly on his own. He must follow the action smoothly and keep the picture framed properly. It's an interesting job, but one that requires good coordination and quick reflexes. In filming our television show we were fortunate in having with us two of the finest camera operators in the business—Bobby Moreno, who is now much in demand as a first camerman, and Bill Fraker, who did the brilliant operating in the chase sequences of *Bullitt* and whose beautiful photography for *Rosemary's Baby* and for *Paint Your Wagon* were worthy of Academy Awards.

The nicest part of any separation, of course, is the getting back together again, and when Harriet arrived at Newark Airport we were all waiting for her—David, Jonesie, Geneva, Harold—all of us. The landing, however, turned out to be a little more spectacular than we had anticipated. We wondered about the firetrucks and ambulance that rushed out and took strategic positions on the airfield, but it wasn't until the plane landed that we learned that something had gone wrong with the landing gear and that all the passengers had been strapped together in the back of the plane in the event of a crash landing. However, big hugs from Harriet's two boyfriends soon made everything all right.

The month of April in 1936 was notable in the family files

for one other reason—the purchase of what we came to refer to as "Nelson's Folly." Actually that was a misnomer. If it was a folly, it was a grand luxurious one. It happened as follows. One day I said to Harold, "I think we're about due for a new car. How about looking around to see if there's anything you especially like."

About three days later, Harold said, "I don't want you to think I'm crazy, but there's a salesman downstairs with a car that nobody in the world can afford, but I finally promised him you'd take a ride around the park in it but that you were definitely not interested in buying it."

Harriet, Harold, and I went downstairs and there it was, standing majestically by the curb—the most beautiful town car I had ever seen in my life. We got in and sank back into the luxurious grey upholstered seats and Harold drove us—not around the park, just around the block.

The salesman was waiting for us in front of the apartment. "Well," he said, "What do you think?

"It's beautiful," Harriet said. Then somebody said, "How much?" Harriet and Harold both swore later that it was me who said it, but I don't think it was.

"Seven thousand dollars," said the salesman casually. (Once again I'd like to remind you of the difference in the value of a dollar then and now. Seven thousand dollars in 1937 was the equivalent of close to twenty-five thousand today.)

Somebody took my checkbook and fountain pen out of my pocket. Harriet and Harold claimed later that that too was me. They may have been right about the checkbook, but I swear it was Harold who handed me the pen.

"What are you doing?" said Harriet.

"What do you think I'm doing?" I said. "I'm writing the man a check for seven thousand dollars." I hesitated a moment and looked up.

"Well, don't stop now," she said. "Keep writing."

"Yeah!" said Harold. "Keep writing."

"You stay out of this, Harold," I said. "You've caused enough trouble for one day."

128

12

John Reber, who was in charge of radio for the J. Walter Thompson ad agency and the liaison between them and Standard Brands (our sponsors on both the Joe Penner and the Bob Ripley shows), was a very nice person. He was a tough businessman and could drive a hard bargain when necessary, but he was also a dedicated family man and was terribly concerned about the fact that Harriet and I were separated so much. He once told Ed Gardner that he had never known two people so much in love or so ideally suited for one another as Harriet and I, and yet he had grave doubts that any marriage could survive two careers separated by three thousand miles.

He phoned me one day and said that he'd like to have dinner with us and discuss plans for the following radio season—the season of 1937–38. Very briefly, his thoughts were as follows: He felt that the Ripley show had run its course, and he was looking for a new star and a new format—and that the new format would include Harriet and me, but he wanted the show to emanate from Hollywood instead of New York because he didn't like the idea of our being separated.

There was one problem: Los Angeles had very little night life. Unlike New York, where there were any number of hotels we could play (including, of course, the Lexington, where we could have stayed forever), there were only three spots in Los Angeles that featured name bands—the Ambassador Hotel, the Biltmore Hotel, and the Palomar Ballroom. What's more, each of these at that time brought in bands for limited engagements of four weeks at most. The problem was whether the radio show could pay enough money so that I could afford to maintain the band without outside work. I made a suggestion that Mr. Reber, fair man that he was, immediately agreed to. I suggested that I write down what I considered to be an equitable salary for Harriet and me and then what I thought would be fair weekly salary for the band personnel and we would total it up and see if we could work out a deal on that basis. He told me to go ahead and write it all down, which I did—on the back of the menu. I then said, "Here, would you like to add it up?"

"No," he said, without looking at the figures. "Do you think these are all equitable amounts?"

"Yes, I do," I said.

"Okay," said Mr. Reber. "You add it up, and whatever it comes to you've got a deal on that basis."

And so in September of 1937, after subletting our Seventy-eighth Street apartment, the entire Nelson entourage moved to California: fourteen musicians; one arranger; one secretary (Myra Wallace, a lovely girl and a dedicated person); one baby nurse, Rose Foster (Jonesie having returned to England); one Harold Lane; plus Harriet, David, and I. The boys in the band drove their cars, and the rest of us went by train—that is, all except Harold: he drove the "Folly." He said it rode beautifully all the way. There was only one problem: it averaged five miles to a gallon.

The house we rented during our stay in California was a charming English Tudor-type house that belonged to Charlie Farrell. It was located on Toluca Lake, and was literally a stone's throw from the first tee of Lakeside Golf Club. Needless to say, I wasted no time in applying for membership.

Lakeside was a pretty great place back in those presmog days of 1937 and 1938. Bob and Bing were members, as were Dick Arlen, Johnny Weissmuller, Jimmy McLarnen, Charlie Barton, Johnny Gallaudet, Ray McCary, Lloyd Nolan—all good people and fine golfers (you had to be or you'd soon find yourself without any pocket money).

It was not a particularly difficult course except for one hole, the thirteenth, which was a par 5 and a tough one. You had to put together two long woods and then hit a long accurate iron shot to reach the green, which was nestled nicely in the middle of a clump of trees across the Los Angeles River. The river was never very deep except after a severe rainstorm, but it was definitely a mental hazard. It got to be a standing gag. Harriet would take a look at my face as I came in the house and say, "I know. You would have had a good score if it hadn't been for that *'goddam thirteenth hole!'* " This last was always said in unison.

I hadn't played a great deal of golf up until then, and I did everything wrong. I gripped the club like a baseball bat, took a short fast backswing, and punched at the ball instead of swinging smoothly. But I played so often (at least eighteen and sometimes twenty-seven holes every day) that my score kept improving in spite of my horrible form. Even so, the first-tee bargaining was so larcenous that by the time I got my handicap down to a 10 I had to shoot in the seventies or lose all bets.

The format finally decided on by John Reber for our 1937-38 season was an interview-type program which gave behind-the-scenes glimpses of some of the outstanding figures of the motion picture industry. The star of the show was Feg Murray, a syndicated cartoonist, and the show itself was patterned after Feg's popular newspaper feature, "Seeing Stars."

Once again Harriet and I were called on, not only for the musical part of the show, but also to help out with the interviews. It was a relaxed show, easy to do, and gave us an opportunity not only to renew our acquaintance with some old friends but also to get to know some people whom we had long admired but had never met. Since the band included several home-movie buffs, we have some wonderful films that would make Harriet's old boss and current Hollywood film historian, Ken Murray, jealous. We ran them recently and it was a real treat to see us with

Humphrey Bogart, George Raft, Tyrone Power, Pat O'Brien, Walt Disney, Ralph Bellamy, Ida Lupino, Billie Burke, John Barrymore, John McCormick, Francis Lederer, Joan Bennett, Bela Lugosi, Boris Karloff—the list could go on and on—and all of us looking so discouragingly young.

Since the radio show only took up two days a week including rehearsals, the fall of 1937 was really a delightful one for Harriet, David, and me. After the hectic years of working day and night and the frustration of being separated so much of our married life, it was wonderful to have our little family together. David was getting sturdier and handsomer by the day. His once-bald head was now covered with beautiful golden curls, and his perpetual angelic smile belied the mischief that he was constantly planning. He was quite a handful. Look away from him for a moment and he would hit you with a baseball. Let him out of your sight for ten seconds and he would disappear. He's the only kid I've ever heard of who ran away from home at the age of fourteen months. How he got three blocks away in two minutes we'll never figure out.

Like all parents, Harriet and I were soon faced with the inevitable problem: to spank or not to spank. The question was answered, as far as one of us was concerned, one afternoon when Harriet was driving and David was sitting in my lap. For lack of something to do, I guess, he decided to pat me on the face. This went on for a little while, and then he gave me one pat just a little harder than the rest. I responded by giving him a sharp little pat on the cheek. He then slapped me a little harder, and I immediately slapped him. He then slapped me really hard and I slapped him right back just as hard. He looked at me and two big tears welled up in his eyes. He buried his little face in my arms and started to cry. I said to Harriet, "I'll never hit this little guy again as long as I live." And I never did. Coward that I am, I left the miserable job to Harriet from then on.

Although we had made a couple of changes in our band (Irving Gellers was now playing piano for us and Bill Stone was on tenor saxophone), our personnel had remained substantially the same through the years. For the first few months in California, the boys had been content to take it easy and just play for the radio show and an occasional record date. But along about December we all started to get restless, so when MCA called us with an offer to play at the Victor Hugo, a new supper club that was opening in Beverly Hills, we decided to accept.

Meanwhile, Harriet had accepted an offer to costar with Fred MacMurray in a picture at Paramount Studios called *Cocoanut Grove.* It was a high-budgeted musical and had a fine cast which included Eve Arden, Ben Blue, the Yacht Club Boys, Rufe Davis, and Harry ("Sweet Leilani") Owens and his Royal Hawaiian Orchestra. One of the songs Harriet got to sing in the picture was a commercial little jingle called "Says My Heart," which became a very big hit and was number one on the "Hit Parade" for several weeks. This, following closely upon George Jessel's "Roses in December," which she had introduced in *Life of the Party,* gave Harriet two big hits in a row.

The Victor Hugo engagement was pleasant enough and business was good, but we were not comfortable in the room. Acoustically it was very bad. Anything that reflects light also reflects sound (or so it seems to me), and since the room was mirrored we had to play "under wraps" most of the time. This was particularly bothersome to the brass, who had to keep the mutes in or play into the music stands. Also, because of the prices, the location, and the general atmosphere of the place, the clientele was largely composed of older people who would have been just as happy with a "society" orchestra or a rhumba band.

Better times were just ahead, however. A couple of months later we went into the Palomar Ballroom, where we could blast away to our hearts' content and play our best arrangements in the knowledge that our audience understood and appreciated what we were doing. Harriet didn't work with us during either of these engagements, but we did have a fine vocalist, a beautiful young lady named Emily Lane who really sang up a storm.

A frightening episode occurred during the first week in March of 1938. Hollywood at that time was separated from the San Fernando Valley by the Los Angeles River. The river, as I mentioned earlier, was actually just a small stream except when there were severe rainstorms, at which time it rose to considerable size. It had been raining very hard for a period of several days and the river was overflowing, so certain areas in the valley were being evacuated.

I had been in Hollywood working with the writers trying to figure out an interesting angle for our interview with Ralph Bellamy, who was to be one of the guests on the Feg Murray show the following Sunday.

Harold had picked me up at the J. Walter Thompson office at about four o'clock. When we reached the bridge at Barham Boulevard near the Warner Brothers studio, however, we discovered that it had been washed away, so we decided to drive south a few miles and see if the bridge at Lankershim Boulevard was still passable.

Meanwhile, the river was rising at an alarming rate, and the news coming over the car radio was getting progressively worse. Houses were being washed away not only in the valley but in many other areas throughout Los Angeles County, and the toll of the dead and missing was mounting steadily.

All telephones were out in the Toluca Lake area, and even though no serious flooding had been reported there, I was still concerned about Harriet and David and I knew that she was concerned about me.

When Harold and I arrived at the bridge near Universal, it was still holding, but the river at that point was rushing with such velocity that we weren't sure if it would be safe to drive the car across. Also, we couldn't tell how deep the water was in the streets on the other side, so we decided that Harold should wait in the car while I walked across the bridge to investigate.

As soon as I got across the bridge I realized that there was no way a car could get through. The water was knee-deep in some places and waist-deep in others. I figured I'd better go back with Harold and try to find some other place to cross. I turned to go back and I couldn't believe what I saw: the bridge was gone! Not just part of it, but the entire bridge. The roar of the rushing water was so loud that I hadn't heard it being swept away, although it had been only fifteen or twenty feet in back of me. If I had crossed it ten or fifteen seconds later I would have been swept away with it.

It was only a little over a mile back to our house at Toluca Lake, but it seemed much longer trudging through the mud and water. We were lucky. Although the water in the lake rose up close to our house, we experienced no ill effects except for being without our telephone and electricity for a couple of days. Some of our friends, however, were not so fortunate—for instance, Ralph Bellamy. He had plenty to talk about when he came on the show the following Sunday. His entire house, all his furniture—everything he owned, even the property on which his house had been standing—all of it had been swept away.

About the only good that came out of the whole debacle was that my old nemesis, the thirteenth hole at Lakeside, had been washed into the river. When they rebuilt it, they put it on the near side and it immediately took two strokes off my score: I now got an 8 on it instead of a 10.

One day shortly after we had finished our engagement at the Palomar Ballroom—I would guess it was near the end of April or the early part of May—Hardy said, "I just want you to know, sir, that Gladys and I were terribly sorry to hear that your radio program had been cancelled."

Hardy was our butler, and Gladys, his wife, worked as cook and upstairs maid. They were a delightful couple and had joined our household shortly after we arrived in California. Hardy, who looked like he had just stepped out of an English movie, was the absolute, perfect butler, and Gladys was a sensational cook. Harriet has often said that practically everything she knows about running a household she learned from Hardy.

One day when she and Hardy were preparing for a dinner party to be given that night and she was overcome with the usual last-minute panic so familiar to every young hostess, Harriet said

135

"Oh, Hardy, do you think I will ever be a really good house-keeper?"

"No, madam," answered Hardy, "you are much too nice. But it will always be a great pleasure for people to work for you."

If it seems a bit ludicrous for a couple as young as Harriet and I to have been living this high on the hog, I can only reply that it certainly was. We realized it and enjoyed every minute of it. One of the many areas where Harriet and I have always been in complete agreement is in the determination of a life style. We both feel that we are willing to work long hours and with total dedication, but as compensation we like to live well and enjoy the good things of life. This is true today, and it was true back in 1938 at Toluca Lake.

I remember one night we were lying in bed—there was no activity of any sort going on, we were just lying there—when suddenly the bed gave way. We both got to laughing. I remember Harriet's saying, "This is really ridiculous. Here we are, you and I and one small boy with a staff of a butler, a maid, a gardener, a chauffeur, a nurse, and a secretary, and we don't even have a bed to sleep in."

"Well," I said, "I guess we'll just have to hire a handyman and get it fixed."

When Hardy had expressed his regets that our radio show had been cancelled, I wasn't quite sure how to respond, because this was the first I had heard of it. As I recall, I mumbled my thanks for his kind thoughts and immediately phoned the guys at the Hollywood office of J. Walter Thompson, only to discover that they had heard nothing about the cancellation either. Although I never did get adjusted to Hardy's calling me "sir," I was well-enough acquainted with the protocol to know that butlers, along with reporters and police informers, should never be called on to reveal the source of their information. I also knew that the backstairs grapevine was seldom wrong. Sure enough, about three or four days later I received a letter from John Reber confirming the unhappy news.

In show business, when the show closes, you hit the road. We had had five wonderful years with the same sponsor, Standard Brands. They had given us the opportunity to live at home like a normal family while broadcasting to millions of people week after week. As a result of this constant exposure, plus our recordings and hotel broadcasts, we were well known in just about every area of the United States. There was no problem about getting bookings. There were any number of fine theaters, ballrooms, hotels, and nightclubs with not enough name attractions to fill their schedules. Our only problem was one of readjustment. We had become used to living a normal life, and now we had to face the fact that show business is anything but normal. It's interesting, even fascinating, and its financial returns, when you hit it right, are fantastic. But there comes a time when you have to get your behind up off the sofa and get moving. At least that's what I told Harriet—or maybe it was Harriet who said it to me. At any rate, along about the middle of August we said goodbye to Hardy and Gladys, Feg Murray, Toluca Lake, and the Lakeside Golf Club, and headed back to New York. It would be three long years before we returned to California, but then we would be back to stay.

13

We opened a two-week engagement at the Strand Theater in New York City in September of 1938. Vaudeville theaters—or presentation houses, as they were often called—furnished an especially good medium for us. Harriet and I were basically entertainers rather than straight singers, and yet our orchestra was well-enough established as a "name band" for us to qualify in that category during a time when most theaters had established a "name band" policy in booking their attractions.

Benny Goodman, Artie Shaw, Tommy and Jimmy Dorsey, Duke Ellington, Count Basie, Woody Herman, and Glenn Miller had all become big box-office names in the preceding few years, but since the drawing power of each of these bands was based on the tremendous musical talent of the leader, it followed that their stage shows were mainly in the nature of expertly played concerts where the leader himself rarely talked to the audience except to announce the title of the next number or to introduce a vocalist or one of the accompanying acts. These acts, which usually included some sort of dance team and a stand-up comic, were booked by the individual theater managements and were brought on as a change of pace between musical numbers.

Since I could hardly be classed as a saxophone virtuoso, there was no way I could compete on a straight musical basis, so I tried to construct our stage shows like miniature musical comedies. Also, since we had been visiting people in their homes via radio for the past eight or nine years, I felt that the audiences thought of us as friends as well as entertainers.

Rather than have each theater furnish acts to work with us, we made it a practice to select our own acts so that we could integrate them into our overall production.

In order to get our show working smoothly before playing the New York Strand, we booked the week of September 1 at the State Theater in Hartford. We had already decided on Don Cummings, who had worked with us several times before and was to work with us many times in the future. Don was a brilliant young comic from the West Coast who, as a teenager, had won several roping contests. His act consisted mainly of clever comedy bits interspersed with some really sensational roping tricks. He and I had worked out so many routines together that it finally reached a point where he had a tough job reconstructing his act when he wasn't working with us.

When I heard we had been booked into the Strand, I asked Bill Kent, who was still handling theater bookings for us, to get us a girl dancer to work in the early part of the show. I explained that she didn't have to be a Ginger Rogers or a Ruby Keeler—just as long as she was young and attractive. As it turned out, the girl he got for us was very young—about sixteen—and looked great. Her dance routine was nothing to get excited about except for her finish, which was a succession of back flips where she landed on one foot. This, too, would have been rather commonplace, except that she did the entire routine on a small platform about the size of a card table. This not only made the act exciting but presented us with a problem. How do we get that damn table out to the middle of the stage without a "stage wait" or at least an awkward light change?

Fortunately, two stagehands at the second show in Hartford gave us the answer when they got their cues mixed up and brought the table out after our second band number instead of at the end of our third band number, where it had been scheduled. The resulting confusion proved to be so hilarious (the audience always loves it when something goes wrong on stage) that we enlarged on

139

it and made it a planned "accidental" routine. Here's the way we did it the next show and for all the shows that followed. At the end of our first band number, and just as I was starting to announce the second number, our piano player, Irv Gellers, would walk off stage and immediately return carrying the table, assisted by good old Harold Lane. (Yes, Harold also did stage bits.) The other guys in the band would wave them back and I would join in, calling out, in a stage whisper, "Not yet . . . later." This would be repeated at the end of the second number with my again waving them back and their registering disgust and embarrassment, much to the delight of the audience. At the end of the next band number I would announce something to this effect: "And now we'd like to introduce to you a lovely and talented young lady who has just joined our organization. Her name is Mary Lou and she does a sensational dance on a table. I would then gesture toward Gellers. This time, however, he would be absentmindedly staring into space. The band guys would try unsuccessfully to get his attention, and I would repeat, much louder, "She does a sensational dance on a *table!*" By now the audience would be joining in, trying to get Irv's attention, and I'd finally call out, "Tyrone! Will you please get the table!"

The routine never missed, and Mary Lou played all our vaudeville dates for the next two years.

Other acts that worked with us many times with great success were Bob Dupont, a tremendously clever comedy juggler; the Ghezzi Brothers, who did a show-stopping hand-balancing act; Stone and Barton, brilliant tap dancers; and three really great comedy dance teams, Armanda and Lita, Grace and Nikko, and the sensational team of Harris and Shore. Then, of course, there were the famous Hartmans, Paul and Grace—but more about them later.

Ballroom dance teams were extremely popular in the thirties, especially in nightclub and hotel floor shows. They were also notorious among bandleaders for being temperamental, especially as to how their music was played. Strangely enough, although we must have worked with thirty-five or forty dance teams with all sorts of varying tempos and rhythms, we never had any difficulty accompanying any of them. There was one act, however, that we never could seem to satisfy. It was called Pansy the Horse and consisted of two guys in a horse costume and a shapely girl, who acted as the trainer, putting the horse through its paces. At the end of the act the horse went into a little dance, and there was where we ran into trouble.

The owner of the act was a guy named Andy Mayo, a pleasant enough fellow offstage, but once he got inside that horse outfit he became a changed man. No matter how we played the music, Andy didn't like it and he would let us know about it—right on stage. All of a sudden we'd hear a voice bellowing out from under the horse, "Faster! Faster! Slower! Louder! Softer!" People in the first couple of rows would look around in bewilderment, wondering where the voice was coming from. Fortunately, Andy played the front end of the horse. A voice coming out of the horse's rear end would have been just too much.

Oh, yes—you might be interested to know that the shapely girl came out to Hollywood a few years later and made quite a name for herself as Virginia Mayo.

Our engagement at the Strand was memorable for a couple of reasons: it was our first New York theater engagement in over two years, and it marked David's first stage appearance.

Wayne Morris and Johnny ("Scat") Davis were both under contract to Warner Brothers at that time, and since the Strand was a Warner Brothers theater they appeared on the bill with us to plug their latest pictures. Since they were both personable and talented young guys, they were a valuable addition, not only to the entertainment but to the box office as well.

David's nurse, Rose Foster—or "Nana," as she preferred to be called—used to bring David over to the matinee performances, and he'd stand in the wings and bounce up and down, fascinated with the lights and the music. At the end of each performance, the entire company would come on stage for the final "curtain," which actually was effected by the stage lowering as the lights dimmed out. One afternoon, much to our surprise, as Wayne came

141

on for the finale he brought David with him, carrying a bunch of flowers. Evidently, our young son enjoyed the tremendous applause his appearance had engendered, because the next afternoon, right after Harriet had finished singing "The Kid in the Three-Cornered Pants" (a novelty song that had been written especially for us a few months after David was born), we heard a fresh burst of applause followed by "oohs" and "ahs" from the audience, and there, over by the wings but well out on the stage, stood David, smiling and bowing, just as he had seen his Mommy and Daddy do.

Needless to say, Nana kept a closer watch on him from then on, and his bowing was restricted to backstage for the stagehands. We felt that he was a bit young to embark on a stage career at twenty-three months. Besides, he didn't have a union card.

By one of those strokes of good fortune, a fan in the audience happened to be taking pictures of the show that afternoon (contrary to theater regulations) and sent us a photograph of the event. I still have it hanging on the wall of my office.

At the conclusion of the Strand engagement, Wayne and Johnny went back to Hollywood, but the Nelson entourage hopped a train to Richmond, Virginia, where we opened at the National Theater the next day. The following week we were in Fort Wayne, then Indianapolis, then Toledo, then Columbus, followed by Youngstown, Akron, Cleveland, Philadelphia, Baltimore, and Washington. It was a little like those montages you see on the "Late Show" movies with Dan Dailey, Alice Faye, and June Haver, with the train wheels speeding down the tracks superimposed over copies of *Variety* and flashes of theater marquees.

In case you're wondering where David was all this time, he was right with us. We have some wonderful movies of his second birthday party in Columbus, Ohio. There were no other children there, but David seemed delighted with the whole affair because he was surrounded by all his best friends. Somehow, I don't think he thought of himself as a little boy anyway—I think he considered himself one of the musicians.

Even with Nana along, Harriet had a busy time of it because

David was the most tireless, energetic little guy I've ever seen. A reporter who interviewed Harriet for the *Fort Wayne Sentinel* on October 3 wrote as follows:

"Ozzie handles the business and I handle the domestic problems," Harriet said in an interview today. And she will tell you that a two year old boy is a real problem.

David, who is blond and tousled-haired, is a real boy—into everything. The interview was interrupted briefly when David managed to open the door of the hotel room and escape down the hall. His mother quickly brought him back and locked the door to prevent any further explorations.

The theater tour was rewarding in many ways. Business was excellent, the audiences were warm and enthusiastic, and the reviews, without exception, were most flattering—but it was also tiring and confining. The least number of shows we ever did was four a day, and since there was never quite enough time to go anywhere between shows, we were virtually prisoners in our dressing rooms. As a result, we were very happy to settle down for awhile at the Gold Coast Room of the Drake Hotel in Chicago, where we opened November 5.

Rose Anne Stevens joined us at the Drake. Rose Anne—or "Rosie," as we called her—was a great-looking teenager with a terrific personality. She had sung with a few local bands in Fort Wayne and had come over to audition for us when we played the Lyric Theater in Indianapolis. We billed her as the "Indiana Hep-cat" ("hep" being the 1939 equivalent of "hip").

Rosie fit in perfectly with the organization and was to be with us as band vocalist for almost three years, enabling Harriet to limit her performances to special appearances.

As I recall, we were at the Drake for almost six or seven weeks. I know for sure that we closed there in time to spend Christmas back home. Well, not exactly "home"—we spent it at the Essex House (our Seventy-eighth Street apartment was still being rented), but at least it was in New York and gave us a chance

143

to visit our family during the holidays. It also gave David a chance to renew acquaintances with some of his animal friends at the Central Park Zoo.

The start of 1939 found us hitting the theater circuit again. We played Brooklyn, Newark, Chicago, Providence, and Dayton and then returned to New York in time to open with a big show on February 19 at Billy Rose's Casa Mañana—a huge, Broadway-type theater-restaurant on Seventh Avenue in New York City.

Billy Rose was a dour, arrogant little man, but he was a great showman who did things on a lavish scale. The show was set up originally in straight vaudeville style, but after four weeks he dropped some of the acts and set up the production as more of a musical revue. John Murray Anderson staged the show and directed it. The chorus of forty-eight dancers included some fantastically talented kids, among them Vera Ellen, who later starred in many musicals at Twentieth Century Fox, and Miriam Nelson, who became one of Hollywood's leading choreographers.

The acts included some of the biggest names in show business, such as Willie and Eugene Howard, the Andrew Sisters—at the height of their popularity with "Bei Mir Bist Du Schön" and "Begin the Beguine"—Gene Austin with his ever-popular "My Blue Heaven," Gil Lamb, Mario and Floria, Gloria Gilbert—all great entertainers.

The job, for me at least, was interesting but exhausting. I emceed the entire proceedings and joined Harriet singing a couple of duets during her appearance in the show.

A twelve-piece house band accompanied the other acts, but our band played for the dancing and, of course, accompanied Harriet and me. The band started at seven o'clock and finished at three. It made for a long, long night.

It was a source of great satisfaction that, even surrounded by all these "socko" acts, as *Variety* would put it, and playing to what was acknowledged to be the toughest audience in the world —a New York nightclub audience—Harriet with her quiet effectiveness and great charm managed to stop the show at every performance.

144

The show ran for twelve weeks and could probably have run longer, but by this time Billy had become involved in staging his Aquacade at the World's Fair. The World's Fair was situated in Flushing Meadows, on Long Island, which was just far enough out of town to hurt New York City theater and restaurant business, so Billy, understandably, figured the smart thing to do was close down the Casa Mañana while he was still ahead.

Show closings are always sad occasions anyway, but this one was especially so for the dancers and showgirls who had rehearsed diligently for many weeks and had expected the show to run at least through the summer. Since business had been good, it came as quite a surprise when a notice was posted on the bulletin board that the show would close in one week. It was especially surprising to me, because our contract carried a four weeks' cancellation clause, and I so informed the stage manager.

The next morning my phone rang at about eleven o'clock. It was Billy Rose. "I hope I didn't wake you up, Oz," he said solicitously. This was the first time he had ever acknowledged that he knew my name. He then went on to explain that he hadn't realized that we had the four-week clause in our contract, but that he had looked it up and I was absolutely correct. "You've got me over a barrel, Oz," he went on, "but if I keep the show open I stand to lose a fortune. All I can do is appeal to your kindness and generosity. Everybody in town says you're a hell of a fine guy. If you could see your way clear to let me off the hook I'd feel indebted to you for the rest of my life." I could almost hear the violins playing in the background.

I immediately assured him that it would be fine with me—that we hadn't had a vacation in three years and would actually look forward to having a little time off.

"I can't tell you how much I appreciate this," said Billy. "You're a real friend. As I say, I'd love to keep the show open, but I just can't afford it. I'm sure you understand."

By this time it was getting a little embarrassing, so I thought I'd change the subject.

"How are things going at the Aquacade?"

"Terrific," he answered. "Just between you and me, I'll make

145

a million dollars on it before the summer is over. And thanks again, Oz," he added. "I'll never forget you for this."

A couple of hours later I went down to Lindy's Restaurant to get something to eat. There was Billy sitting at his usual table near the window. (There is an old Broadway legend that you get bigger portions if you sit near the window.) I said, "Hi, Billy!" Billy didn't even look up. He just kept right on eating. He did, however, acknowledge my greeting by raising one finger from his fork as he raised it to his mouth, and I must say he did it with flair. He stayed right in rhythm. He didn't miss a beat.

The two weeks' vacation proved to be a welcome relief. We went to Miami Beach and just swam, played tennis, and lay around in the sun. Since it was the first time off we had had since we were married, we called it our honeymoon. David went along with us, of course. We often told him in later years that we hoped he appreciated the fact that he was the only kid we had ever heard of who had gone along on his parents' honeymoon. Of course, that was quite a few years ago.

14

The summer of 1939 was "hit the road" time again, but actually it was one we all remember quite pleasantly. We played very few one-nighters and not too many theaters. Mostly we played one-week stands at vacation-type places like Cedar Point, Ohio; Buckeye Lake, Ohio; Virginia Beach; Atlantic City's Steel Pier (where, twenty years later, Ricky would make a personal appearance and set an all-time attendance record that still stands); West - wood Gardens near Dearborn, Michigan; the Totem Pole at Norumbego, Massachusetts—places where we could swim or play tennis or softball. The summer ended all too soon, however, and by September we were back on the theater circuit.

You might well ask why so many theater dates. The answer was one of simple economics. Because of the demand for good musicians, salaries had gone up and up until it had become impossible for a name band to meet its payroll on a hotel job alone. Until we could get ourselves on another commercially sponsored radio program to add to our income, we really had no alternative except to play theaters in order to cover our overhead.

On the other hand, I realized that we couldn't continue indefinitely without some sort of radio exposure, so we tried to balance out our bookings by scheduling a couple of months of theater appearances and then settling down for a while at a steady location where we could catch our breath and do some broadcasting on a nightly, noncommercial basis.

Following four weeks at the Strand Theater in New York we

147

headed west for appearances at the State and Lake Theater in Chicago and a return engagement at the Lyric Theater in Indianapolis. Smaller theaters, like the Lyric, were especially good for us financially, because we would play them on a percentage basis. The theater would take out the first thousand or fifteen hundred dollars, and from there on we would split fifty-fifty. Naturally, with this type of deal we would always ask to have our own accountant checking the box office to protect our interests. Harold Lane wasn't really an accountant, but when he took off his chauffeur's cap he could pass for one.

Our lease on the Seventy-eighth Street apartment had expired, so we moved our little entourage to Brinkerhoff Manor, an attractive apartment complex that had just been built in Englewood, New Jersey. We rented an apartment in the next building for Hazel, Harriet's mother, and with my mother and Al, Kay, and Don living just a few blocks away we had the feeling that our family was indeed a closely knit group. It's always nice to have your family nearby, but it's especially comforting when you're expecting a baby—and Harriet and I were expecting a playmate for David sometime in April.

I opened with the band at the Blackhawk Restaurant in Chicago on February 14, 1940, to begin a ten-week engagement. Harriet remained at Brinkerhoff Manor to await the new arrival. Needless to say, it was a difficult time for both of us. I realized that Harriet was getting the best possible care and attention, but I missed both her and David terribly and felt extremely guilty about being so far away from her during those last few months of her pregnancy.

This was also a worrisome time financially, because our band payroll was running about five hundred dollars a week more than we were being paid. As I suggested earlier, the justification for this type of booking was that the Blackhawk had an arrangement with radio station WGN (which blanketed the Midwest) whereby the bands that played there would broadcast at least twice

148

nightly in choice time periods. As a result, I knew I would make up the loss in a couple of weeks of one-nighters or theaters, as soon as we finished the engagement, but nevertheless it didn't exactly contribute to my peace of mind to write out those deficit checks every week.

Most of the members of the band stayed at the Croydon Hotel, which at that time was the "in" place for musicians and entertainers. The Croydon Bar stayed open all night—in fact, it really didn't start swinging until about five in the morning. There were usually parties in progress on every floor. If anyone happened to be one of those oddballs who go to sleep before six o'clock in the morning—forget it.

I have always considered myself a "night person" and someone who likes to be where the action is, but the Croydon proved a little too much, even for me. And so when they murdered a guy at seven o'clock one morning in the bar, I moved out and checked into the Ambassador East. To be completely factual, I guess you couldn't say they murdered him in the bar—somebody shot him there but he managed to stagger outside and die on the sidewalk.

During our engagement at the Blackhawk, we recorded three sides that proved to be among our biggest-selling hits. One was a Count Basie instrumental called "Riff Interlude," another was a novelty song called "The Man Who Comes to Our House," and the third was one I wrote as an inside trade joke, but which soon caught on with just about every disc jockey in the nation and which quickly became our most requested number. I wrote two verses and two choruses. It was originally recorded with Rose Anne singing the girl's part, but when Harriet came back with us, she picked up on it and it became a standard with us for years.

The song was inspired by the fact that, due to the increase in the number of dance bands springing up all over the country and the compulsory military-service law that had just gone into effect, there was an acute shortage of top-flight musicians. As a result, many bandleaders found themselves in the position of suddenly having to replace guys who were practically irreplaceable.

149

I called it "I'm Looking for a Guy Who Plays Alto and Baritone and Doubles on a Clarinet and Wears a Size 37 Suit." The words are as follows:

First Verse (OZZIE)

While walking down the street I chanced to meet
  a friend of mine who leads a band.
He seemed a bit perplexed, in fact, I'd say com-
  pletely vexed and when I tell you what was
  wrong, you'll understand.
I said, my friend, you're looking slightly on the
  worried side.
He heaved a heavy sigh and then replied.

Chorus

I'm looking for a guy who plays alto and baritone
  and doubles on a clarinet and wears a size 37 suit.
Of course, we'd expect him to do some arranging
  and perhaps a bit of copying and double oboe
  and some flute.
He may sing the vocals just in case we get stuck.
Oh yes, and he's the guy who shines the shoes and
  drives the truck.
I'm looking for a guy who plays alto and baritone
  and doubles on a clarinet and wears a size 37 suit.

Second Verse (ROSE ANNE *or* HARRIET)

It happened in Gary, Indiana,
We were playing a one night stand.
As Ozzie tapped off number three, a gal stepped up
  and said to me,
I'd like a good look at the members of your band.
I'm looking for a certain young musician.
I met him at a dance a year ago.
I can't recall if he was with B.G. or Tommy D.
But I'll tell you all about him so you'll know:

150

My dad and mom.

The Pugeot A. C. I'm the 10 year old front and center—not because I was captain, but because I owned the football. My brother Alfred is standing on the extreme left.

The Ridgefield Park delegation to the Boy Scout Jamboree: In back are Laurence MacDonough, Alfred, Harry Fisher, and Milt Emerson; in front, myself and George Alberque.

On the practice field at Rutgers.

The band in 1935: *back row,* Bill Nelson, Elmer Smathers, Sandy Wolf, Joe Bohan, Sid Brokaw, Harry Murphy, Charles Bubeck, Bo Ashford, Harry Johnson, Holly Humphreys, *front row,* Abe Lincoln, Bill Stone, Fred Whiteside, Chauncey Grey.

In 1932 a beautiful vocalist joined the band: Harriet Hilliard checks her script.

Before sparring with World's Light-Heavyweight Champion, Tommy Loughran. He hit me 3,642 times and I hit him 3 times.

Early radio days with Believe-It-or-Not Bob Ripley.

My kid brother Don and I in 1937.

Harriet and I standing beside "Nelson's Folly."

With Humphrey Bogart at the Strand Theatre in New York.

David Ozzie Nelson at age 1.

David meets Ricky for the first time.

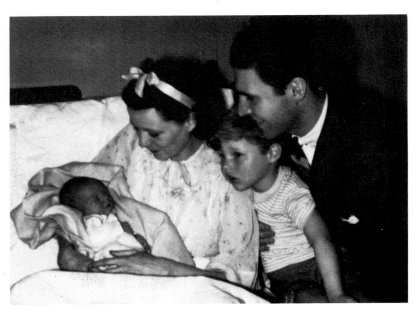

David's unscheduled appearance on stage.

With the boys at Hermosa Beach, 1941.

"The Adventures of Ozzie and Harriet": A typical on-camera scene of the family at breakfast.

"The Adventures of Ozzie and Harriet": A typical off-camera scene during one of those interminable waits between "takes."

I'm especially fond of this picture of the boys and me taken at Juan-les-Pins in 1954.

Ricky recording "Poor Little Fool."

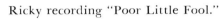

David and Ricky: The Daring Young Men on the Flying
Trapeze.

David and June's wedding. Rick was best man.

Rick and Kris.

The cast of "Ozzie's Girls." The girls are Susan Sennett (l.) and Brenda Sykes (r).

The youngest generation of Nelsons. Tracy and Danny are standing in back; Gunnar, Matthew, and Jamie, in front.

Second Chorus

I'm looking for a guy who plays alto and baritone
and doubles on a clarinet and wears a size 37 suit.
I can't find him listed in Downbeat or Metronome,
Billboard or Variety
But oh my goodness, was he cute.
I don't remember if his hair was dark or light
'Cause he didn't take his hat off when he kissed me
goodnight.
I'm looking for a guy who plays alto and baritone
and doubles on a clarinet and wears a size 37 suit.

The new baby was expected about April 15, but as so often
happens, he wasn't quite ready to make his appearance at that
time. We had Monday nights off at the Blackhawk, so I flew back
home twice near the end of the engagement, hoping I might get
lucky, but he still hadn't arrived by the time we closed on May 1
and started on the road.

We played a couple of one-nighters and then opened at the
Riverside Theater in Milwaukee on May 5. Naturally, I phoned
home every night, and although Harriet was feeling fine there
was still no news. Then, the afternoon of May 8, immediately
following our first show, Don Cummings and I were sitting talking in my dressing room when the phone rang and it was Al
calling to report that David now had a baby brother. We named
him Eric Hilliard Nelson. He was born at Holy Name Hospital
in Teaneck, New Jersey, where Al was in charge of the dental
staff and where Kay had been head nurse.

I didn't get to see the little guy until four days later. Luckily,
we had two days off between Milwaukee and the Cotton Carnival
Ball in Memphis, so I made another quick flight home, and David
and I went over to the hospital and met little Ricky for the first
time. Dr. Prather, our obstetrician, stopped by with his camera
and took a picture to commemorate the event. After all, it was
the first get-together of our entire cast.

The summer of 1940 was a hectic one for our little family.

Harriet flew down to visit me while we were playing at the Peabody Hotel in Memphis, and I made a couple of quick trips home to see her and the boys. But for the most part they were in Englewood, New Jersey, and I was in Alabama, Mississippi, Texas, Virginia, and points east, west, north, and south.

I remember one dismal, rainy night when we were en route from someplace to someplace and I was so tired I checked into a dingy little hotel in a small town in Missouri. As I was lying on the bed talking on the phone to Harriet, I happened to glance over in the corner and there was a mousetrap with a dead mouse in it. Yes sir! There's nothing like the glamor of show business!

By the end of the summer, we had decided that it was time we established roots someplace so that we would at least have a place that we could call our permanent home. We were lucky to find what could only be described as a dream house. It was about a year-and-a-half old and was located at the edge of a beautiful wooded area in Tenafly, New Jersey. Some years later, Streeter Blair, one of America's foremost primitive painters, would paint a picture of it which hangs in our living room in Hollywood.

The next house down the road from us was a charming little eighty-year-old farmhouse which we also bought and remodeled for my mother and Don, who was now thirteen.

As fate would have it, we lived in the Tenafly house for only a short time. (Al and Kay bought it from us and lived in it for thirty years while they raised a fine family of five sons), but we did spend an unforgettable Christmas Eve there.

In order to spend Christmas in our new home, we had arranged a six week's booking at our old stomping grounds, the Strand Theater in New York, starting November 22. David, now four years old, was at an age where Christmas was beginning to have a real meaning for him.

Christmas Eve of 1940 was a clear, starry night. The ground was covered with snow, making the whole area look like a beautiful Christmas card. It was a little after two in the morning, and Harriet and I, following our last show at the theater, had just finished trimming the tree and setting out the presents. We were upstairs getting ready for bed when suddenly we heard the sound of voices singing outside our front door. They were singing "Little Town of Bethlehem." Coming across the snow through the clear winter night, it had a dreamy, angelic quality. I've never heard anything so beautiful. We opened the bedroom window and looked out, and there were the King Sisters—Alice, Louise, Donna, and Yvonne—together with Alvino Rey and all the boys in his band. We had met Alvino and the girls in Chicago a few years before, when they were with Horace Heidt, but we hadn't seen them since that time. They had been playing at the nearby Rustic Cabin (where Frank Sinatra got his start) and had decided to surprise us. And what a wonderful surprise!

Naturally, they all came in and we had sandwiches, cookies, and coffee and hot chocolate and lots of laughs. There were a few tears, too. The girls insisted that Harriet and I open some of our presents. Among the presents I had gotten for Harriet were some lace handkerchiefs. She read the card aloud. I had written on it, "Just in case I make you cry sometime." Whereupon all the girls immediately burst into tears.

The mention of Christmas presents reminds me of the time about 1945 or '46 when I decided to surprise Harriet by buying her a Persian lamb coat at I. Magnin's in Los Angeles. It was a beautiful coat and quite expensive. The more I looked at it, however, the more I realized that, while it was a perfect coat for New York City, it was much too heavy for the mild winters we have in California. So I bought a revolver and put it in the pocket of the coat, and then wrote out a card which said, "In case you don't like the coat, there's a revolver in the pocket so you can shoot me."

I realize it would make a much better story if she had shot me, but she didn't. For one thing, I made sure that there were no bullets in the gun—but I really don't think she would have shot me anyway.

She did, however, share my concern that she wouldn't get much opportunity to wear the coat in California, so, after expressing her appreciation for my thoughtfulness and modeling it around the house for a few days, she decided to exchange it and get a credit.

I had bought it just before Christmas when everything was

153

marked up, and Harriet, smart shopper that she is, waited for the January sales and then went on a buying spree. She said it was the best Christmas present I ever gave her.

The engagement at the Strand proved to be especially interesting because Humphrey Bogart appeared on the bill with us to plug his latest film. He came east without an act but with a series of film clips, each one depicting a scene where he and his mobster buddies got shot. From there we worked out a routine where he confided to me that, since his old mob had been shot full of holes, he had to come to New York to get some new men. He then looked over various members of the band and called them down front to interview them. Since practically every guy in the band was a comedian, the routine proved to be hilarious. The audience loved it and so did Bogie. In fact, he had such a good time that he postponed the start of his next picture so he could go to Philadelphia with us. I think he would have followed us all around the country if the studio hadn't started screaming for him to come back.

Like most genuinely talented people, Bogie was a completely unaffected, really nice person. He was also an easy "break-up" on stage, and as a result we used to pull some awful stunts on him. We had a routine where he and I would talk about his experiences in Hollywood. While he was talking to me, I would look at his ear instead of his eyes, and if that didn't break him up I'd glance down at his fly and give a little gasp as if he'd forgotten to zip up his pants. This never missed. Naturally, the audience couldn't see these things, but they sensed that we were having fun and joined in even though they weren't sure what was going on.

During our conversation, one of the boys in the band would come on stage with a telegram, supposedly from Jack Warner, which congratulated Bogie on the fact that his latest film (I forgot which one it was) had broken all box-office records. This of course would always elicit great applause from the audience. After the first few days, however, the boys in the band started "improving" on the text of the message until it finally bore no re-

154

semblance to the original telegram. Poor Bogie had to ad lib his way through it while pretending to read what was on the telegram. If he had read aloud what the guys had written there, he would have closed the theater in five minutes.

Naturally, Bogie wasn't always the "patsy," but he was usually part of the action. He always hung out in my dressing room between shows and loved to answer the phone as my secretary or valet. As my secretary, he was very British, but if he decided he was my valet he was either Continental or Mexican. Needless to say, I always tried to reach the phone before he did, especially after the time I walked in while he was explaining to a lady caller (who turned out to be my high school mathematics teacher) that I was busy auditioning chorus girls for the next stage show.

February of 1941 found us at the Roosevelt Hotel in New Orleans for the Mardi Gras season. We had left Ricky in Tenafly with his two grandmothers and a nurse, but David, who was now four years old, came along with us, since by now he considered himself a member of the band.

Howard Bruno, who had replaced Joe Bohan as our drummer, used to let David "play drums" during the luncheon sessions, which made our band the only one I'd ever seen with two drummers—one sitting on the other's lap.

Since our dinner sessions started at seven, we would all eat dinner in the coffee shop at six, David included. He, of course, ate at a table with the other musicians and could never quite understand why the waitresses always brought him cereal instead of a regular dinner.

One night he was seated a few tables away from us with Howard and our bass player, Bobby Domas. They each ordered steaks and beer and David said, "I'll have the same." The waitress came over and asked Harriet what to bring him and she said, "Cream of Wheat and a glass of milk." A few minutes later, when the waitress came back with the orders, we heard a little fist pounding on the table and a little voice protesting, "This is not what I ordered!"

It was in New Orleans that David gave us a scare that to this

155

day shakes me up every time I think of it. David's nurse at that time was a young girl just out of college, who traveled with us and who took care of David when Harriet was busy. He had just learned to ride a two-wheeler, so she used to drive out to Lake Pontchartrain with him every afternoon and they would rent bicycles and ride them around the shore of the lake.

One afternoon, on her day off, David asked me if I would take him out there. I had never been to the lake before, but of course he had no trouble directing me to the bicycle shop. I picked out a bike for myself and took care of the necessary arrangements. In the meantime, David had gone outside with the little bicycle that he always rode, and I assumed he was waiting there for me. When I came out of the shop, however, he was nowhere to be seen. I called and called and got no answer, so I started down the path that led to the lake. All of a sudden, from around the bend came this little guy, dripping wet and covered from head to toe with mud. He was shivering from the cold and sobbing—more from anger, as it turned out, than from fright.

He had been riding down the path, he explained, when he heard a bird singing in a tree. He looked up to see the bird and went over the bank and into the lake. "I went down and down right to the bottom," he said, "and I grabbed hold of some roots and pulled myself up. I tried to climb out but I kept slipping in the mud. I kept calling for help, but nobody heard me."

"They'll never find the bicycle," he said. "It's way down at the bottom of the lake." Then he added, "What a stupid place to put a lake. Right where people ride bicycles!"

I wrapped him in a blanket and had him lie down in the back of the car. I told the man at the shop what happened and that I'd be back the next day to pay for the bike in case they couldn't find it. David immediately fell asleep and slept all the way back to the hotel. He woke up as I was carrying him up in the elevator and said, "Don't tell the boys in the band about this—they'll think I'm dumb."

I went back to the bicycle shop the next day and the man told me that they had found the bike. It was in six feet of water.

156

How a little boy just four years old could have swum out of there fully clothed and pulled himself up that muddy bank, I'll never know. But thank God he did.

One more incident connected with David's falling into the lake comes to mind. When we got up to the hotel room, I ran a bath for him and said, "I want you to lie in this hot water for a while, and then you won't catch a cold."

About a week later, I said to Harriet, "It's amazing that, after falling into that icy water and riding all the way back to the hotel in the car, he didn't catch cold."

David came in from the next room and said, "Don't you remember, Daddy? You said if I took the hot bath I wouldn't catch cold. So I didn't." A little boy's unquestioning faith in his father is a beautiful thing to behold. And an awful responsibility.

From New Orleans we headed west. We played a couple of one-nighters in Louisiana and Texas and a week of vaudeville in Houston, and then moved on to Hollywood, where we had been signed to costar in a movie with Ruby Keeler. We knew about this, of course, but what we didn't know was that California was to be our home from then on.

PART THREE

The Adventures of Ozzie and Harriet

15

The movie Harriet and I made was called *Sweethearts of the Campus* and was produced by Columbia Studios. It wasn't good and it wasn't bad. It was a typical little musical just like dozens of others that were being turned out by Columbia, Paramount, and Universal during the 1940s. It was a college story, and the campus scenes were shot at Occidental College. Ruby sang and danced. Harriet sang, and I sang and led the band through some unexciting songs that had been written for us. Eddie Dymtryk, who has since directed some very important pictures, was the director.

Immediately following the completion of the film we opened at the Palace Hotel in San Francisco. Harriet found a charming little house, at the top of a mountain in San Rafael, which we rented for the duration of our engagement.

There were three hotels that featured name bands in the Bay Area in those days: the Palace Hotel, the Mark Hopkins, and the St. Francis. The preceding year, while we were playing at the Blackhawk in Chicago, I had mentioned to Russ Fachine, who was head man of the Chicago office of MCA, that we would like to play San Francisco sometime, since we had never been there. Russ said that he was sure it could be arranged and that he could get us very good money, since there would be three hotels bidding for our services.

Later in the day Russ called back and said, "Do you remember, one night last week, throwing a man off the bandstand?"

I thought for a moment and then recalled that there had been a nicely dressed but very drunk middle-aged man who had come up on the bandstand and insisted that he play the drums. Since we only had one set of drums and the man would have looked ridiculous sitting in Howard Bruno's lap, I was equally insistent that he get off the bandstand. He proved to be a stubborn old goat, so I finally had to give him a little physical assistance so that we could get on with the music.

"Yes," I said to Russ, "but it was no big deal. It was just a drunk who wanted to play the drums. It happens all the time."

"Do you remember my saying that you had three hotels to choose from in San Francisco?" said Russ. "Now you have two. The drunk you threw off the bandstand is the general manager of the St. Francis."

The Palace Hotel engagement proved to be most pleasant. Sharing the billing with us were Paul and Grace Hartman, whom we had known from our Park Central Hotel days nine years previously. Since then they had starred in several Broadway hits and leading nightclubs and were considered the outstanding comedy dance team in the country. The basis of their comedy was a satire of the ballroom dancing that was so much in vogue during the 1930s and '40s. Paul and Grace were actually very fine dancers, so they would begin their act by dancing "straight" and very beautifully. But then little things would start to go wrong—she would trip over his foot, his pants would start to sag—and they would slowly but surely progress from the sublime to the ridiculous.

While we were rehearsing their music for opening night, Paul suggested that it might be funny if he should "accidently" misjudge his distance and fall backwards into the bandstand while I was leading the band. I said I thought it was a funny idea, but why not go a little further and actually fall into me and I would fall down over him. He thought that would be great and suggested that I not mention it to the guys in the band to make sure that their reactions would be spontaneous and not anticipated.

We had a packed house for the opening, and the Hartmans' first number was received most enthusiastically. During their second number, as we had planned, Paul twirled gracefully away

162

from Grace and backed into the bandstand, as we had planned, and I fell over on top of him, as we had planned. However, what we hadn't figured on was that the bandstand, although three tiers high, was not quite as steady as it should have been.

Bobby Domas, our bass player, was on the top tier. As Paul and I fell down, the entire bandstand shook, and poor Bobby *and* his bass fiddle fell over backwards and simply disappeared. There was a terrible crash as they hit the floor, and a moment later, much to our relief, Bobby came climbing back, lugging his fiddle behind him. The audience, thinking it was all part of the act, was hysterical. The laughter went on and on, and finally Paul whispered to me, "How do we follow that?"

Fortunately, neither Bobby nor the bass suffered any ill effects, and although Paul backed into the bandstand and I fell over him every show after that, we never could coax Bobby to repeat his sensational disappearing act. He always used to tell us that it was okay with him, but his bass fiddle didn't like the idea.

The highlight of our stay in San Francisco was the reuniting of our family when Hazel and Ricky arrived by train a few days before his first birthday. In honor of the event, we had a big celebration at San Rafael with the guys in the band and their wives in attendance. Evidently Ricky sensed that something special was expected of him, so he selected the occasion to take his first steps. He walked clear across the kitchen from his mother to the outstretched arms of David.

We all loved the house at San Rafael. As I mentioned, it was on the top of a mountain and was surrounded by fields and woods, with the nearest house about a mile away. However, 1941 seemed to be our year for frightening experiences, and we had our second scare one sunny afternoon about two weeks after Ricky arrived.

We had bought David a little red wagon, and he would sit his little brother in front of him and go speeding down the path from the house and turn up into a dirt road at the foot of the hill. Since ours was the last house on the mountain, there was never any traffic on the road, although it continued on for another half mile or so.

This one day as Harriet and I were watching from the porch, the boys went zooming down the hill as usual when suddenly a car appeared around the bend. Obviously the driver of the car wasn't aware of David and David wasn't aware of the car, but from where we were sitting we could see both headed for each other. It was terrifying, especially since we were too far away to do anything but yell and run toward them.

The car couldn't have been more than twenty feet away from David when he finally saw it and, with amazing presence of mind, turned his wheels sharply to the left and rolled the wagon over, pulling little Ricky over on top of him.

Harriet and I each said an extra prayer of thanks when we went to bed that night.

The week before we closed our engagement at the Palace Hotel, I got a call that Ed Fishman, who headed the band department of the William Morris office, was flying up to talk to me about something very important. It proved to be very important indeed. The Brown and Williamson Tobacco Company was going to sponsor a radio program starting in the fall, which would star Red Skelton, and they were very interested in having Harriet, the band, and me on the show with him. Harriet and I would sing our special-material duets and would also play various characters in the sketches with Red.

We didn't know Red very well at the time, but we had appeared on the bill with him at several benefit performances and were well aware of his tremendous talents, so it took us about five minutes to say yes and ten minutes more to work out the details.

We rented a house at Hermosa Beach for the balance of the summer, while Harriet made a couple of pictures at Columbia (*Boston Blackie* and *Canal Zone*) and the band and I appeared at the Casa Mañana Ballroom, which was located on Washington Boulevard in Culver City.

On October 7, the stentorian tones of Truman Bradley announced, "The Raleigh Cigarette Program! Starring Red Skelton! With Ozzie Nelson and his music! And Harriet Hilliard!"

It proved to be the start of a whole new phase in our careers.

It's very difficult to write briefly about someone as complex as Red Skelton. Like most comics, he is a very moody man, subject to periods of great elation and of deep depression. He had very little formal education, but he has a brilliant comedy mind and an uncanny ability to develop an instant rapport with an audience.

I don't think I have ever met anyone who so loves to entertain people as Red. Whether it's an audience of thousands in an auditorium or five or six people in a room, he feels that it is his mission in life to keep everyone happy. Harriet and I would always have dinner with Red and Edna, his wife at the time, at the Brown Derby after our radio shows, and on many occasions I have seen him pour water over his head or butter his hand and the sleeve of a good suit just to get a laugh from a couple of tourists who had stopped by for autographs.

Working with him was an education in comedy. The format for the radio show ran as follows. After the opening theme Red would be introduced, and then there would be an exchange of topical jokes among Red, our announcer, and Harriet and me. This would be followed by an instrumental band number and then a series of sketches where Red would portray various characters and Harriet and/or I would play various and assorted characters to match. It was not unusual for us each to play six or seven different characters on one show.

It was in this area that Harriet's early vaudeville training with great comics like Bert Lahr, Ken Murray, and Danny Duncan made her such a valuable asset to Red and the radio show. She originated the character of Daisy June opposite his Clem Kadiddlehopper, Calamity Jane opposite his Dead-Eye, and, most important of all, the mother of Junior, the "mean widdle kid." Some of the routines between Junior and his mother were masterpieces, and I'm sure Red would be the first to agree that Har-

165

riet's comedy timing and delivery were absolutely brilliant and matched his to perfection.

Immediately following the middle commercial break, Harriet and I would sing a special-material duet. On such occasions, Red, instead of leaving the stage, would stand off to the side, laughing uproariously at the comedy lines and leading the applause at the end. It was as if to say, "These people are my friends. I like them and I enjoy what they do and I hope you do, too." We worked with Red for three seasons, and never at any time was there the slightest friction or unpleasantness of any kind —just lots of laughs. It was a wonderfully warm and rewarding relationship.

The Red Skelton show proved to be an immediate hit, so Harriet and I started looking for a house in the Hollywood Hills area. One afternoon we drove up a beautiful street called Camino Palmero. It was a wide street, lined on either side with comfortable-looking homes. Just north of Franklin Avenue where the street dead-ended, we saw a colonial-type shingled house—white with green shutters. It was set back aways among some friendly-looking old trees that almost hid the For Sale sign. The big green lawn and the vacant lots in back that ran clear to the next street seemed to send out an invitation for two little boys to come and play. From the first moment we saw it, we knew it was the house we wanted. It was love at first sight.

We moved in in November of 1941. Now, thirty-two years later, the big beautiful homes that used to line the street from Hollywood Boulevard to Franklin Avenue have all been swept away by the bulldozers, but the houses north of Franklin still look pretty much the same. There are apartment houses now where the vacant lots used to be, and the little boys who used to play with David and Ricky have grown up and have little boys and girls of their own. The big swimming pool has been filled in and replaced by a smaller one, and a few more trees have been added, but otherwise the place looks the same, and Danny, Tracy, Jamie, Matthew and Gunnar now slide down the same bannister that David and Ricky used to slide down.

166

We had our furniture shipped out from New Jersey, but we moved in before it arrived and slept on mattresses in front of the big fireplace in the den. Grace Johnson came to work for us as our housekeeper and stayed for thirteen years.

We enrolled David in the kindergarten at Gardner Street Public School, which was just a few blocks down the hill. While rummaging through some old things the other day, we came across his first report card. It was quite remarkable. Among the grades he received were "Unsatisfactory" for Effort and "Outstanding" for Courtesy, which meant, I guess, that he wouldn't do any work but he was very polite about refusing.

The NBC Tuesday night lineup was one of the most powerful in the history of radio, with Fibber McGee and Molly followed by Bob Hope followed by Red Skelton. As a result, the program proved to be a great showcase, not only for Harriet and me, but also for the band as a musical unit. This was a source of great satisfaction to me because, as I mentioned earlier, I had always felt that, because of the emphasis that had been placed on Harriet and me as singers and entertainers, our band, although highly respected by other musicians, has never gotten the full credit it deserved from either the press or the public.

For that reason, I was extremely pleased to read the following Gil Hinckley's column in the November 1941 issue of *Orchestra World*:

> If by rubbing Aladdin's lamp, I were to have my choice of bands to direct, all things being equal, I'd hot foot it to the bandstand of the Ozzie Nelson crew. Steady work and good locations, all based on fine performances, have put this band in an enviable position. Arrangements are written within the band and possess a distinctive, original touch.

A few months later, *Downbeat,* in a review of the band, had these nice words to say:

> The band sounded clean, in tune, at ease with the music. The brass was especially bright toned. Trumpet and trombone

spots, tenor and piano solos satisfied because they were in good taste. There was no drum solo, h'ray. And h'ray generally for Ozzie and his band, encouraging proof that a band can stick to pleasing, easy-riding music and sell without any trouble.

Due to the tremendous exposure on the show, three original instrumental sides that I had writtern while we were in New Orleans—"Swinging on the Golden Gate," "Jersey Jive," and "Central Avenue Shuffle"—were starting to get a lot of play by the disc jockeys. With the advent of World War II in December of '41, however, one by one the boys in our band were drafted into the service bands. By the time we followed Paul Whiteman into the Florentine Gardens in February of 1942, we had experienced about a 90 percent turnover in personnel from the previous year, and the only ones left from our Glen Island Casino days were Holly Humphreys and Charlie Bubeck.

The Florentine Gardens was a showy nightclub on Hollywood Boulevard which was presided over by our old friend N.T.G. and which featured a chorus of extremely beautiful and talented girls, among whom were Doris Houck, Joy Barlow, and Yvonne De-Carlo—who, of course, went on to star in many motion pictures.

During the early months of 1942, while I was still at the Gardens, Harriet appeared in *Juke Box Jenny,* a musical at Universal with Ken Murray and Charlie Barnett's orchestra, and I appeared with the band in a musical called *Strictly in the Groove* and also very briefly in a picture at Paramount called *Big Street,* which starred Henry Fonda and Lucille Ball. Neither picture had an especially long shooting schedule, which was fortunate for me because I was literally working night and day with very little time left for sleeping.

The cast of *Strictly in the Groove* included two fine vocalists, Martha Tilton and Mary Healy, as well as Jimmy Davis, who was not only the writer of "You Are My Sunshine" but also the governor of Louisiana. Also featured in the picture was another well-known country-and-western artist, Spade Cooley, who died in San Quentin Prison a few years ago while serving a life sentence for murdering his wife. It was quite a mixed bag.

168

Although we knew from our fan mail and the audience ratings that the Skelton show was being well received, we really didn't fully appreciate its tremendous impact until we went on a vaudeville tour during our summer hiatus. From our opening show at the Golden Gate Theater in San Francisco in June until we closed at the Orpheum in Davenport, Iowa, in September, business was really great and the audiences most appreciative.

As usual, we carried our own acts with us throughout the tour and integrated them into the show so that we got the feeling of a musical revue rather than a series of individual vaudeville acts. Lew Wood—who had been one of the original members of the California Collegians, with whom Harriet had worked as a teenager—went along with us as stage manager and supervised the lighting and staging.

The accompanying acts were all showstoppers and also nice people, so, except for the fact that we missed our little boys terribly, it was a pleasant summer and certainly rewarding financially.

The acts were Barton and Stone, Armando and Lita, and our old friend Bob Dupont, the juggler. Bernie Jones, who had joined us the year before on tenor saxophone, came out of the band and sang some very funny Swedish-dialect songs, and of course Harriet appeared in the next-to-closing spot, where I joined her to sing a couple of our special-material duets.

We had one piece of business we used during her singing of a Spanish number called "Conchita Lopez" that always did well for us. In introducing the song, I would explain to the audience that one of the lines in the lyric was "Mandolins were softly playing" and that in that spot it would be nice if we had a couple of mandolins to play a little cadenza, but that unfortunately we didn't have any mandolins in the band. "However," I continued, "we do have three trombones, so if you'll just imagine that the trombones are mandolins then everything will be fine." This always got a good laugh, and then Harriet would start to sing the song. When she reached the line "Mandolins were softly playing," the three trombone players would stand up, play a cadenza on their trombones, and then sit down again. The audi-

169

ence really loved it. I guess the sheer absurdity of it struck a responsive note. At any rate, it never missed.

Paul Smith, who had taken Don Ferris's place on piano, was featured on some great solos and also wrote the arrangements for the instrumental numbers. Don and Paul, both tremendously talented musicians, are still doing extremely well—Don as arranger and conductor for Red Skelton and Paul with his Paul Smith Trio, who have turned out some really fine albums.

The 1942 vaudeville tour lasted the entire summer and took us to San Francisco, Kansas City, Omaha, Minneapolis, Chicago, Pittsburgh, Cleveland, Dayton, Milwaukee, Indianapolis, and Davenport. With appearances at service bases and band rallies between shows, it was a busy time, so arriving home and going back on the Skelton show seemed like a vacation by comparison.

16

The second season with Red followed much the same pattern as the first. The ratings continued to be high and the formula continued to be successful, so there was really no reason to change anything.

We opened for an extended engagement at the famed Biltmore Bowl at the Biltmore Hotel in Los Angeles on December 24, 1942. Harriet appeared in the floor show and as usual stopped the show every night, and Liz Tilton, sister of Martha and also a fine singer, handled the vocals on the bandstand.

The acoustics at the Bowl were really excellent, and I still enjoy listening to some of the air-checks taken off the line from our remote broadcasts from there. We were able to get a great band balance, and our rhythm section of Ted Repay, Jud de-Naut, and Spencer Prinz was, I think, as fine as any ever assembled.

We were at the Biltmore until about March or April, and immediately following the engagement Red decided that he'd like to do a couple of his broadcasts from New York City, so we arranged to have ourselves booked into the Capitol Theater for two weeks.

The opening show there was one for the memory book—that is, if you enjoy recalling nightmares. Opening days are difficult enough anyway, but we had to rehearse the acts early in the morning before the theater opened, and as a result, nobody got more than a couple of hours sleep.

Harriet's opening number was planned so that she would sing the verse very quietly with just the piano accompanying her. In order to give an intimate effect, the stage was to be blacked out and there were to be two spotlights, one on her and one on Ted Repay, our pianist. We had used this technique before and it had proved very effective.

As I mentioned earlier, we were all very tired and had had very little sleep, so Ted decided, as he explained later, to take a couple of quick drinks to pick him up for the opening show.

As it turned out, they had just the opposite effect. He was fine during the band numbers, and so I had no advance warning as to what was to follow.

I introduced Harriet with the usual full-band introductory music (a few bars of "Sweet and Lovely"), then the lights faded down and two spotlights came on: one on Harriet, smiling center stage, awaiting the piano arpeggio which was to lead her into the verse, and the other on Ted. Unfortunately, however, he had passed out and was lying across the piano keyboard.

Harriet, great trouper that she is, didn't even glance toward the piano. She went ahead and sang the verse, all by herself, just as if it had been planned that way. She had also managed to pick the key out of the air, so that when the band came in on the chorus she was in perfect pitch.

The summer of 1943 found us on our usual vaudeville tour, playing mostly theaters we had played before but with an entirely new show. This time, however, perhaps due to the Red Skelton influence, we emphasised comedy even more than previously. In fact, most of the newspaper reviews likened our presentation to *Hellzapoppin'*, although, of course, it was not quite as zany. It was just that we had lots of running gags going through the show—little comedy bits that created a feeling of intimacy and good-natured fun. Most of these just involved the guys in the band and the various acts that worked with us, but frequently we would also involve members of the audience.

The shows in the presentation houses ran continuously—that is, there would be a stage show, then the feature picture, then a newsreel or a short subject, and then another stage show. As a result, it was not unusual for people to come in or leave while the stage show was going on. (It was also not unusual for kids to bring their lunches and sit through two or three shows.)

When someone would come down the aisle to take a seat in one of the front rows, I would stop whatever was going on and say, "How do you do. We waited as long as we could but we had to go on with the show." Then as the person or persons would start moving into the row, which of course would cause everyone along the line to stand up, we would start a drum roll. And as the person sat down, our drummer would hit the tympani either lightly or with a thud, depending on the weight of the person. If he was having difficulty squeezing past the other people, I would say, "Don't get up, make him jump."

Strangely enough, this routine would get bigger laughs the more times it was repeated, with people in the audience often calling my attention to latecomers. Sometimes when several groups of people would be coming in at once, the result would be a veritable barrage of assorted tympani beats, much to the delights of the audience.

Of course, all of this was done in a spirit of god-natured fun and accepted in the same way. I don't recall anyone's ever complaining about suddenly becoming part of the show—in fact, they all seemed to enjoy it.

My kid brother Don, who was now sixteen years old, came along with us as one of the band boys, setting up the instruments and assisting with lights and props backstage, and occasionally sitting in on saxophone or even coming down front and playing some great jazz solos.

Harriet just read this last segment and reminded me that the summer of 1943 provided a couple of traumatic experiences for David and Ricky, who were now aged six and three.

My mother hadn't seen the boys for over a year, so we thought it would be nice to have them go back and visit with her in Tenafly for a few weeks. This would coincide with the conclusion of our vaudeville tour, since our last engagement would be at the Michigan Theater in Detroit, following which we could pick up the boys in New Jersey and come back with them on the *Super Chief*, arriving in time for the season's opening show with Red.

It was decided that Grace Johnson, our housekeeper, would accompany the boys on the train from California to New York where my brother Al would meet them and take them over to Tenafly.

The confusion started soon after their train pulled out of the Union Station in Los Angeles. It suddenly occurred to Grace that, in the excitement of saying goodbye and getting the baggage into the drawing room, Grandma Hilliard had forgotten to give her the tickets. Feeling sure that they all would be put off the train at the next stop, Grace started to cry and was soon joined by David and Ricky. Fortunately, however, Grandma discovered the oversight just as the train was pulling out, so she immediately reported it to the station master, who phoned ahead to Pasadena to tell the conductor that the lady and the two little boys were not stowaways or international jewel thieves but were legitimate passengers and that their fare had been paid.

The next nerve-shattering experience that our two young travelers were exposed to was after their Tenafly visit when they were on their way home with Harriet and me. Al was driving us to Grand Central Station where we were going to board the *Twentieth Century Limited,* the train that connected with the *Super Chief* in Chicago, which in turn would take us to Los Angeles.

In anticipation of the heavy New York City traffic, we had left Tenafly at four o'clock to give ourselves plenty of time to make the *Twentieth Century,* which left at six.

As we were crossing the George Washington Bridge, I said to Harriet, "You do have the tickets, don't you?" And she said, "Oh, yes—right here" and took them out of her handbag to show me.

174

She suddenly gave them a double-take and burst into tears. She had four tickets, all right, but they weren't for the *Twentieth Century Limited*. They were for the *Commodore*, a train which left at four o'clock. Lew Wood, our band manager, had given them to Harriet in Detroit, and she had assumed they were for the *Twentieth Century* since that was the train we had always taken, and he had assumed that—well, anyway, here it was about four-ten and our tickets were for a train that had left Grand Central at four o'clock.

Suddenly someone got a bright idea. We can board the train at 125th Street if we get there in ten minutes! Al stepped on the gas and we screeched and skidded to the 125th Street Station in record time. The tracks there are elevated, and we all grabbed bags and rushed madly up the stairs and got there just in time to see the *Commodore* go whizzing through the station. Obviously, it didn't make a stop at 125th Street.

By now the boys had joined Harriet in the crying brigade, and I was ready to join them any minute. There was only one thing left for us to do. Since we had to get to Chicago in time to get on the *Super Chief* or we'd miss our radio show, the only way to make the connection was to somehow get on the *Twentieth Century*. What was so difficult about that? It was Labor Day weekend, there was a war going on, and the *Twentieth Century* even during normal times was always completely booked up weeks in advance. As to any thoughts about flying, we didn't even consider it, since air transportation was totally unpredictable in those days.

It was almost five-thirty by the time we got to Grand Central Station, so Al told us to hurry on down there and that he would meet us at the gate and bring the bags down to us as soon as he could find a place to park the car.

The station was jammed. We went over to the gate and I said to Harriet, "You wait here with the kids and I'll see what I can do."

"And don't be afraid to tell people who you are," she shouted after me, in a voice that could only be described as hysterical.

This, of course, is easy to say but not easy to do. I don't care if you're Bing Crosby, Muhammad Ali, or Howard Cosell, there's always the chance that the other guy will say "So what?" or "Who cares?" or "I never heard of you."

This, however, was obviously a situation that called for drastic measures, so I went over to one of the uniformed station men standing nearby, took a deep breath and said, "I'm Ozzie Nelson. Here's a twenty-dollar bill for openers. There are four of us and it's absolutely essential that we get on the *Twentieth Century* or we'll miss our opening broadcast with Red Skelton."

The man said, "The train's been sold out for weeks but I'll see what I can do."

When I went back to report to Harriet and the boys, I found her holding an absolutely gigantic basket of flowers. A young man from the William Morris office had brought them down as a going-away present. I said, "Any sign of Al?" She said, "Not yet."

The train man came back. "I'm terribly sorry," he reported, "but there's not a thing I can do. The train is absolutely full."

"Okay," I said, "then give me my twenty dollars back." The man hesitated for a moment, so I said, just like the private eyes do in the movies, "Here's ten more, try again."

They were just yelling the final "All aboard" when our man came rushing up. "We had a cancellation and I got you one roomette," he said. "This is really against the law. We're not supposed to let anyone on without sleeping accommodations, but maybe the conductor can make some arrangements on the train."

As they were holding the gate open for us to go through, Billy Kent, our theater agent, came rushing up with another big basket of flowers. And so we got on the train with no bags— just two big baskets of flowers.

For the benefit of those who are too young to know about train accommodations, a roomette is about the size of a broom closet. So, there we sat, the four of us jammed into this little cubicle. We weren't sure whether to laugh or to cry, but suddenly we all looked at each other and began to laugh. I think Harriet was

176

the one who started it, and it's lucky she did because it could have gone either way.

Just as the train got underway, the porter came up with two bags. "A man shoved these on the last car just as we were pulling out," he said. "He said they were yours."

We learned later that Al had had to park about five blocks from the station, so he had grabbed two of our bags and planned to ship the rest of them on to us. When we opened the bags we discovered that one of them contained the boys' toys and the other, the heavy one, was filled with old books of mine.

The trip back home was uneventful—that is, except for the incident in Albuquerque. There was a stopover there, and David and I got off the train to buy some Indian beads. When we got back the train was gone. It had been shifted over to another track and nobody seemed to know where. By the time we found it, it was pulling away. We chased after it, David hanging onto to my hand, his little legs barely touching the ground. We just did make it as the conductor reached down and grabbed David and I swung up after him. David told me he had nightmares about that for years after.

When we got home, Grandma Hilliard asked Ricky if he had had a good time. "It was okay," he said, "but I just don't like traveling on trains." I wonder why??

During the spring of 1944, Red Skelton received notice from his draft board that he was being inducted into the army, so I decided that the time might be right for Harriet and me to try for a radio show of our own.

The West Coast representative for the advertising agency that produced the Skelton show was a dynamic young guy named John Guedel, who had created "People Are Funny" with Art Linkletter and who would later create "You Bet Your Life" with Groucho Marx and "House Party" in conjunction with Art.

It was John who encouraged us to go ahead with the project and who later joined with us in financing the audition record that served as the "pilot" to sell the show to a sponsor.

177

Although I had written almost all of the special material for the band and for Harriet and me and had made occasional contributions to the Skelton show, I had never actually sat down and written a script all by myself.

After considerable discussion, it was agreed that the story line would be based on a situation where Harriet and I would inherit a drugstore from a distant relative of mine. We would decide that we had had enough of one-night stands and cross-country tours and that we would settle down and manage the store. The drugstore would be handled more or less like the general store in a small town, with various characters coming in and out for comedy bits.

Our first plan was for John and me to collaborate on writing the script, but we soon found out that, even though we were the best of friends, we were both basically "loners" and not tempermentally suited to collaborate with each other—or anyone else for that matter. So we quickly abandoned that idea and agreed that I would write the script and John would handle the casting and other business arrangements.

I can still feel the butterflies that were tickling my stomach as Harriet and I waited in the wings while the audience filed into Studio B at NBC, where we had rented the facilities to make our audition record.

"Suppose they don't laugh?" whispered Harriet. "Suppose they just sit there and stare at us?"

I would like to have given her a reassuring answer of some sort, but the truth is that I had been wondering the same thing myself. We both knew that audiences would laugh when we were doing sketches with Red, and we knew that they would laugh at the funny lines in our songs or at the jokes that I would tell on stage with the band. But this was different. Now we were completely on our own—actors doing situation comedy.

We had had the foresight to keep our friends out of there. On an occasion like this, your friends will just sit there and worry.

I'll never forget the thrill as that first big laugh came rolling in and the feeling of relief and pleasure as the show gathered momentum and we realized that the audience had accepted us and liked us all by ourselves.

We were still under contract to the William Morris office, so our first move was to play the record for Wally Jordan, a bright, young guy just out of Dartmouth who was the West Coast head of the radio department.

Wally's reaction was immediate and enthusiastic. "This is terrific!" he said. "I'm going to fly back to New York with this on the first plane tomorrow morning. I'll have it sold before the week is over!"

He almost made it, too. He sold it to the International Silver Company (who would be our sponsors for the five happy years) in about ten days.

I think Wally would have sold it within the week, just as he had promised, if it hadn't been for a slight delay. He flew out on the morning plane, just as he said he would, but, in his excitement, he forgot to take the record with him.

The summer of 1944 was the last time we toured with the band. We played most of the same presentation houses that we had played during the two previous tours and once again emphasized comedy and, of course, our special-material duets.

Brother Don came with us again, but this time as a regular member of the band, playing tenor saxophone and taking most of the jazz solos. He had played football on Tenafly High School's championship team the previous season and had been elected captain for the coming year, so we were all very proud of him.

At the conclusion of our tour, the band went back to the coast, but Harriet and I came on to New York to meet our sponsors and to discuss promotion activities for the radio show.

The account executive for Young and Rubicam, the advertising agency that handled the International Silver account, proved to be a good friend of ours named Joe Moran. I had

179

known Joe for just a few years, but Harriet and her mother had known him and his wife, Thelma Ritter, even before they were married when they all worked together in stock. Thelma, of course, would come to Hollywood later and have a brilliant career in motion pictures.

Joe is a very intelligent, personable guy and served as the liason between us and the sponsor, which was one of the main reasons why our five years with them were so pleasant.

I was terribly concerned about the coming meeting, however, for one specific reason. As I mentioned earlier, the audition record, on the basis of which the sponsor had bought the show, had Harriet and me inheriting a drugstore, which was to be the locale for future episodes. The more I thought about it, the more I became convinced that this was a mistake. Most of the program structure was true. I was a bandleader and Harriet sang with the band. We were married and were eager to settle down and raise our two boys in a normal environment. This, as I say, was true—but it was not true that we had inherited a drugstore. It struck me that it would be much better and much more honest to throw out the drugstore idea and have the situations adhere as closely as possible to our own home life.

The question was, would our sponsors feel that they had bought one premise and were being given something else? I soon found out.

Joe had called and asked to have lunch with me, so I figured I'd broach the subject to him and get his reaction first before approaching the sponsor. So, as soon as the social amenities were over, I said, "Joe, I want to drop this bombshell right away so you'll have time to think about it and perhaps suggest what my next move should be." I then launched into my feelings about throwing out the drugstore concept.

A big smile spread over Joe's Irish face. "Mr. Stevens [President of International Silver] called me the other day," said Joe, "and said to me, 'I don't want Ozzie to think we're trying to tell him how to run his show, but do you think there's any way

180

of getting him to drop the drugstore idea? That's the only thing about the program we don't like.' So I'll call him this afternoon and tell him that it was a tough job, but I finally convinced you."

17

Sunday, October 8, 1944 was our ninth wedding anniversary. It was also the night that Jack Bailey first announced:

From Hollywood—International Silver Company presents "The Adventures of Ozzie and Harriet!" Starring young America's favorite couple—*Ozzie Nelson and Harriet Hilliard!*

Music: (*Theme.*)
(*Applause—hits simultaneously with theme—fades on cue*)

ANNOUNCER: Ozzie and Harriet have just finished their usual summer orchestra tour with the many annoyances and discomforts that go with a theatrical career on the road. . . . As our scene opens they are getting settled in their new home at 1847 Rogers Road. Here they are . . .

OZZIE: The living room looks great the way you've arranged it.

HARRIET: Thanks. I'm glad you like it. I tried to make it look as near as possible to page fifty-three in House Beautiful.

OZZIE: It sure feels good to be off the road and in our own home. How did everything go today?

HARRIET: Well, the sink got stopped up . . . there was a leak in the water heater . . . the pilot light in the stove won't work . . . a fuse blew out in the refrigerator and there are moths in the clothes closet.

OZZIE: Isn't it wonderful to be living like human beings again?

HARRIET: I still can't seem to realize we've finally settled down— I'm so used to living in hotels, I start packing our grips every afternoon around four o'clock.

182

OZZIE: Yeah, me too. I guess it'll take a little time to get used to it.
HARRIET: Try to remember that this is our own home and stop putting the towels in your suitcase. . . .

This is how it started. And I'm sure nobody, most especially Harriet and I, dreamed that "The Adventures of Ozzie and Harriet" would continue, in one medium or another, for twenty-two years.

We purposely avoided doing any singing on our opening program because we wanted to establish right at the outset that we weren't doing a musical variety show but rather a situation comedy. However, for the balance of the year, we sang one or two songs whenever we felt that they could be integrated smoothly into the framework of the show, much as songs are interpolated into musical comedies in the theater.

Our script writers for the first season were John P. Medbury and Jack Douglas, two of the top comedy writers in the business. John had a fine reputation as a sketch writer for New York shows and had written a successful newspaper column for many years. Jack, who has written several hilarious books and whom you have probably seen with his charming wife Reiko on any number of talk shows, had been the mainstay of the Red Skelton show, and prior to that, a writer for Bob Hope and Eddie Cantor.

Since both John and Jack were basically joke writers and since I had just come off of three years with Skelton, the general character of the show leaned heavily on jokes and sketch comedy rather than having the humor evolve from the situation itself.

We used to preview our shows on Friday nights in order to test the material before going on the air with it on Sunday. Each week I would promise myself to eliminate the jokes and stick to straight situations, but then we would do our preview and the jokes would get such tremendous laughs that I couldn't bring myself to cut them out of the script. Jack, especially, wrote outlandish jokes that were totally unbelievable but which never missed with the audience. As an example, one joke of his

183

that has been quoted many times was that my mother-in-law was bowlegged because she hitch-hiked out here from the East on oil trucks. In another scene, where I was having an argument with a neighbor who was belittling my musical ability, Jack had the man say, "Who do you think you are, the great Leiderkranz?" and I said, "That shows how much you know about music—Leiderkranz is a cheese," and the man said, "You're just jealous!"

On another occasion, the following conversation took place between Gloria, our lugubrious maid (played by Bea Benadaret), and myself:

GLORIA: I suppose Mrs. Nelson has told you that I'm going to my sister's wedding. She's marrying a soldier.
OZZIE: That's fine. Is he an officer?
GLORIA: No. He's a Second Lieutenant.
OZZIE: A Second Lieutenant?
GLORIA: Yes, the first one got away.

Now, these are very funny lines, the kind that always get big laughs, especially when told by someone with a funny delivery. But they are essentially jokes, and I realized that eventually we would have to get into more believable situations with stronger audience identification rather than jokes per se.

For the first few weeks of our show we used only a few outside characters, and these were for the most part rather broadly drawn. For example, Bea Benadaret, in playing Gloria the maid, used a mournful, whining, "adenoidal" type of delivery which was so funny in itself that when she made her entrance she always got a huge laugh merely by saying, "Did you call me, Mrs. Nelson?"

Bea also played a domineering lady named Mrs. Waddington whom we matched up with a little character actor named Dink Trout, whose voice and appearance made him perfectly typecast for her henpecked husband, Roger. Roger's lines consisted of a series of "Yes, my dears"—until the end of the scene when

184

he would strike back with one devastating remark, after which she would drag him off with a "Come along, Roger!"

These characters, however, funny as they were (and they never failed to get big audience laughs), were too exaggerated to match Harriet and me, so we had to gradually write them out and replace them with more believable characters. We didn't have to look far to find what we needed.

In our early shows, we often referred to David and Ricky in the scripts. But except for a running gag of a deep-voiced man (Jack Douglas) saying "Goodnight, Dad" as if it were Ricky—after which I would say, "We've gotta get that kid's tonsils taken out"—we never had anyone actually playing either of the boys in a scene. However, now we brought in Joel Davis, who was about thirteen, to play the part of David, who at this time was actually eight.

David's real-life friend was a little boy named Will Thornbury who, with his parents, Syd and Katherine Thornbury, lived next door to us. And so our actual neighbor became our radio neighbor, "Thorny," played by John Brown (and later on television by Don DeFore).

Harriet's mother, Hazel, who was now living a couple of blocks from us at North Vista, across the street from the Gardner Street School, was the next of family and friends to be depicted (or maligned, or what have you). Her part, played by a fine, versatile actress named Lurene Tuttle, was not too difficult to write because all we had to do was depict her just about the same as she was in real life. Hazel, in person, was a delightful, affectionate lady and just nutty enough to be totally unpredictable. A brief example: My brother Don had enlisted in the navy when he became eighteen and after getting out had enrolled at the University of Southern California. While attending classes there, he stayed at Grandma Hilliard's house, and after he had moved out he continued to get his service checks at that address. One morning he phoned Hazel to ask if there was any mail there for him. She said, "I'll go out and see if the mail has been delivered yet. Just hang on."

185

Don waited and waited, but Hazel never came back to the phone. So he started to worry about her and decided to drive over to her house to make sure nothing was wrong.

He drove up to the front of the house and there she was, talking to a neighbor lady. She said, "Hi, Don."

Don said, "Just tell me one thing, Aunt Hazel. Is your phone off the hook?"

Hazel said, "Oh, for goodness sakes," and started to laugh till the tears ran down her face. Do you see what I mean when I say she was easy to write for?

Rounding out our cast of regulars was a breathless fourteen-year-old, played by Janet Waldo. We called her character Emmy Lou, and she was a composite of about four or five teenagers who frequented the Los Angeles Tennis Club's swimming pool during vacation time. Emmy Lou was played very dramatically and emotionally with a contagious enthusiasm that often swept me right along with her. The character was an exaggerated one, but Janet played it so expertly that it always maintained its believability.

At the same time Janet was appearing with us, she was starring in the series "Corliss Archer." Because of a conflict in schedules, she eventually had to leave us and was replaced by another excellent young actress named Barbara Eiler, who later became our sister-in-law by marrying Don. Together they became the parents of two lovely daughters, Kathy and Laurie.

Although our responsibilities were heavy during the radio years, the actual time devoted to our weekly show left us plenty of free time to devote to each other and to the boys. We built a big swimming pool that took up most of the back yard and which was constantly filled with kids of all ages, sizes and shapes.

We converted an upstairs bedroom and sitting room into an office for me so I could sit up as late as I wanted while working on the radio scripts. As I've said, I'm a night person: I hate to go to bed before four or five and I hate to get up before noon.

186

Fortunately, Harriet is the same type, or we'd never get to see each other.

About this time, Tommy Dulin, a friend of Grace Johnson, joined our household. And what a great addition he was! Tommy had been a waiter on the Southern Pacific and had a fantastic sense of humor. He and Ricky had so many inside gags going between them that all they had to do was exchange looks and they would both break up.

One time at dinner, I happened to look up at Tommy, who was standing in back of my chair. He was gently rocking back and forth and had a faraway look in his eye. I said, "What time do we get to Kansas City, Tommy?" and from then on it became a byword in our house. Any time anyone would be caught deep in thought or daydreaming, someone would ask, "What time do we get to Kansas City?"

That dining room of ours is filled with memories—so many birthday parties and anniversaries and Thanksgivings and Christmases, not to mention a few surprises. Like the night we had six or eight guests for dinner and Ricky, who was then three years old, decided to sneak downstairs and join the party. Harriet carried him right back up again, explaining on the way that, no matter how warm it is, you don't come down into the dining room with no clothes on.

Then there was the night during Christmas week when David came dancing into the room making all sorts of silly faces. We finally discovered that he had been in the living room draining the bottoms of the Tom and Jerry glasses. We felt that six years old was a little young to get smashed, even during Christmas week.

I remember one night, when the boys were very young, we were playing a little game during dinner. Someone would name a city and the next person would have to name the state it was in. Harriet said, "Philadelphia," and David quickly piped up with, "Penicillin!"

Aside from the little games and jokes, which were usually a

187

part of the regular dinner fare, dinnertime was filled with conversation and questions—many, many questions. And like most parents, we occasionally encountered one that was not too easy to answer.

I recall one night when David suddenly said, "Pop, do you have a thousand dollars?"

I said, "Well, Dave, a person's value isn't determined just by the number of dollars he happens to have in his pocket or in the bank. People own automobiles and houses and clothes and furniture. But the most important asset is a man's character, his reputation and his skills, his ability to do things. So when you add all those things up I would say that just about everybody you know has a thousand dollars."

There was a small pause, and then he said, "You mean everybody except you?"

Then there was the night when both boys came down to dinner, their faces aglow with excitement. "You won't believe this!" said David, "but Ricky can read!" Since Ricky was only five at the time, we had our doubts until David produced a first-grade reader and stood by, beaming, while his little brother read the entire book aloud to us. We never were quite sure whether he really could read or whether he had memorized the book by having David read it to him.

Most little boys are willing to be subjected to almost anything rather than to put out their lights and go to sleep, and David and Ricky were no exceptions. I used to take advantage of this by reading aloud to them excerpts from Dickens or Goldsmith or short stories by Saki and a few like "The Freshest Kid" and "The Baby Party" from F. Scott Fitzgerald—things that I thought might stimulate their interest in something other than the ever-present comic books.

We also had an almost-nightly game of hide and seek. The boys' wing of the house consisted of two large bedrooms and baths with a hall in between and several closets and storage spaces, so there were plenty of good places to hide, especially if you were little and could roll up into a small ball.

188

There was sort of an unwritten law that, if I should happen to discover one of the boys a bit too soon, I would make believe I hadn't seen him in order to prolong the game to a respectable length.

On the other hand, on those occasions when they would be so well hidden that I had trouble finding them, I had a sure-fire, though slightly unsportsmanlike, way of uncovering them. I would walk into one of the bathrooms and say, in a loud voice, "No, he isn't in there," whereupon I would flush the toilet.

In the old days when there were theatrical stock companies in practically every city in the United States, the scripts would have copious stage directions to help the actor assimilate his part more quickly. An old favorite was the admonition to "wait for the laugh that is sure to follow." That was the way it was with our hide-go-seek routine. If you are a father playing the game with one of your small fry and you want to discover where he is hiding, just say, "No, he isn't in there," then flush the toilet and "wait for the laugh that is sure to follow."

The grand finale of the evening ritual, after the boys had been tucked in, was the singing of the Lord's Prayer, which had been learned from a well-worn disc recorded by John Charles Thomas. An added fillip to the vocal rendition was that Harriet and I were expected to assist the boys in achieving the proper vibrato when they reached the high notes at the finish. This was accomplished by placing a hand on each boy's diaphram and vibrating it up and down as one would play a musical saw. A bit sacrilegious, perhaps, but it created an interesting effect.

In contrast to David, who had always been an outgoing little boy, Ricky was a quiet little fellow and very private person even at the age of five or six. We had a large console radio in our living room with a speaker at the bottom, directed at the floor. It was in a corner of the room where one of the heat registers was located. Ricky would tune in to the classical music station, then open the heat register and lie under there, for hours at a time, completely lost in his own little world. I have often harbored the suspicion that many of those who profess a great in-

189

terest in opera or symphony music would really rather be listening to Lawrence Welk or Guy Lombardo, but Ricky at the age of five or six wasn't trying to impress anybody. As I said to Harriet one day, "He's one classical music lover that I'm sure of."

My working habits during the radio years were unorthodox, to say the least, but they worked fine for me. I usually got up about noon, and our secretary would come in at one o'clock and work until about five-thirty. Jackie Brundage was an attractive young girl who had just graduated from Pasadena Junior College and who could type faster than anyone I had ever known in my life. While working on scripts, I would write in longhand and then Jackie would type the final copy.

As she was typing she would laugh out loud if something struck her as being funny. Naturally, when this happened I would immediately look up from what I was doing and ask her what line she was laughing at, and invariably it would be either a straight line or some line that I didn't think was especially funny. It got so puzzling that I would make a mental note of these lines, and, sure enough, when we tried them at the preview the audience didn't think they were funny either. It got so I was almost afraid to ask what she was laughing at, because if it happened to be a favorite line of mine, it was too discouraging to learn that the audience wasn't going to laugh at it—that's how dependable she was at laughing at the wrong things. But then gradually a change started to take place. Whether it was from typing so many scripts or listening to so many shows—whatever it was—Jackie's batting average started to get better and better until by the time she left us to get married eight years later, I'd get worried about the lines she didn't laugh at.

Thursday night was the toughie. Jackie would come in at about five in the afternoon, have dinner with us, and since I had to drop the finished script off at the radio station's mimeo department early Friday morning, we'd work right through until five or six o'clock, at which time I'd drive her home. I often wondered what her mother thought she did for a living.

190

I played tennis at the Los Angeles Tennis Club almost every afternoon from about four until six, and the boys went ice skating with Harriet at the Polar Place three or four times a week and also managed to squeeze in some horseback riding at Griffith Park.

The Los Angeles Tennis Club was a great place in the 1940s and '50s. Just about every name tennis player in the United States could be seen playing there any afternoon in the week: Don Budge, Bobby Riggs, Jack Kramer, Pancho Segura, Gene Mako, Frank Parker, Pancho Gonzales, Ted Schroeder—all the great ones. And the nicest part about it all was that the "B" players like me got to play with them occasionally. There was only one problem about that: Some pretty fancy betting went on over there, and when, for instance, Don Budge and I teamed up against, say, Frank Parker and another "B" player, and there was a hundred dollars riding on the match, you can imagine who they hit all the balls at.

There were some really weird matches played over there, too. Bobby Riggs beat me in a close singles match that was played on the center court one day. In fairness to Bobby, I have to admit that he was wearing a top coat and gave me the alleys and fifteen points a game.

At the risk of sounding immodest, I'd like to report at this time my most rewarding victory on the tennis courts. Actually, it wasn't a victory in the true sense of the word—it was a moral victory, which is a nice way of saying that we lost, but only after a struggle that can aptly be described as heroic.

My partner was Bill Self, who is now and has been for the past eight or ten years in charge of all television for Twentieth Century–Fox. Bill had been an outstanding player in college, and although he still played a good steady game he had been out of active competition for several years. As to my game, it could best be described as "enthusiastic"—or perhaps, at times, "acrobatic."

The tournament we were playing in, the Pacific Southwest, was one of the most prestigious in the United States and drew the top players from all over the world.

191

Our opponents in the second round were Drobny and Cernic, of the Czechoslovakian Davis Cup team, who had been top-seeded and who were heavy favorites to win the tournament. In fact Drobny would, a few years later, win the singles crown at Wimbledon.

Urged on by the highly partisan crowd, consisting mostly of personal friends of ours, Bill and I played way over our heads, and the issue was actually in doubt until the final point. The cheers brought Perry Jones, the czar of West Coast tennis, over to Court 4, where we were playing, and I could guess what was going through his mind: "If those two clowns should, by some fluke, luck this out, the whole tournament goes down the drain."

The tournament was saved, however, because Drobny and Cernic finally beat us by breaking my service twice. Bill didn't hold it against me, though—although, now that I think of it, the only studio in town where Harriet and I have never worked is Twentieth Century–Fox. You don't think . . . oh, no—I'm sure it's just a coincidence.

Our contract with our sponsors called for us to furnish an eleven-piece orchestra, but there were certain effects that I wanted to get in our background and underscoring music that could only be achieved with a bigger band, so we augmented our standard instrumentation of seven brass, five woodwinds, and four rhythm by adding a five-piece string section (three violins, a viola, and a cello) and a harp.

During our last season with Red Skelton, Billy May, formerly with Glenn Miller, had joined us to play first trumpet and write arrangements, so when we started our own show I asked Billy to continue with us in the same capacity. It was soon evident that he not only wrote brilliant dance arrangements but also had a great talent for writing "bridges" (musical interludes to blend one scene into another) and underscoring or "mood" music.

Billy and I had our own unique method of working together. Saturday evening, after I had finished editing the script following the Friday-night preview, I would call him on the phone and say, for instance, "On page 4 we need about an eight-bar bridge that goes something like this"—and I would whistle a few bars (usually something stolen from Rimski-Korsakov or Khachaturian). Billy would say, "I've gotcha," and have it written down as fast as I could whistle it. We'd go through the entire script whistling or humming back and forth, and the whole process would take no more than ten or fifteen minutes.

Billy, who, like me, was also a night person, would have all the scores in the hands of the copyists by morning, and they would have the arrangements ready for the rehearsal that afternoon.

Fortunately, our show was received extremely well from the start, both by the critics and by the public, so our renewal by our sponsors for the second year was assured almost from the outset.

October of 1945 found us making several changes in the show. Tommy Bernard replaced Joel Davis in the part of David, and Henry Blair came in to play Ricky. Henry was about thirteen, but he managed to pitch his voice high enough so that a listener would believe he was five, which was Ricky's age at the time.

In order to provide a musical interlude between acts, we brought in the King Sisters, who did a fine job with extraordinary arrangements and a great blend of voices. Also, for the first time I was able to talk Billy into conducting the band. Prior to that I had conducted the musical bridges with my left hand while reading the script, which was being held in my right hand. This of course made no sense at all, and must have looked pretty silly to the studio audience. As was to be expected, Billy soon became just as expert at conducting as he was at arranging.

The big change as we moved into our second year, however, was in our script preparation. Jack Douglas moved over to the "Jack Carson Show" and John P. Medbury went back east to write for Martha Ray, and I brought in Sol Sax and Sherwood Schwartz to work on scripts and Ben Gershman to work on story lines.

Ben is an interesting guy with a very sound literary background and a wry sense of humor. Writers as a group are notoriously insecure people anyway, and Ben—at least when he worked for us—was no exception.

Our weekly routine began when Ben would phone me with a story idea. He and I would discuss it and usually have several phone conversations where we would get it into a workable form. Then Ben would type up a two- or three-page outline, which he would bring to our story meeting to be further discussed by the entire staff.

I could always judge by the tone of Ben's voice on the phone whether he thought he had a good story idea. Sometimes I'd just have to say, "It sounds good. I'll see you Monday night." Then again, there would be those days when our phone dialogue would run something like this:

OzziE: Hello.
BEN: Hi. This is Ben.
OzziE: Hi, Ben. What have you got?
BEN: Well, I've got a little something here, it seems fresh to me but it's probably been kicked around before.
OzziE: Maybe not. Let's hear it.
BEN: You know, a guy does his best. You keep trying, sometimes you feel like you're taking money under false pretenses. Sometimes you get lucky, sometimes you come up empty.
OzziE: Not very often. Not with you. What have you got there?
BEN: Well, it's really not much more than an idea.
OzziE: Maybe we can work something out from it. What is it?
BEN: Well, it's . . . it's really lousy. I'll call you back later. (*He hangs up.*)

As you can infer from the above, Ben was hardly a bundle of self-confidence, and yet week after week for the entire ten years we were on radio, he managed to come up with a viable story premise.

During the ten years of our radio show's existence we had a veritable army of writers working on the scripts for varying lengths of time. They included (besides Ben, Sol, and Sher-

194

wood) John L. Greene, Paul West, Bill Davenport, Frank Fox, Bill Manhoff, Poot Pray, Rik Vollaerts, and Selma Diamond. Also joining us the last few years on radio and carrying over into television were Jay Sommers, Dick Bensfield, Perry Grant, and my brother Don.

The story meetings for the radio show were held at our house on Monday evenings. We usually had about five writers working at one time, although some of them worked as two-man teams, delivering one script between them.

Our meetings started at eight-thirty, and the first hour was usually devoted to social conversation and discussions of topics of the day. Then Ben would hand out the story outlines that he had drawn up as a result of our phone conversations, and the general discussion would begin and continue, except for the ice cream break, until two or three o'clock in the morning.

The ice cream break had to be seen to be believed. The delivery boy from Schwab's Drug Store would show up at about eleven o'clock with four or five quarts of ice cream, usually vanilla, chocolate, and strawberry, which would all be dumped together into a huge silver bowl. Each writer had his own bowl with his name on it and would serve himself with a big silver ladle. I'm sure ours was the only writing staff in show business history with a collection of ice cream freaks.

The discussions got to be quite spirited at times, but we always managed to hammer out a complete story before the evening was over. Each writer would then write a complete script and bring it in to the meeting the following week. I would then take what I considered the best parts of each script and blend them into one master script, which we would preview before a live audience. This preview was put on discs which I would take home and use as a guide for my final editing and rewriting. It was a long and tedious process, but I do think we wound up with some of the finest scripts in the history of situation comedy.

For the next few years our domestic lives followed much the same pattern as any average family, and our notebook of activities and memories was, I'm sure, quite typical: David joined the Cub Scouts and Harriet and Katherine Thornbury became den mothers, while Ricky (whose favorite radio program was, according to him, "The Lone Stranger") wondered why he too couldn't be a "Club Scout"; David saw smoke drifting up over the hill and sent in a fire alarm at the corner of Franklin and Camino Palmero—at least it looked like smoke, but you really couldn't tell because it had disappeared by the time the fire-trucks arrived; Ricky fell out of a tree and broke his arm; David threw a make-believe hand grenade (actually a rock) in the direction of the enemy trenches while they were playing "war" in the back lot and scored a direct hit on Anthony Love-man, raising a lump the size of a baseball on poor Anthony's head; Ricky suddenly started to get asthma attacks of frightening intensity, which after three or four years just as suddenly disappeared.

There were the usual birthday parties, trips to the Griffith Park Zoo, innumerable visits to the Ferris wheel and carnival rides on La Cienaga and Beverly Boulevard; and picnics and lunches at the Farmer's Market.

Harriet just reminded me that once when she was driving the boys over to the Farmer's Market for lunch, an ambulance sped by them and Ricky shouted, "There goes an anulope!"

"Don't be stupid," said David, with that certain disdain that older boys reserve for their younger brothers on such occasions, "that's not an anulope, that's an ambliance."

Our professional lives were moving along in fine fashion. Our ratings remained steady, and Maury Foladare, who had come with us to handle publicity, was doing an excellent job with the press and public relations. By 1946 we had dispensed with our singing and band numbers altogether, and the only music remaining in our show was the underscoring and "bridges." These, I must add, were still being scored in a most imaginative and interesting way by Billy May, whose great creative talents added much to the production values and to the subliminal enjoyment of the listener.

The change in image to a point where the public and our fellow performers no longer thought of us as a bandleader and vocalist actually took place so naturally and gradually that we weren't aware of it ourselves. In fact, I still recall that it came as a bit of a shock the first time a little friend of David's said to me, "Is it true that you used to be a bandleader?"

Of course this was years ago, long before the battered cliché of "What does Ozzie do for a living?" became a standard ploy of unimaginative nightclub comics and newspaper writers in search of a column. I thought I had put the old bromide to rest when Harriet and I did a sketch on the "Johnny Carson Show" a couple of years ago and I inserted the following dialogue:

HARRIET: Would you mind answering a personal question? It's something that's been bothering me for years.
OZZIE: Of course not. You know we have no secrets from each other. What is it?
HARRIET: What do you do for a living?

It got a very big laugh from the audience, of course, and, as I said, I thought that would be the end of it. But to this day scarcely a week goes by that somebody doesn't sidle up to me and hit me with the same old line. As you can well imagine, after all these years I can always see it coming. A sort of self-satisfied little smile comes over the person's face as he says, "There's one thing I always wondered about your show"— whereupon I say to myself, "Here it comes"—and then, sure enough: "It was never explained. What did you do for a living?"

If I have had a good night's sleep and have plenty of time, I will carefully explain that we have always tried to keep the show honest—that when we started on radio back in 1944 I was a bandleader both on the show and in real life, and that if I were suddenly to become a plumber or an insurance salesman it would simply not ring true, also I would further explain that our scenes were almost always played as if it were a Saturday or Sunday, and that we were careful never to have me at home while the

197

boys went off to school—that I did occasionally go downtown to an office, but I never designated the kind of work I did because by my not designating a specific job people were able to identify with me more readily.

As I say, this is the explanation I give if I have had plenty of rest and am not especially rushed for time. Otherwise, I simply smile and say, "I was a bum."

I find that I give that latter answer more and more, lately. Not that I'm usually rushed for time and don't get enough sleep. It's just that I find that it's shorter and enables us to move on to something else and that the person really didn't expect an answer anyway.

18

Sunday, February 20, 1949, was a very, very important day in the lives of the Nelson family. On that day we broadcast a show called "Invitation to Dinner," and the script started as follows:

ANNOUNCER [*Verne Smith*]: At 1847 Rogers Road where the Nelsons live, there's usually an air of happiness prevailing. . . . It starts at the big friendly welcome mat on the front porch and continues clear through the big friendly house to the big friendly back yard where Nick, the family setter, lives—He's the big friendly dog with the laugh in his bark. But today, there's one face that doesn't fit in with this happy atmosphere. . . . Young David Nelson seems to have something on his mind.

HARRIET: What's wrong David? You've hardly said a word all morning.

DAVID: It's nothing, Mom.

HARRIET: There's something bothering you. . . . What is it?

DAVID: It's nothing, really, Mom.

HARRIET: David. . . .

OZZIE: Harriet, please. You say it's nothing, David, is that right?

DAVID: That's right, Pop.

OZZIE: All right, if it's nothing, it's nothing. . . . We'll just forget it. (*Sighs.*) Let's see what's here in the paper.

DAVID: (*Pause.*) Well . . . it *is* something.

OZZIE: Oh. . . . (*Puts paper down.*) I kinda thought you'd like to tell us about it. What seems to be the trouble?

DAVID: It's . . . nothing, Pop.

OZZIE: Look, David. . . . We're not trying to pry into your personal affairs, but why don't you just tell us about it. Maybe we can help you. . . .

DAVID: It's kinda silly, I guess. . . . Grace Anderson invited me to her party Friday night and I told her I'd come.

HARRIET: That sounds very nice.

DAVID: Yeah, but our team is supposed to play basketball Friday night. . . . So I gotta tell her I can't make it.

RICKY: Is David a dope, Pop?

OZZIE: No, Ricky, read your comic book. In other words, David, you mean you forgot you had to play basketball and that's why you accepted her invitation?

DAVID: Oh no. . . . I remembered it.

OZZIE: You mean when you accepted Grace's invitation you knew you couldn't make it . . . that it was the same night as your basketball game?

DAVID: Yessir.

RICKY: *Now* is David a dope, Pop?

HARRIET: Ricky! . . . Then why did you accept it, David?

DAVID: Well, golly, Mom, she seemed so excited about the party. . . . I just didn't have the heart to disappoint her.

OZZIE: I realize how you must have felt, David . . . but you're going to have to tell her sometime and now it'll be a bigger disappointment. You'll find it's much better to tell people the truth right off. . . . Otherwise you wind up in an embarrassing situation for everybody.

RICKY: Are they gonna have ice cream at the party?

DAVID: Oh sure . . . gallons of it. . . . That's another thing, Pop. I'd feel awful silly if I turned down the party and then the basketball game was called off.

HARRIET: Do you think that's possible?

RICKY: They never called one off yet.

DAVID: Oh Ricky, you keep quiet.

OZZIE: Do you think it may be called off, David?

DAVID: I don't know. . . . There's always a chance . . . lots of things could happen.

OZZIE: Like what? . . .

DAVID: Well . . . suppose the captain of the other team gets the measles.

200

OZZIE: That sounds to me like a pretty remote possibility.
DAVID: Maybe not, Pop. . . . A couple of weeks ago, we were supposed to take an arithmetic test and the teacher got the appendicitis.
OZZIE: That was just a rare coincidence. . . . I think the safest thing for you to do is call Grace on the phone and tell her you can't make it.
DAVID: Maybe I could go to the party first and then play basketball.
HARRIET: I think you'd be too full of ice cream and cake to play much of a game.
RICKY: He could be the basketball.
DAVID: I guess I'll think it over.
OZZIE: It's your problem, David. . . . But you know the old proverb . . . Never put off until tomorrow what you can do today. . . . Procrastination is the thief of time. . . .
HARRIET: Oh. . . .
OZZIE: Were you going to say something, Harriet?
HARRIET: Yes . . . did you go downtown and pay the gas bill yesterday? You said you would.
OZZIE: I'm glad you mentioned that, Harriet. . . . Here is a perfect example of the point I'm trying to make, David. Your mother asked me to pay the gas bill yesterday, and instead of putting it off until tomorrow, I'm going down and pay it today.
(*Music: bridge.*)

What's so special about this particular script and this particular date? It's simply that, for the first time the part of David was played by David Nelson, age twelve, and the part of Ricky was played by Ricky Nelson, age eight.

Between the years 1945 and 1948 Harriet and I had made guest appearances with Jack Benny, Eddie Cantor, Fred Allen, Frank Sinatra, Ken Murray, Al Jolson, Art Linkletter, Charles Laughton and Elsa Lanchester, Dinah Shore, Tallulah Bankhead, and just about everyone else who used guest stars, including Bing Crosby.

201

Our appearance with Bing stands out in my memory for a couple of reasons. Along with millions of others, I had always admired him not only for his singing and acting ability, but most especially because of his nonchalant, totally relaxed manner. Perhaps "envied" would be a better word. I had thought to myself many times, "Why do I always get these little butterflies in my stomach every time I perform and yet Bing just stands there completely at ease and as comfortable as if he were in his own living room?"

I said to myself, "At least I'm not going to let him see that I'm nervous."

The red light went on to signify that we were on the air, and there was old Bing, nonchalant as usual, up there just having a good time.

Now it was our turn, and as we came up to the microphone to read our lines I looked over at the old crooner and noticed just the slightest bit of a tremor in the area of his upper lip. I said to myself, "God bless you, Bing Crosby."

A couple of days after our appearance on the Crosby show, Maury Foladare, who also handled publicity for Bing, called me and said, "Bing told me that he really enjoyed working with you and Harriet and that if you could come up with a story idea for him and one of his boys he'd love to come on your show with you."

This of course was wonderful news, and we immediately went to work on a script for Bing and his youngest son, Lindsay, who was about the same age as our David.

When David and Ricky heard that Linny was coming on our show they immediately wanted to know why they couldn't come on, too. They had been playing tennis with the Crosby boys over at Bing's, and evidently they had all talked it over and had decided it would be a swell idea. Harriet and I weren't so sure. It was okay for Harriet and me to get butterflies in our stomachs every week, and for Bing to get twitching face muscles—or even for Linny, for that matter, since for him it would be a one-time shot—but we knew that once David and Ricky came on the show, that would be it: they would be professional performers from then on with all the pressures and heartaches inherent in our business.

We finally reached a compromise. We agreed that they could do the preview show but not the actual broadcast. In that way they could give the thing a try without making a final commitment.

Before we had gone more than two or three minutes into the show we knew what the decision would be. David and Ricky were knocking off their lines like seasoned veterans, and the laughs were rolling in like tidal waves.

This happened in December of 1948. We talked over the whole situation at great length—first just Harriet and I, and then all four of us. We pointed out the hard work and the responsibilities involved, but David said that he and Ricky had always known that sooner or later they would go on the show— that it was what they had always really wanted and yes, they were sure.

And so in February of 1949, for the first time, the billboard read "THE ADVENTURES OF OZZIE AND HARRIET, starring the entire Nelson family: Ozzie, Harriet, David, and Ricky."

The addition of David and Ricky to our radio cast proved to be a tremendous asset to the show. Both boys were quick students and seemed to have instinctive comedy timing. They were also of great help in the preparation of the scripts. I found myself asking them more and more, "Is this the way you would say this?" If their speeches sounded awkward or stilted or not phrased properly for their age group, we would catch it at the first reading rehearsal. I would try to pick up their speech mannerisms and write them into the scripts just as we had always done with Harriet and me. Of great value to us in this area was the fact that Don, who was now at the University of Southern California, had joined our writing staff and was especially adept at writing for the boys, because he of course knew them so well and spent so much time with them. It was Don who first wrote

203

the line, "I don't mess around, boy," which proved to be a great catch phrase for Ricky and which got a tremendous laugh every time he said it.

I remember that Ricky had always pronounced "unusual" as "unusural." It was so typical of an eight-year-old and sounded so natural that we had never corrected him. One day, however, our regular network producer was sick and a new man was sitting in for him. He was in the booth and we were rehearsing on stage. We had purposely written the word "unusual" in one of Ricky's lines, and he of course read it "unusural"—as usual. The new producer, trying to be helpful, pressed the talk-back button and called out, "No, no, Ricky. The word is 'unusual.' You're saying 'unusural.'" It reminded me vaguely of an item I had once read in the *New Yorker* magazine about a light that had been burning continuously in a cathedral in Rome for 350 years until one day in 1938 when an American tourist blew it out.

Prior to 1949, the three major networks had had an absurd ruling that all radio broadcasts had to be done completely "live" —that is, nothing could be recorded and played back at another time. With the advent of tape, however, Bing Crosby and others, including ourselves, started to pressure the networks to allow us to tape the shows ahead of time and then edit them in order to get the best possible result. Fortunately, the networks gave in just as David and Ricky joined the show, so we were able to tape the programs at a time that wouldn't interfere too much with their schoolwork. This was fortunate because neither boy was exactly enamored of school anyway. In fact, I remember one night when Harriet was putting a little pressure on Ricky to get him going on his homework, he maintained that it was a waste of time. "I'll probably be a radio actor all my life anyway," he argued, "and I can read the scripts okay now, so why should I have to go to school anymore?"

David, along about this time, was experiencing all the difficulties that older brothers have known—probably since civilization began—with the little guy getting the lion's share of the attention. It has happened with the Osmond Brothers and the

Jackson Five, it happened with my brother Al and me when we were little guys, and it happened with David and Ricky.

It's a cruel, hard fact that a punchline delivered by a little guy of eight will get a much bigger laugh than the same line delivered by a boy of twelve. As a result, Ricky was getting more and more of the laugh lines and David was getting more and more of the straight lines.

It's amazing how thoughtless people can be about other people's children. Time and again when we were on radio, and even more so after we had gone on to television, perfectly normal-looking people would come up to the four of us and say something like, "Of course, David is okay, but *this little Ricky!*" —whereupon they would literally push Dave aside to get at Rick. Harriet used to say, "It'll be a wonder if David doesn't murder Ricky in his bed some night."

To David's credit it must be said that if he ever felt any jealousy toward his little brother he didn't show it. And to Ricky's credit it must be said that, at that time, and even later when he was accorded the kind of frantic adulation that few people ever experience, he always remained well aware of his tremendous stature but genuinely modest about it.

One night a few months ago when Rick was on the Carson show, Johnny was asking him about his reaction to that "teen-age idol" period, and Rick said that it was really weird—that he would come off a tour of one-nighters where the girls would be screaming and fainting and trying to tear his clothes off and he'd get back home and his mother would call out, "Ricky! Come back upstairs here and pick up this wet towel!" He said he'd say to himself, "Doesn't she realize who I am??" But as he told it, he had a twinkle in his eye.

We have recently talked to Dave and Rick at great length about their relationship during those years, and David has said that because of the difference in their ages (about three-and-a-half years) he had never really felt a sense of competition between them, but rather had felt a deep sense of pride in his brother's accomplishments. Also, he said that the mere fact of his being older than Ricky had given him a sort of number-one status—an edge that Rick could never overcome.

Like all brothers, they of course had their little set-tos, some of them funny and a few that were not so funny.

We had never allowed the boys to have guns, but one Christmas a neighbor gave David a BB gun. We told him he could keep it on condition that he promise not to shoot at anything that moved. The next morning Harriet discovered a series of small indentations, forming a semicircle, in the headboard of Ricky's bed (something like this: .•˙   ˙•.). Astute maternal detective work disclosed the frightening fact that Ricky had awakened that morning to find the BB gun pointed at his head. David had said, "Hold still and I'll show you what a good marksman I am," and had proceded to shoot a small semicircle of BBs around Ricky's head. In spite of David's claim that he hadn't broken his promise—since Ricky hadn't moved (thank goodness) —the BB gun was immediately heaved into the trash can. About a week later, however, it reappeared. We were going to the beach for a few days, and as I started to back the car out of the driveway I heard this loud crunching noise under the car. Investigation turned up a mangled BB gun. David had tied it to the drive shaft in order to smuggle it out to the beach, but had neglected to take into account the fact that when the car moves the drive shaft turns with it. So if you have a BB gun that you want crunched up, I can think of no more effective method.

There was another rather frightening little escapade of David's that we didn't hear about until years later. It seems that David, Ricky, and a bunch of the neighborhood kids were fooling around in Bobby Vitto's back yard when David picked up a pitchfork that was lying there and playfully jabbed it down on Ricky's foot, expecting him to jump away. Something went wrong with the timing, however, and Ricky wound up stapled to the ground. The prongs of the pitchfork had gone right through his shoe—but had miraculously missed his toes.

Lest you get the idea that David was trying to do away with

his little brother in those early years, I must say that he more than made up for it one afternoon when Ricky was riding his bicycle around the swimming pool (which incidentally was against the house rules). He had borrowed a pair of Harriet's boots to make himself look more like a motorcycle rider, and was wearing his football helmet to complete the costume. He had attached playing cards to the wheel of his bike, and the clickity-clack of the spokes spinning against the cards was supposed to approximate the sound of the motor.

Evidently he got going too fast or became too daring in his turns, because the bike skidded and Ricky was dumped into the pool. The boots, a few sizes too big for him, immediately filled up with water and pulled him down to the bottom like an anchor. He most certainly would have drowned if David hadn't dived in, fully clothed, and pulled him out.

Ricky, from the time he was a little fellow, had always been very big on costumes. One day, when he was about four, he was dressed up in his Indian suit and David decided to add to the overall effect by daubing on some warpaint. Getting the paint was no problem, since the Thornburys' house was being painted and Will was a willing conspirator. The green housepaint worked so well on Ricky's face that they decided to do his chest and stomach as well. This gave them a really brilliant idea, and little Ricky wound up as the smallest jolly green giant on record. I'm not sure he was so jolly about it, but he certainly was green—all over. Have you ever tried to get housepaint off a four-year-old boy?

A few years later when we got a television set, Ricky would change clothes according to the show he was watching. It was not unusual during an early fall Saturday afternoon for him to change from a cowboy suit to a clown suit to a baseball suit to a football suit within the space of an hour. Of course, when he was watching ice hockey or the roller derby it required a little improvising.

I hasten to add, however, that Ricky's fascination with dressing up didn't extend to wearing a necktie. I recall one time

207

when he was nine or ten, we had been invited to have dinner at Romanoff's (which was, at the time, one of the most prestigious restaurants in town) with a group of network executives and their wives. Usually we spared the boys this kind of ordeal, but this was a very special occasion, and they were interesting people, and we thought the boys might enjoy it. We didn't encounter too much resistance until Harriet started to put a tie on Ricky. "This Romanoff's," he suddenly exploded, "is it a good place to eat?"

19

At the end of the 1948–49 season we had completed our fifth year of the radio show, and our sponsors, the International Silver Company, no longer had options on our services. They were willing to continue on a year-to-year basis, but I felt that I wanted to hold out for the security of a five-year deal with no options. They didn't feel that they wanted to commit themselves for that length of time, so, with handshakes, kind words, a few tears, and a complete set of beautiful silver that we still cherish, we came to a friendly parting of the ways. We would have many sponsors in the years to follow, several of whom (like the people at Hotpoint, Eastman Kodak, Quaker Oats, and American Dairy) we enjoyed a close relationship with, but none could ever quite replace in our affections the good people from Meriden, Connecticut, who gave us our first opportunity.

At the same time that our contract with International Silver ran out, I negotiated a settlement to terminate our agency agreement with the William Morris office. Here again, our relationship had been a friendly one. In fact, years later we would again have them represent us when Norman Brokaw (younger brother of Sid, who was one of the original members of our band) became head of their television department.

In the late spring of 1949, however, I had a special kind of deal in mind, and I wanted us to be represented by a special kind of guy with a special kind of talent. So we flew to New

209

York, signed with Music Corporation of America, and put ourselves in the hands of our old friend Sonny Werblin.

Sonny and I had at least two things in common. He too was a Rutgers graduate, and he too was married to a beautiful exband singer (his wife, the lovely and talented Leah Ray, had been the featured vocalist with Phil Harris's band). Our thinking processes were also quite alike, as was evidenced by our first meeting in his office.

I don't remember our conversation word for word, but I recall that I explained to him that I thought I could do a better job creatively if I could be relieved of the constant pressure of options coming up every year—that it was as if we were constantly on trial. I said I realized that this was standard procedure in the business but that I'd like to try to negotiate a deal directly with one of the networks whereby they would guarantee us a firm five years and relieve us of the worrying as to whether the sponsor was going to pick us up or not.

"That sounds great," said Sonny, "but while we're at it, let's go all the way. Let's make it for ten years—the first noncancellable ten-year contract in the history of show business." And that was the deal we signed with the American Broadcasting Company on July 14, 1949.

The contract was for the four of us and guaranteed us a basic salary for ten years whether we worked or not. ABC had the option of putting us on television after the second year, with additional income to be negotiated at that time. Since the boys were only nine and twelve years of age, it was agreed that their contracts would be cancellable at any time by either boy.

The negotiating was on a very friendly basis, with Bob Kintner and Charles ("Bud") Barry representing ABC and Sonny and I representing us. One very important clause that they (fortunately) readily agreed to was that I would have complete artistic control of the shows on both radio and television. This proved to be invaluable in that it insulated me from any interference on the part of sponsors, advertising agencies, or network

210

executives. I have always felt that a continuing series should represent the thinking of one person in order to preserve the consistency not only in the characterizations but in the general style of the show. I believe the most successful shows are those where the producer has surrounded himself with the best possible talent, but where the decisions are in the hands of one person rather than a committee.

We knew that we would eventually make the transition to television, but we also wanted to make sure that we didn't make the move prematurely. Aaron Rosenberg, a former All-American football player from USC, was at the time a producer at Universal studios and since he had evinced some interest in doing a motion picture based on our radio series, we decided that this would give us an opportunity to see how the family came across on film. As a result, we authorized Arthur Park of M.C.A. to work out a deal as quickly as possible.

In the meantime, we had bought a big old Mediterranean-type beach house at Camel Point in South Laguna and headed down there almost every Friday night immediately following the taping of our radio show. David told me a year or so ago that some of his most pleasant memories are of the four of us driving down to the beach, singing songs and telling jokes or listening to the car radio—all of us relaxed in the knowledge that we had the weekend to ourselves with no responsibilities.

The surf at Camel Point is unusually rough, and the riptides there can be quite treacherous at times. There was no life guard station at that part of the beach, so on more than a few occasions I had to pull someone out. It was usually a female who would not necessarily be in really deep water but who would get knocked off her feet by a wave and then start to panic as she felt the undertow pulling her out. It also seemed that invariably she would lose the top to her bathing suit when the wave hit her, which made for some interesting but rather awkward rescues.

Rick's most vivid recollection of Camel Point is of an incident

211

that occurred when he was about nine or ten. He and I were in one of those little navy surplus life rafts. I was rowing, facing shore, and he was sitting opposite me facing out to sea. Suddenly he yelled, "Turn around quick, there's a whale!"

I said, "Come on, Ricky, if you want to go back just say so, don't make up a story like that."

He said, "I'm not kidding. I just saw a whale as big as a house! There it is again!"

I turned around and sure enough, there was the biggest whale I'd ever seen in my life, not more than fifty feet in front of us—that is, he was the biggest I'd ever seen until another one surfaced right alongside him. He was even bigger. Needless to say, I wasted no time in turning the raft around and heading back to shore. I know that whales are supposed to be very friendly, but somehow it just didn't seem like the right time to stop and find out.

David was selected as quarterback on the All-Star team of the YMCA Junior High School touch football league in 1950, and Ricky won his first tennis trophy when he and his partner were runners-up in the eleven-and-under division at Altadena. Their most interesting match—from a spectator's point of view —was in the quarter-finals when one of Ricky's opponents ran into a rather unusual problem—his pants kept falling down.

My brother Don, Bill Davenport, and I wrote the screenplay for the motion picture at Universal, and we called it *Here Come the Nelsons*. We wrote it during the spring of 1951, and it was filmed in August of that same year. It was, of course, the first picture for David and Ricky. And it was also one of the first for a handsome young leading man who had just changed his name from Roy Fitzgerald to Rock Hudson. Others in the cast were Gale Gordon, Jim Backus, Sheldon Leonard, Barbara Lawrence, Frank Nelson, and Ed Max.

Although the picture was made on a modest budget, it was well directed by Fred de Cordova and seemed to come off amazingly well, especially those scenes involving the boys. Most importantly from our standpoint, however, was that it demonstrated to us that our type of comedy projected just as well on the screen as it did on radio and that the transition from radio to television would not be too difficult.

The first telecast of "The Adventures of Ozzie and Harriet" was on October 3, 1952. We had started filming the show in August, and, needless to say, that first season was a hectic one. In order to keep our production costs at a minimum, Harriet and I each took on a few extra duties in addition to our acting chores. I functioned as producer, director, story editor, and head writer, while Harriet supervised the boys' wardrobe and was responsible for most of the original set decorating.

We filmed the show at General Service Studios, which is located at Las Palmas near Santa Monica Boulevard in Hollywood. This was most convenient for us because it was only a ten-minute drive from our house and just a few blocks from Hollywood High School, where David was a sophomore, and even closer to Bancroft Junior High, where Ricky went to school.

In retrospect, I don't know how we found time to fulfill all our obligations. We not only were filming the television show every week, but were also taping the weekly radio show with an entirely different script. It makes me tired just thinking about it.

ABC had engaged a production company called Volcano Productions to produce the show and had appointed Leo Pepin, who had formerly been with CBS and MGM, as their representative to supervise costs and to act as coordinator between the production company and the network.

It's hard to realize in these days when we take for granted the clear, beautiful pictures we see on our television screens that, back in the early fifties, the technical difficulties encountered in getting an acceptable picture transmitted seemed almost insurmountable. All the networks seemed to be agreed on one thing: the best results could be obtained by "flat" pho-

213

tography—that is, by filming with the backgrounds brightly lighted to afford little contrast and to minimize, as much as possible, any shadows or dark areas. The theory was that the television projection itself would accentuate any contrast in lighting.

Actually, this type of lighting was not new. It was employed by Chaplin and Mack Sennett in the early days in order to give a vaudeville or "music hall" look to their films and to compensate for the faulty projectors in the old movie theaters.

Our film crew, like most other television crews in the early days, was composed mostly of people who had worked at Monogram, PRC, Republic, and so on—studios that had specialized in turning out "quickies"—the theory being that these people, being used to short schedules, could more easily meet the demand for speed that filming for television required.

After a few months of filming, however, I decided to make a drastic change in procedure. Our cameraman, Fred Gately, was leaving to go on another show, so it was necessary to find someone to replace him. About this time, Harriet and I happened to see a film called *A Place in the Sun,* which was directed by George Stevens and starred Montgomery Clift and Elizabeth Taylor. The photography, especially the exteriors filmed at Lake Arrowhead, was the most beautiful I had ever seen. The cinematographer, I noted, was a man named William Mellor, who would be rewarded for his fine work by winning an Academy Award that year. I called Leo Pepin and asked him if he would call Mellor, who I learned was a friend of Leo's, to find out if there was any possibility of luring him away from MGM.

Union scale for cameramen in those days was about four hundred dollars per week. I learned that Bill Mellor's salary was seven hundred and fifty, so I suggested that we offer him a thousand dollars a week with a guarantee of forty weeks, feeling that with his expertise not only would we get beautiful photography, but he could save us the difference between his salary and union scale by making speedy lighting setups and eliminating the need for retakes. To our great delight, Bill accepted—

214

but with the condition that he bring with him his own gaffer (background lighting man). This gave me a further thought. I said, "Just as the sportswriters pick an All-American football team each year, suppose you pick the best operator, the best assistant, the best second assistant, the best head grip, and so on —the best men you've ever worked with in every area, and we'll see if we can get them to come to work for us."

Fortunately, Leo Pepin was willing to put his job with ABC on the line, and so by the start of our second season we were paying higher salaries than the major studios, but we had assembled a crew of the finest, most talented people in the industry, and our photography and overall production values were the equivalent of any "A" motion picture.

As I mentioned earlier, it has been my experience that arrogance usually accompanies incompetence and that the most talented, most competent people are the nicest and the easiest to get along with. And so it was, year after year, with our crew.

I wish there were time and space to name all the fine people who worked with us throughout the fourteen years we filmed our show. It was truly like a big happy family, and regardless of the tremendous pressures and the long hours involved I can't remember not looking forward to going to work in the morning nor can I remember any unpleasantness of any kind.

As to the edicts from the network concerning "flat" lighting, we decided to simply ignore them. For a fine cameraman like Bill Mellor to make compromises in his lighting to accommodate the inefficiency of the transmission equipment seemed to me like the tail wagging the dog. We both reasoned that sooner or later equipment would be devised to handle normal-contrast lighting—since otherwise the great motion pictures, past, present, and future, would never find their way to the television screen.

Nevertheless, the fact that our shows were initially well photographed was no guarantee that they would look good on the home screen. In fact, during those early years the opposite was usually the case, much to our frustration. It was a terribly dis-

215

heartening experience, week after week, first viewing our completed film in a projection room where it looked like a beautifully photographed motion picture and then watching this same film at home on our television screen after it had been projected against a white wall at the television studio, then flashed out to the transmitter, and then to the home sets. Meanwhile, both at the television studio and at the transmitter there would be a guy with a panel full of knobs adjusting the contrast to suit his particular taste. His instructions were to keep the contrast within a certain range, so it was not unusual for him to bring up a dark area in the corner of a room—oblivious to the fact that by so doing he had completely obliterated the faces of the people.

We finally worked out a scheme where Leo Pepin or Frank McKelvy, our music editor, would go up to the television studio on the night of the broadcast and engage the engineer in conversation or bring him a sandwich—anything to keep his hands off those knobs. Meanwhile, I would phone the guy out at the transmitter to keep him away from his panel. Of course, this only helped in Los Angeles. I hate to think of what went on throughout the rest of the country. I suppose the reason the public accepted this poor quality was because television was such a novelty that most people were thrilled at the idea of getting any sort of picture in their living room.

The set we built on Stage 5 at General Service was an exact replica of the front of our own home (in fact, we sometimes photographed a long shot in front of our own house and then moved to the studio for the closer shots), but the interior, although similar in general layout and furnishings, was quite different from our own home. Throughout the fourteen years we filmed the show, however, we spent so much time on the set that the boys often said it was difficult to figure which was our real home—the one at General Service or the one at Camino Palmero.

The character of Thorny, our next door neighbor, had become such an important adjunct to our radio show that we decided to carry it over to television, and we chose Don DeFore to play the part. Besides being a skillful actor, Don is a pleasant, effervescent guy, both on and off the screen, and proved to be a happy choice. Some of our "Thorny spots" were among the highlights of our early shows. Although he was only with us for the first four years, Don told me recently that people still call out, "Hello, Thorny!" to him.

Our sponsors for the first few years were Hotpoint and Listerine. Old-timers may remember that we opened the show with a huge Hotpoint sign and a cute little teenager would dance around on it and sing out, "I'm Happy Hotpoint!" The cute little teenager is now a very fine comedienne and the star of one of the best shows on television. Everyone loves Mary Tyler Moore.

David and Ricky proved to be just as big a hit on television as they were on radio, and they took their success completely in stride. Besides doing both the television and the radio show, David managed to find time to play quarterback on the "B" football team at Hollywood High School during his sophomore and junior years and to play tailback on the varsity his senior year. He also swam backstroke on the swimming team and pitched on the baseball team.

I remember one afternoon I decided to swing around to Hollywood High while the camera crew was setting the lights for the next scene, so that I could watch a couple of innings of a game David was playing in. As luck would have it, he was just coming to bat as I turned the corner. There was no place to park, so I drove slowly down the street. I was almost a block away, but he recognized the car and waved to me and then smashed a long drive up against the fence for what was obviously an "inside the park" home run. I headed back to the studio to spread the good news, and he waved to me once again as he circled the bases.

When he arrived on the set about an hour later, Harriet rushed over to congratulate him. "Dad told us about the home run!" she said.

217

"Only thing, though," said Dave gloomily, "it wasn't a home run. I was so busy waving to Dad I forgot to touch second base."

The highlight of Dave's baseball career was, strangely enough, a game where Hollywood High lost to Van Nuys. In fact, the opposing pitcher almost pitched a no-hitter. David got the only hit—a single in the ninth inning. The Van Nuys pitcher was Don Drysdale.

Meanwhile, Ricky was busy playing tennis and basketball and taking lessons on the clarinet and drums. He hadn't been hit by the rock 'n' roll bug yet—that would come later.

Because of the difference in the boys' ages they usually traveled with different groups. But one night when Ricky was twelve and Dave was sixteen, Dave told Ricky he could go along with him to one of the dances at the high school. "I might as well warn you, though," said Dave. "Nobody'll dance with you because the girls will all be from sixteen to eighteen years old."

"That's okay," said Ricky. "I'll just listen to the band."

When they got home Dave said, "You won't believe this, but the girls all wanted to dance with Ricky. He danced every dance."

"How did you manage it, Ricky?" I asked.

"It was easy," said Rick. "I told them I was thirteen."

Almost everyone has financial problems of one kind or another. Ours was not exactly a shortage of money (although I tend to agree with the guy who first said that there is no such thing as being too rich or too thin). It was a question of how to put money in its proper perspective at our house.

The laws of California require that all contracts with minors be approved by the courts to make sure that the compensation is equitable and that the money that the minor receives is being invested properly. The California law also states that half of the money that the child earns belongs to his parents, so Harriet and I made a gift of this amount each year and had it placed in a trust fund for each boy.

218

Once each year we would have a family meeting with Donald Kelley, a brilliant attorney and close friend who has handled these matters for us throughout the years, where he would explain these procedures in detail to the boys.

In the meantime I would try to make it clear to them, not only that show business was the most precarious form of making a living known to man, where everyone wants you today and no one wants you tomorrow, but also that the lion's share of the money we were all making was going to the government in taxes.

It would have been the height of hypocrisy to try to suggest to the boys that we were under any economic pressure, but on the other hand we didn't want them to feel that any amount of money they wanted was theirs for the asking. So we tried to reach a compromise by giving them a reasonable weekly allowance with extras for special occasions.

Actually, the question of money rarely came up until an article appeared in *Time* magazine which mentioned, for some reason I never could figure out, that our boys were each making more money than the president of the United States.

That night at dinner Ricky, who was then thirteen, said, "I know I'm making a lot of money and I know all about the trust fund, but that won't come due until I'm twenty-one. I'd sure like to have about a hundred dollars right now."

I said, "What would you do with it?"

Ricky said, "I don't know. I'd just like to have it."

David said, "Yeah, me too."

I said, "Okay, tomorrow night I'm going to give you each a one-hundred-dollar bond, and any time you want to cash it in just ask your mother and she'll get it cashed for you."

David said, "And we can spend it any way we want?"

"That's right," I said. "It's all yours. You can do whatever you want with it."

A couple of nights later Harriet said to me, "Come up to the boys' room for a second. I want you to see something." I went up there, and there were the two bonds tacked up on the wall.

"It's just as I thought," I said. "They can't figure out what to do with them."

I spoke too soon. About a week later they cashed them in, and late that afternoon David came roaring up on a second-hand motorcycle with Ricky riding on the back. "Isn't it a beauty?" said Dave. "We bought it this afternoon."

Little did we realize that this was just the start of what we later came to refer to as the "Let's live dangerously" syndrome, which would involve not only motorcycles, but racing cars, a demolition derby, and finally a flying-trapeze act.

20

In the summer of 1954 we went to Europe for six weeks. David had just graduated from high school and Rick had just had his fourteenth birthday, so we figured this might be the last summer we'd get a chance to do something together—as a family. We discussed going to Hawaii but finally decided on Europe, mainly, I suppose, because I have always felt that my trip there to the Boy Scout Jamboree in 1920 had been such a rewarding experience, at least in retrospect.

We sailed on the *Kungsholm* of the Swedish American line. I must confess that I am not what you'd call a good sailor. I don't get seasick to the point where I lean over the rail and feed the fishes ("I see you have a weak stomach." "What do you mean, 'weak'? I'm throwing it as far as the rest of them!"), but neither do I ever feel quite comfortable. From the moment the ship leaves the harbor until it docks, I am always aware of the ship's motion and the constant vibration of the engines. A big ship always looks so romantic and inviting when you're seeing someone else off or when you see it steaming majestically out of the harbor, but somehow, to me, it loses its allure when I'm on it.

Thirty years had passed since I had been on a ship, but the moment I went down the stairs to the lower decks a certain unpleasant recollection of familiar sights and smells came back to me like a bad dream—certain memories that I had managed to

221

hide away, but which now resurfaced and which seemed to say, "*Now* do you remember?"

The fact that the *Kungsholm* is sort of a tubby-type ship with a great deal of roll to it didn't help much, and it started to give ample evidence of what was in store for us shortly after we got out of sight of land. In fact, on the occasion of the first lifeboat drill, when several of the passengers came up with the old stand-and joke—"I hope it's for real"—I had a feeling it was entirely possible that they weren't kidding.

As I said, I was never entirely comfortable, and Rick also had a few queasy moments, but Harriet and David had several really bad days. David's misery was compounded by the fact that he was actually not too happy about going on the trip in the first place, since he was romantically involved with one of his high school girlfriends. Naturally, we weren't aware of this at the time.

The dance music on the *Kungsholm* was provided by a small combo comprised of five excellent musicians who played on alternate nights in the two salons—first-class and tourist. For some unexplained reason they had a set of drums, but no drummer. The second night out we looked up on the bandstand and noted that they now had a drummer—Ricky. Rick reported later that when he first sat in he was greeted with an understandable lack of enthusiasm by the other musicians. It didn't take them long to realize, however, that he played like a professional. From then on, if he didn't show up, they went looking for him. They spoke no English and he spoke no Swedish, but their smiles of appreciation and the mutual satisfaction of playing good music together transcended any language barrier.

Although there was an Old World atmosphere about the *Kungsholm,* and although the personnel and even the food was typically Swedish, the menus were in English and everyone we came in contact with spoke English. It wasn't until we pulled into the harbor at Göteborg that it dawned on us that we were actually in a strange country where we were the foreigners who would have to cope with someone else's language. Suddenly,

222

there we were, standing on the dock with hundreds of people milling about and our not knowing quite where to turn or even how to find our baggage, let alone get it through customs. Then a very pleasant thing happened. A nice-looking young man in a chauffeur's uniform came up to me and said, in remarkably good English, "Mr. Nelson?"

I said, "Yes," and he said, "My name is Anderson. They told me at the hotel that you would be arriving, and I thought maybe I could be of some help to you."

I said, "You certainly can. Have you any idea where I'm supposed to take these?"—and I showed him my baggage claim checks.

"Just give them to me," said Anderson. "I have a cousin who works here." He took the checks, and in what couldn't have been more than a couple of minutes reappeared with a man pulling a hand truck with our bags neatly stacked on it.

"We'll go out this side door," said Anderson. "I have the car parked in the alley."

I said, "What about the customs?"

"That's all been taken care of," said Anderson.

I took one look at the long line of people waiting to have their baggage inspected and felt a twinge of conscience. It lasted for maybe two or three seconds, and then I quickly followed Anderson out the side door.

As we settled back in the comfortable limousine and headed for the hotel, I said, "Mr. Anderson, what are you doing the rest of the week?"

"I'm at your service, sir," said Anderson.

I turned to the boys and said, "Now you see, fellahs, how easy traveling can be when you've got everything well organized?"

When I was a small boy, my Grandmother Nelson used to tell Alfred and me about Lysekil, a summer vacation village where her father owned a hotel and where she had learned to swim as a young girl. ("Could you swim, Grandma?" a little boy asked. "Like a fish.") It sounded like a fascinating place so we decided

223

to make it one of our side trips while in Sweden. We discovered that it was not too far from Göteborg, so we asked Anderson to drive us over there one morning.

It proved to be a pleasant drive of only a couple of hours (with a stopover at Marstrand, a beautiful seaport vacation spot). Lysekil, surprisingly enough, turned out to be just about as I had pictured it. We decided to spend a little time there, so we arranged to have Anderson return to Göteborg and come back to pick us up again in a few days. This turned out to be a little more daring than we had first imagined, because we soon discovered that practically no one in Lysekil spoke any English.

We checked into the only hotel in town and all went down to the main dining room to have dinner. We had been seated there only a few minutes when a nice-looking, well-dressed man of about fifty came over to our table and introduced himself to us. He proved to be a most charming gentleman by the name of Ivar Heulegren. He said he had read in the local newspaper that we might be visiting Lysekil and wanted to welcome us to the town. (We learned subsequently that a Swedish masseuse who used to give Harriet massages had written to some of her relatives about the possibility of our coming there to visit.) The article had mentioned that my grandmother had lived in Lysekil as a child and also that her family name was Stolhanska. It so happened that there were some members of the Stolhanska family living in Lysekil who were friends of Mr. Heulegren, and he said he would like very much to have us meet them.

Bright and early one morning a few days later, Mr. Heulegren phoned to say that my relatives (if indeed they were) had invited us over to their house for breakfast. He would drive us there and act as interpreter—which was pretty funny, since Ivar himself could barely make himself understood with the aid of a small English-Swedish pocket dictionary.

The Stolhanskas proved to be a very pleasant, round, shiny-faced couple and most hospitable. She had evidently been baking since dawn, because her dining room table was filled with the most fantastic assortment of pastries I have ever seen. It was a little difficult to figure out what to do. We didn't want to offend our charming hostess by not eating enough after she had gone to all this trouble, and yet we didn't want to seem like we were stuffing ourselves.

As for me, I took one bite of some sort of apple strudel and instantly made up my mind. I decided to stuff myself. Harriet, David, and Ricky, noting the broad smiles of approval from our host and hostess, decided to stuff themselves, too. And so we all just sat there—smiling, laughing, and stuffing ourselves. The language barrier didn't seem to bother us at all, and, besides, it's pretty difficult to talk with your mouth full anyway.

We reciprocated by inviting them to join us for dinner at the hotel the following evening, where we did a lot of smiling, laughing, and dancing—oh, yeah—and some more eating. One more week in Lysekil and we would have gained about fifty pounds apiece.

There was one more incident in Lysekil that had a rather poignant touch to it. Late one afternoon, Harriet, the boys, and I took a walk up to the highest point in the village, which was the courtyard of an old church that looked to be centuries old. From this vantage point we could see for miles in all directions. Suddenly the church bell started to toll and people began arriving and entering the church.

It was obvious from their manner and their somber dress that a funeral service was about to begin. Just as we started to leave, a small delivery truck pulled up and a couple of men got out. One of them came over and started to say something to me in Swedish, meanwhile pointing toward the church and gesturing for me to come with him. I responded, in English of course, and tried to explain that I was an American and that I was about to leave.

The man, however, wouldn't be put off this easily and kept insisting that I come with him. David and Ricky, noting that I was obviously in some sort of difficulty, did what any normal, red-blooded American boys would do in this kind of a situation —they quickly moved away and made believe they didn't know me. Harriet, of course, was halfway down the hill.

By this time, I was involved in what was practically a tug of war, with the man talking in Swedish and pointing toward the church, and me trying to explain in English that I didn't want to attend the funeral—that I didn't even know the deceased.

I evidently finally got through to the second man, who said in halting English, "He wants you to help." He then opened the back of the truck and there was the casket! They were undertakers and they wanted me to help them carry the deceased into the church.

And so, here I was, seven thousand miles from home, acting as a pallbearer for someone I didn't know, at a little church that my grandparents probably attended a hundred years ago.

We flew from Göteborg to Paris on the Scandinavian Air Lines. After our pleasant experience with Anderson we decided to wire ahead to the George V Hotel and request that they have an English-speaking driver meet us at the airport.

Once again, we hit the jackpot and were whisked through customs without so much as a bag being opened.

Our new driver was a most extraordinary young man of about thirty named René Kaddar. We liked him immediately and asked him to drive for us while we were in Paris. We never regretted the decision. Wherever we went, day or night, we just told René, and he took care of all the details, including tickets, reservations, etc. He was our personal, private tourist service.

The scene in the lobby of the George V as contrasted to the lobby of the hotel where we stayed in Göteborg was like coming from a Philadelphia library to Times Square on New Year's Eve. There were wildly hysterical assistant managers everywhere, bumping into each other, shouting at bellhops, sending people to the wrong rooms. It was the damndest welter of confusion I've ever seen in my life. But that's France. If you don't like it—stay home! As Harriet said—and it came to be a family cliché—"The whole country is strung together with chocolate éclairs."

We, all four of us, took in all the tourist sights—Notre Dame, the Eiffel Tower, the Louvre—as well as the nightclubs—the

226

Folies Bergères, the Nouvelle Eve, the Lido. You name it, we saw it.

Our visit to the Louvre was a typical American tourist scene. We had somehow misjudged our time and arrived there rather late. Immediately upon entering the building, we were accosted by one of those independent tour guides who infest the place. For an outrageous fee he offered to cover the high spots for us during the brief time we had before the 5:00 P.M. closing hour.

His sales pitch would have sold us anyway, but when he showed us President Eisenhower's autograph and told us that he had been Ike's personal guide, we felt it would have been downright unpatriotic not to go along with him.

I understand there are all sorts of tourist speed records for going through the Louvre. In fact, that seems to be the object of most tourists, at least the Americans: "See how fast you can go through the Louvre"—without running, that is. Running, I believe, is considered poor sportsmanship except when going up or down stairways.

At any rate, our guide moved along at what I would describe as a brisk walk. We soon found out that slowing down got us dirty looks, and that *really* slowing down brought dirty looks and low grumbling. Stopping, of course, was definitely out.

In desperation, Harriet finally ducked in behind some other people and circled back in order to take another look at a Cellini collection of silver that especially interested her. This display of duplicity really annoyed our friend, and he promptly launched into a speech about how we were never going to make it if we insisted on falling behind and dawdling like that.

It was then that we decided that we had had enough of this nonsense, so we went into what we had come to refer to as our "airport maneuver." We had learned from experience that we attracted more attention and were more easily recognized when we were all together, and as such were easy targets for well-meaning but sometimes overzealous autograph seekers. So we escaped from our man from the Louvre by each suddenly moving off in a different direction and losing himself in the crowd.

227

If you are wondering as to whether he collected his money in advance, you've just never been to Paris.

As I mentioned before, closing time at the Louvre is five o'clock—and that means everybody *out* by five. This is accomplished by a deployment that you have to see to believe. At fifteen minutes before five, you are aware of an eerie rumbling sound—like an approaching tidal wave—in fact, it is a tidal wave, of strange little men in battle formation, pushing brooms in front of them and slowly but surely moving men, women, children, newspapers, pamphlets, cigarette butts—everything and everyone—toward the exits.

Since all the posted signs state that five o'clock is the closing time, I naively assumed that one is allowed to remain in the museum until five. When the charge of the brush brigade started, I was desperately struggling to get close enough to the Mona Lisa to catch her eye. Unfortunately, this being the height of the tourist season, there were a couple of hundred people standing in front of me who had the same idea.

As the little men advanced, however, the crowd soon found themselves being shoved gently toward the hallways, where they met the next phalanx, who pushed them down the hall and, I presume, out into the street.

The thought suddenly occurred to me that I just couldn't leave without seeing the Mona Lisa. ("You mean you went to the Louvre and didn't see the Mona Lisa?" "No, you see there were these little men. . . .") So I pretended to go with the crowd, then suddenly reversed my field, and dodging in and out I straight-armed a couple of would-be tacklers and made my way straight toward the goal.

My adversaries, however, now aware of my determination, brute strength, and fleetness of foot, switched to new tactics. Shouting something that sounded suspiciously like "Allons enfants de la Patrie"—or maybe it was "Yankee go home"—they quickly jumped between me and Mona and started leaping up and down and waving their outstretched arms like semaphores in order to block my view.

228

I responded by dancing back and forth, getting a glimpse here and a little peek there, until finally one of them—a rather elderly man, I must admit—either slipped and fell or decided "the hell with this." Anyway, down he went, and suddenly, *there she was!* —the beautiful Florentine lady, not only looking at me but *smiling* at me! Naturally, I smiled back.

I momentarily considered shaking hands with my worthy opponents, but decided instead to settle for a snappy Foreign Legion–type salute which they returned, accompanied by a little gutteral sound which I like to believe could properly be called a cheer. Anyway, I responded in kind: "Viva la France! Vive la Louvre! Vive les petits hommes!"

Oh, yes—I finally caught up with Harriet and the boys back at the hotel. Harriet made what I thought was a small and inappropriate joke. She said, "Where the hell were you? Your horse got back an hour ago!"

The next stop on our itinerary was a little town called Juan-les-Pins on the French Riviera about midway between Cannes and Nice. After a tearful farewell from our by-now devoted friend and driver, René, we boarded the famous *Blue Train* and headed south. How or why it became famous I never will know, but any train at all seemed a better choice than flying Air France. I'm sure the rumors that they were still using some of the old Lafayette Escadrille planes from World War I were unfounded, but why take a chance?

The train trip was slightly uncomfortable, but it did give us a chance to see some of the French countryside and to taste, for the first time, an unusual flavor of ice cream that I can only describe as "tobacco juice." (Actually most of the ice cream in France is very good, and David and Ricky being third-generation ice cream addicts, the first French words they picked up were "vanilla and chocolate glacé.")

Juan-les-Pins proved to be a free-swinging, happy little town with great swimming and water skiing and lots of good-looking girls in very brief bikinis. We were originally scheduled to go from there to Rome, but we were having such a good time that we held a family meeting and voted three to one to forget about Rome and stay on at Juan-les-Pins for an extra week. Oh, well —Harriet can't win them all!

We stayed at the Provençale, an old-fashioned hotel located right on the beach. It was comfortable and there was a general atmosphere of friendliness about the place, but we encountered one slight difficulty. None of the maids or waiters spoke any English, so I was called upon to act as the family interpreter. I studied French for two years in high school and as a result I speak it fairly well. Also, according to my high school French teacher (a young lady named Bridget Lynch), I speak with an excellent French accent.

Now comes the unfortunate part. I'm sure you've heard people say, "I can understand the language, but I can't speak it very well." Not so with me. As I say, I don't have too much trouble speaking it, but I can't understand a damn word. "Plus lentment, sil vous plait?" I would plead. But regardless of how slowly they spoke—Gernichts helfen! (I also speak a little Yiddish, but I can't understand that either.)

At any rate, the first day at the Provencale, David and Ricky stopped by our room just as Harriet had buzzed for the maid to come up and pick up our laundry. There was a knock at the door and Harriet calmly called out, "Entrez!" I don't know why the boys found that so funny, but for some reason they both started laughing hysterically.

A moment later there was another knock on the door and Harriet again called out, "Entrez." Still no one came in, and by this time the boys were rolling on the floor. I went over and opened the door and *motioned* for the maid to come in.

"Do you speak English?" I asked.

She smiled and shook her head no.

"Okay," said Harriet to me, "here's your big chance."

"What do you want me to tell her?" I asked modestly.

Harriet smiled, took a deep breath, and launched into the damndest list of instructions I have ever heard.

230

After all these years, I can't reconstruct what she said exactly, of course, but it went something like this: "I'd like to have her press these two dresses and have them back this evening, or at least have one back by tomorrow morning but not before ten o'clock because we may want to sleep late. Ask her to please press them by hand and not with a steam iron. Those things over here go to the laundry, one-day service if they have it— that is, all except this blouse that has to be dry-cleaned."

"I said, "Are you kidding? You expect me to say that in French? I can't even remember it in English."

"I thought you studied it for three years."

"I did. But we just learned stuff like 'La plume est sur la table' and 'Fermez la fenêtre.'" With that, the maid went over to the window and started to close it.

"Non, non, merci," I said, trying unsuccessfully to hide the fact that I was rather pleased with myself for having at least established a line of communication. Then, to Harriet, "Would you tell me that again, slowly please?"

Don't ask how I did it, but with the help of many gestures and a lot of pointing, I managed to get the entire message across —that is, all except for one word. For the life of me I couldn't remember, if indeed I had ever heard it, the French word for "blouse."

Finally Harriet remembered that she had a French-English pocket dictionary stashed away someplace, so we looked the word up. Just in case you need to know it sometime, the French word for "blouse" is "blouse." Pronounce it "blooz" though, or you'll be there all day.

There was a little refreshment stand on the beach near our hotel where they served delicious orange sherbet. It was run by two charming people who spoke no English but whose friendly smiles always made us feel especially welcome. One day I indicated by gestures and pointing that I wanted some orange soda pop in a glass with a scoop of orange sherbet in it. I then pointed to it and said "Orange spécialité!" From then on, I merely said, "Orange spécialité," and they served me my special drink.

231

One morning just before we left, I noticed that they were smiling especially broadly and exchanging glances as though they were sharing a private little joke. Finally they could stand it no longer and together they pointed to a brand-new, freshly made sign. It read: "ORANGE SPECIALITE."

A few miles northeast of Juan-les-Pins is Cap d'Antibes, which was the scene of many of the F. Scott Fitzgerald escapades of the twenties. There is a semiprivate beach club located there called Eden Roc where we often went swimming. It was preferable to our hotel beach in that they had a huge swimming pool and diving boards, so you could dive into the sea rather than wading in as you had to do at Juan-les-Pins.

At one end of the swimming pool was a series of natural rock steps that led up to a little ledge from which you could get a beautiful view of the entire area, with the Mediterranean about thirty-five or forty feet below.

This one afternoon I decided to take a walk up there and look around. The view from the ledge was beautiful, all right, but a little scarier than I had imagined. I have always had this thing about heights anyway, so it didn't take me long to decide that I had had enough of all this and that I would be much more comfortable back down there at the swimming pool.

Just as I started for the steps, however, Ricky came running up.

"Where are you going?" he said.

"Back down to the pool."

"I thought you were going to dive off."

"Are you kidding?" I said. "I just came up here to look around. If I ever dove off here I'd get killed. It must be forty feet down there. Besides you'd have to dive way out to clear the rocks."

"Well, okay," said Rick, "but you're going to disappoint an awful lot of people. Everybody down at the pool thinks you're going to dive off."

I looked down there and, sure enough, they were all looking up at me and gesturing for me to go ahead. After all, it isn't every day you see a man commit suicide, not even a crazy Ameri-

232

can tourist. I gestured right back at them, smiling broadly and indicating as best I could that, no, I was just up there to admire the view.

"Isn't that a beautiful view, Rick?" I said, fooling neither one of us. By now a couple of people at the pool had started to applaud.

"This is getting embarrassing, Pop," said Rick. "Will you please go ahead and dive?"

"If it's so embarrassing, go ahead and dive off yourself," I said, which was pretty ridiculous on the face of it because Rick at that time was barely fourteen years old and weighed about 110 pounds.

Then a strange thing happened. Dave came running up the steps and, thinking that I was going to dive off and wanting to be the first one in the family to achieve the honor (?), rushed past me and without even hesitating dove off into space. He made a nice, clean entry into the water, waved up at me as if to say, "Nothing to it!" and swam back to the dock.

"This is ridiculous," I said to myself. "If my son can do it, so can I." I walked quickly up to the edge, took a deep breath, and . . . *whoops*! . . . just caught myself in time. "My God!" I said, "Have I gone crazy?—a man my age? Get out of here before you kill yourself!"

Just then a little boy about eight years old came walking up the steps. He was obviously an American kid because he said to me, "I watch you on television all the time."

"Thank you," I said.

"Are you gonna dive off there?"

"No. I'm just looking around."

The little boy took another good look at me. "You look much older in person than you do on television!" he said.

That did it! Off I went!

I thought I'd never reach the water. It seemed like I was in the air about twenty minutes. Maybe I didn't hit at just the right angle, or maybe I was just too damn old for that kind of nonsense. At any rate, it felt like I had landed in the middle of an asphalt street. My head felt like somebody had hit me with a mallet. I remember, as I went down farther and farther into the sea, wondering whether I had broken just my arms, or my arms and my legs, or maybe just one arm and one leg.

Somehow, in some way, I finally managed to surface and make my way over to the ladder, and there waiting for me were Harriet and Rhonda Fleming.

"That was beautiful!" said Harriet.

"It was great!" said Rhonda.

"Did you hurt yourself?" Harriet asked.

"Are you kidding?" I said. "It was nothing!"

From Juan-les-Pins we flew to London, and once again had no trouble with the customs officials, having wired ahead—this time for an *American*-speaking driver. Although we were there for only about a week, we managed to take in most of the usual tourist scenes: the changing of the Guard, London Bridge, Madame Tussaud's Waxworks, Hyde Park, Trafalgar Square. The only one we missed was the Tower of London. We drove over near there, but there was a line two blocks long, so since there wasn't a beheading scheduled for that day, we decided to skip it.

For my part, the most enjoyable evening we spent in London was the night we went to the Palladium Music Hall. This is old-time vaudeville in its truest sense. We saw a typical variety bill, with Norman Wisdom as the headliner. The audience was refreshingly unsophisticated and enthusiastic, and the whole scene was pleasantly reminiscent of the wonderful evenings when my father would take Alfred and me to the vaudeville shows at Proctor's Fifth Avenue in New York City.

There was an old standard vaudeville joke that went something like this: The question of age would come up between an old maid and the comic. She would ask coyly, "How old do you think I am?" and he would answer, "Oh, about twenty-five." She would wriggle with pleasure and say, "Oh, really?" The comic would then say, "No—but it sure made you feel good for a minute, didn't it?"

This old joke relates, strangely enough, to an interesting experience we had during our last day in England.

For our return voyage home, we had booked reservations on the United States line, which embarked from Southampton, and we had hired a limousine and a chauffeur to drive us down from London. At every intersection where a policeman was stationed, he not only waved us through but drew up to a military salute as we passed. We were, of course, very flattered—and frankly puzzled by all this attention and respect, especially since our television show wasn't even playing in London.

The mystery was solved when we arrived in Southampton, however, and a friend of ours who had come down to see us off explained that the limousine we had been riding in was a Daimler, which was the official car of the British royal family. Obviously, the English police were taking no chances. Anyway, like the old maid, we "sure felt good for a moment."

The *United States* proved to be a luxury liner in every sense of the word. Because it was much larger, it lacked some of the friendliness and informal atmosphere of the *Kungsholm*, but it tossed and rolled in the heavy seas with the same disdain for a settled stomach as its Swedish counterpart.

Also, because it was an American ship, we found ourselves much more vulnerable to that most boring of all social events, the cocktail party. I guess some people must like them, but as for myself I find them confusing, tiring, and generally a waste of time.

First of all, I don't drink, and you can consume just so much ginger ale. When the hors d'oeuvres come around I always manage to pop into my mouth something that tastes entirely different than it looks like it should taste. Add to that the unhappy fact that I have these mental lapses where I introduce people to their ex-wives, or start to introduce two people only to discover that I have forgotten *both* their names—you know, things like that.

I remember I was talking to Rick and his wife Kris at one cocktail party when the president of one of the major networks came over to say hello. After a split second of panic, his name suddenly and miraculously came to mind, so I calmly and confidently introduced him to "Krick and Riss."

If you forget someone's name in Terre Haute, Indiana, or Hackensack, New Jersey, that's bad enough. But in Hollywood, where egos run high, it can be disastrous. I know, having been on the receiving end a few times: I was introduced once as Art Linkletter, once as Red Buttons, and on several occasions as "Mr. Ushrushrushrush" (or however you spell an indistinguishable mumble).

Actually, this doesn't happen to me too often, however, because, being a fellow sufferer, I am constantly on the alert for name-forgetters, so I usually approach anyone who is not a close friend with "Hi, I'm Ozzie Nelson." This gives the other guy a chance to say something nice and make believe he knew who I was all along.

I was getting on a plane once when I felt a tap on my shoulder and heard a familiar voice say, "Ozzie?—Cary Grant." Under the circumstances, I usually say something like "Duh, duh," but I said, "This is great! Now if the plane crashes, there'll be a banner headline on page 1: 'Cary Grant Killed in Plane Crash' —and I'll wind up on page 12." Cary smiled modestly and said, "You're very kind."

Of course, anyone who has been on television or in motion pictures for any length of time has had innumerable experiences of trying to field questions like "Are you 'what's his name'?" or "Now, don't tell me . . .," or, the most often asked and definitely the toughest to answer, "Are you who I think you are?"

As Harriet has often said, most people consider that she and I are joined at the hip and, as a result, several times when I have been alone someone has asked, "Aren't you Ozzie and Harriet?" She is often called "Mrs. Ozzie," and even more alarmingly I have several times been asked if I were "Mr. Harriet."

We had a beach house at Hermosa Beach some years ago, and early one afternoon there was a knock at the back door. Harriet answered it, and a little four-year-old girl wearing a bikini the size of a postage stamp was standing there. She said, "Can Ozzie come out and play?" Harriet told her I was taking my nap.

I've always liked the story of the guy who stopped Groucho Marx outside the Hollywood Brown Derby and said, "Are you

236

Harpo Marx?" Groucho said, "No. Are you?" I really feel, though, that the first time someone says to me, "Didn't you used to be Ozzie Nelson?" I'll know it's time to quit.

Edgar Bergen eliminates a lot of problems by the simple process of never calling anyone by name. He once told me he has discovered that, if you wait long enough, people will eventually introduce themselves to one another. Then all you have to do is smile and say, "Oh, I thought you two knew each other." In fact, according to Edgar, that's how Charlie McCarthy met Mortimer Snerd.

Social life for the boys on the trip home seemed to be a big success. David, having made a remarkable recovery from the pangs of being separated from his Hollywood High School sweetheart, made some sort of mysterious romantic connection that kept him below decks for most of the trip. As for Ricky—well, it seems there were about twenty-five kids on board whose ages ranged from twelve to fifteen and who decided that Ricky was their leader. About three of four times a day, someone would say, "Here comes Ricky and his disciples!" And sure enough, there would be Ricky with his loyal followers close on his heels. They walked like Ricky, talked like Ricky, dressed like him, combed their hair in the same "eggbeater" style, and did whatever he did. I'm sure if he had jumped overboard, they would have followed him without a moment's hesitation.

For some reason, I don't remember too much about our arrival in New York or the flight home to California. I guess by that time Harriet and I were thinking more about starting back on the weekly grind of filming the television show and the boys were thinking about returning to school.

One thing is for sure: I think we all knew that the end of the summer of '54 was the end of a phase in our lives. We would always be a family, but never again in quite the same way. I think we all knew, although two of us made believe we didn't, that this was the last summer we would spend together—as a family.

That's the way it was and that's the way it should be. As Mom used to say, "That's life!"

21

There were a few changes in our life style when we resumed filming in the fall of 1954. David had moved into an apartment near the USC campus, where he had enrolled as a freshman but with not quite enough credits to allow him to go out for athletics, and Ricky had entered Hollywood High School, where his limited weight (115 pounds) had barely qualified him for the "B" football team but where he performed valiantly until he was sidelined with a broken hand.

Our personnel on the home front and in the office had undergone a couple of changes, too. Tommy Dulin had left to get married and go to work as the personal driver for a good friend of ours, and Grace Johnson, our housekeeper, who had left to start her own catering business, had been replaced by Erma Watson, who is still with us and whose friendship and affection we have treasured throughout the years.

Jackie Brundage, our secretary, had also left to get married and was replaced by Sally Hughes, an attractive and talented Phi Beta Kappa from Pomona College whom we knew from the Bel-Air Bay Club. Sally had done considerable theater work at college, and so whenever we needed someone for a few lines on the television show, we'd yank Sally away from the typewriter to join the acting team. She became so good at it that we started to give her bigger and bigger parts until after a few years she began doing commercials and parts on other shows and finally left us to devote full time to her acting career, which she has successfully combined with a happy marriage.

The year before we took the trip to Europe, we had sold the Camel Point beach house (Harriet had tried and tried, but it just didn't seem to respond to her efforts to make it feel like it was "ours") and had taken, as part payment, a beach-front lot in Lagunita, a small community about a mile north of Camel Point.

We had never driven down to see the property, but when we started to get offers from people who wanted to buy it, including one from the vice-president of a Laguna Beach bank, we decided to go down and take a look at it.

It proved to be located on a rocky cliff about twenty feet above the ocean with a beautiful view of the beach and the water on all sides. The air smelled clean and fresh, and the golden sun glistening on the waves painted one of those magical pictures that only nature can conjure up.

Harriet took a little book from her handbag. "What's that?" I asked.

"These are my notes of all the things that were wrong with the Camel Point house and the things I'd like in our new house when we build it here."

"You mean like next summer?" I asked.

"I mean like right now," she said.

Organizing a project like that is no small task, but somehow Harriet managed to find the time. So miraculously, by late spring our beautiful beach house, our home away from home, was ready for us to move into and enjoy. We are constantly being besieged by people who want to buy it, offering us four or five times what it cost us, but Harriet always says that she'd sell me first. Of course, she's kidding, but she seems to say it with more and more conviction as the years go by.

For David, enrolling at USC was like entering a new world. At Hollywood High School he had been among kids he had grown up with and with whom he felt comfortable. At USC, however, he said he felt conspicuous and self-conscious, as if the other students were staring at him and saying to themselves, "What's he doing here?" Then one afternoon a new student enrolled in one of his classes and was seated right next to David. He was a Korean War veteran and a little older than most of the other students. He had been wounded in the war and, as a result, had a badly scarred face. Regardless of this, however, he was well adjusted and seemed totally unselfconscious about his misfortune. David said it suddenly occurred to him that if his new classmate could handle this kind of a situation without losing his poise, certainly he, David, could take a few stares and whispers without falling apart. He said he then remembered something Harriet and I had told him and Ricky when they first started on the radio show: "The best way to have people forget that you are a celebrity is to forget it yourself."

Working out a shooting schedule for the television show had become increasingly difficult and wouldn't get any easier as time went on. Because of his classes, David was only available on a part-time basis, and Ricky was trying to play football and, later in the year, in tennis tournaments while attending classes and acting in the show. The fact that David was doing his commuting on the freeway on his motorcycle didn't add any to our peace of mind. Later in the season, Dave started attending night sessions for several of his classes and Rick started to work with a tutor on the set so that he could apportion his time better.

Rick was still officially enrolled at Hollywood High School and as a result was able to represent them in interscholastic tennis matches. Meanwhile, he was starting to collect a roomful of trophies, and by his junior year he was ranked fifth in Southern California in the fifteen-and-under division.

In the fall of 1955, David entered USC as a fullfledged student, having made up all his credits, and as a result he was eligible to play freshman football. He weighed only 170 pounds and was the only man on the squad who wasn't in school on an athletic scholarship, but he was such an excellent passer that he played in every game and scored a touchdown against the freshman of the University of California at Berkeley.

240

We all went to see him play against the Stanford frosh at the Coliseum, where he threw a game-winning touchdown—only to have it called back because one of his teammates had jumped offside. The game ended in a tie, as did the UCLA game.

If you're wondering how David managed to play football, do the television show, and keep up his studies, the answer is—he didn't. To add to his already overcrowded schedule, he joined a fraternity (Kappa Sigma) and, after the first of the year, started waiting on tables at a sorority house so he could meet more girls.

At the end of the spring semester, the roof caved in, and despite the best efforts of the Athletic Department (they desperately needed a passing quarterback for the next season), our overly ambitious number-one boy flunked out. There simply weren't enough hours in the day for him to do all the things he was trying to do.

With the start of the 1956 season, the show took on a more expansive look and we filmed many more scenes outdoors, principally because of a change in sponsors.

Nowadays there is a great deal of "spot" buying of advertising time on television whereby a sponsor will buy spots on several different shows rather than buy all the commercial time on a particular show. This was not the usual practice back in the '50s, however, and as a result we had two sponsors, Hotpoint and Listerine, who split the tab for the first four years, and then Eastman Kodak came in as our sole sponsor in the fall of 1956.

One of the big advantages of being the only sponsor or of being co-sponsor was that it was possible for us, perfectly legitimately, to give them a great deal of subliminal advertising in addition to their paid commercial blurbs. For example, while we were sponsored by Hotpoint, they furnished the kitchen with all the latest Hotpoint appliances, and if we had a choice of where to play a scene we'd move it into the kitchen where Harriet could be cooking dinner or putting dishes in the dishwasher or taking clothes out of the dryer. Or even if we were eating dinner in the dining room, the Hotpoint appliances could still be seen in the

241

background. The Listerine people, of course, were not so lucky. We weren't quite ready to write in any gargling scenes—not that they didn't try to coax us (in a nice way, of course).

When Sonny Werblin, Mickey Rockford (head of television for MCA on the West Coast at the time), and I met with the executives of the Eastman Kodak Company, one of the main points in our sales pitch was the fact that we were especially adept at working these subliminal plugs into our shows. Of course, with a product like a camera this was easy, since cameras are so much a part of our everyday lives.

Just to make sure we didn't forget, Phil de Lacy of the J. Walter Thompson Company (Kodak's advertising agency) would always be on the set armed with a bunch of cameras ready to hang one around the neck of anybody who could conceivably be wearing one. I didn't mind if it was a scene that called for us to go on a picnic, or even if it was a party scene or a special occasion of some sort, but I had to draw the line on carrying a camera if I were merely mowing the lawn or sitting reading the paper—just as a few years later I had to convince the Aunt Jemima people that we didn't eat pancakes for dinner, and the Coca-Cola people that we didn't drink Cokes for breakfast, and the Dairy Association people that not *all* the men at a poker party would be drinking milk.

The start of the '56 season saw us lose a character (Don DeFore had requested to leave the show so as to devote his full time to motion pictures) and gain one.

Our first show that year was one that I wrote called "The Kappa Sig Party" and was, like so many of our stories, based on an actual incident. The script involved a fraternity rush party that was given at our home, and I had written in a character of a chubby guy who was a happy "life of the party" type and who loved to eat.

In order to maintain a natural quality to the show, we rarely used professional actors to play the young people, preferring instead to use friends of the boys. Throughout the years we were especially fortunate in the use of athletes, since they are usually well coordinated, very intelligent, and used to taking direction. As a result, our main sources of supply for our fraternity scenes were the USC and UCLA football teams and the Los Angeles Rams.

The day we started filming "The Kappa Sig Party," a very personable young man about David's age appeared on the set and requested an interview. He said he had heard that we were looking for a chubby boy who loved to eat and that he met both qualifications. He said he had had no film experience but that he was currently appearing on the stage at Knott's Berry Farm in a revival of *The Drunkard*. He had been using the name Skip Young, but his real name was Plumstead, which to my mind fit him much better. So we dubbed him "Wally," and from then on Wally Plumstead became a regular member of our cast and soon developed into one of the finest young comedic actors in our business and a very special friend of all of us Nelsons.

Later that same season, two more excellent actors and close friends of long standing also joined our cast as regulars; Lyle Talbot and Mary Jane Croft, playing the parts of Joe and Clara Randolph. Mary Jane had played Clara on our radio show even before David and Ricky were in the cast—when their parts were played by other boys. In fact, we have often repeated a priceless line of Mary Jane's. Somebody once asked her, "Have you met Ricky Nelson?" and Mary Jane said, "Are you kidding? I knew him when he was Henry Blair."

Lyle, of course, had costarred in countless numbers of motion pictures as a leading man, but I really feel that on our show his fine comedic talents were evident for the first time. I know it was always a delight for Harriet and me to work with Lyle and Mary Jane—true professionals and nice people.

I remember Lyle's telling me an incident that occurred on one of the first films he had ever made. He made an entrance, as directed, and the director immediately called "cut" and then went over and said, "Lyle, I want you to make that entrance again and this time *bring something with you*." Lyle and Mary Jane always

243

"brought something with them"—an indefinable extra dimension that distinguishes the really fine actor from one who is merely adequate and brings nothing to the part.

Of course, there is such a thing as "bringing *too much* with you." There is nothing worse than the actor who makes a two-minute emotional scene out of a line like "Please pass the potatoes." In fact, "Would anybody like some more coffee?" is often more difficult to say naturally than "My God, I've been shot!" If you don't believe it, ask Harriet. She got stuck with those nondescript "coffee lines" week after week. I'm sure if one of the writers, including me, had suddenly called out, "My God, I've been shot!" it probably would have been Harriet who shot him.

Among the other fine actors who started to appear on the show with more or less regularity were Parley Baer as Dunkel, Frank Cady as Doc Williams, Lloyd Corrigan as Wally Dipple, Gordon Jones as Butch, and the very versatile and talented Jack Wagner, who appeared in a variety of roles until we finally settled him down as the manager of the Malt Shop.

This, of course, was the group that we referred to as the "older posse." The fraternity group gradually developed their own cast of regulars whom we'll discuss a bit later.

Before leaving "The Kappa Sig Party," I must confess that it was one of my favorite episodes, not because I happened to have written it but because there is a scene just before the second-act curtain that I especially like. I have a feeling that it expresses not only my thoughts but also the thoughts of almost all fathers toward their teenage sons.

The rush party has been a big success even though Harriet, Ricky, and I have broken our promises to each other to stay out of the way and let the fraternity kids have their party without our joining in. The script reads as follows:

Scene 22—Interior Nelson Front Hall—Night.

The party is breaking up. The Nelsons are lined up at the door, saying goodbye. We hear ad libs: "Goodnight. . . . Thank

244

you very much. . . . Goodnight . . . Goodnight," *as the kids file out.*

DAVE: Chuck, do you want to bring the car around? (*To Cathy, his date.*) I'll be right out, Cathy.

CATHY: (*Off stage.*) Okay.

DAVE: Gee, Mom, Pop, I don't know how to thank you. Everybody said this was the best party the Kappa Sigs ever had.

HARRIET: That's good. Well, I'm glad everybody had a good time.

DAVE: Yeah. So am I. And even if you do look young enough to be my sister, I'm glad you're my mother.

OZZIE: Yeah, I think she's pretty special too. You know, Dave, sometimes parents like us are a little reluctant to let you guys go. But if we seem to hang on to you, you've got to be a little understanding about us. See, we want you to grow up and get along without us and yet we hate to lose our little boys. It seems like yesterday when I'd go into the bedroom at night and there'd be a couple of little towheaded guys asleep there, and I'd go over and kiss you goodnight. Now, I have to shake hands with you.

DAVE: I know what you mean, Pop.

HARRIET: Well, you'd better not keep the others waiting, dear.

DAVE: Yeah, thanks again. Goodnight Mom. (*He kisses her.*)

HARRIET: Goodnight, dear.

DAVE: Goodnight, Pop.

OZZIE: Goodnight, son.

He shakes hands with Dave. Dave hesitates a moment and then reaches over and gives his dad a kiss on the cheek. He goes to the door then turns and looks at Ricky.

RICKY: You wouldn't dare!

This breaks it up and as Dave goes out the front door we
FADE OUT: CURTAIN.

22

Ricky's tennis game improved steadily until, by the time he was sixteen, his bedroom began to look like a trophy shop. In the fall of '56 he went to St. Louis with his partner Allen Fox, and they reached the semifinals of the National Indoor Junior Championship. This was no small accomplishment in view of the fact that they were competing against the best players in the nation, most of whom were eighteen. It was also getting extremely difficult for Rick to play in tournaments because of the crowds he would attract, especially when he played out of town. He was also competing in interscholastic matches representing Hollywood High School, and not only did he and his partner Bruce Campbell win all their matches, but neither of them ever lost a set in either singles or doubles in league competition.

David meanwhile was engaged in a much more dangerous pastime, which we didn't learn about until he had been involved in it for several months.

One day Bill Mellor (whom you will recall was our head cameraman) came to me and said, "I hate to sound like a squealer, but there's something I think you should know about. I was out at the Gardena Raceway last night where they have the Midget Auto Races, and one of the winners was announced as 'Mike Sullivan,' but when he took his helmet off I could swear it was David." "I wouldn't say anything," continued Bill, "but it's a three-quarter-mile dirt track and very dangerous. I've seen some really bad accidents out there."

It was David, all right, and two weeks later he went over the side of the railing but miraculously escaped injury. Fortunately, it scared him enough so that he sold his car and gave up racing —that is, he gave up auto racing and took up a new hobby, motorcycle racing.

About two weeks later it was Ricky's turn. The Porsche he was driving skidded out of control while he was doing eighty miles an hour on Sunset Boulevard at three o'clock one morning. Ricky wound up in St. Joseph's Hospital with a bump on his head and a cracked vertebra. The car, which had hit the curb and rolled over three times, wound up in the scrap heap—completely demolished.

Although David took part in any number of motorcycle races —including the Big Bear Run, an annual event with over five hundred entrants riding over unbelievably rough terrain—the only motorcycle injury he ever sustained was while filming a scene for one of our shows.

As was the case with most of the boys' activities, we wrote an episode around Dave's motorcycle racing. The script called for him to be involved in a hill-climbing contest where he would hit a bad bump and get thrown off the bike. We had never before used a double for any of us on the show, but in this particular case we hired a stunt man (over David's protests) to take the fall. It took us only two or three takes to realize that we had hired the wrong guy. He was willing enough, but he just wasn't a good enough motorcycle rider. Dave said, "Please, Dad, let me do it before he kills himself and wrecks my bike."

We had one camera stationed at the bottom of the hill for the long shot and another camera in a trench, near the spot where the fall was to take place. This, of course, was for the closer angle.

David went zooming up the hill, hit the bump, went flying over the handlebars, and disappeared from sight. A moment later, much to our relief, he waved to us to indicate that he was okay. This was true—up to a point. As it turned out, he had wrenched his knee and suffered a bad gash across his forehead. Unfortunately, the stunt doesn't look too exciting on film, since we could

247

only use the longer angle. The close-up camera operator, seeing David fly through the air and fearing that he was seriously hurt, shut off the camera and rushed over to pick Dave up.

As I mentioned earlier, neither David, Ricky, nor I had ever used a double—which was quite remarkable as far as the boys were concerned, because they were involved in some really exciting fight scenes where all the other participants were professional stunt men.

As far as old Dad was concerned, my stunts were limited for the most part to falling into mudholes, having buckets of water dumped on me, jumping into a fire net, getting pelted with tomatoes—fun things like that, which were messy but not dangerous. Twice, however, I got hurt—not seriously, but enough to make me uncomfortable for a while. And once I almost got scared to death.

The scary one was a scene that required some careful planning and split-second timing. It called for the boys and me to be playing baseball in the back yard (our simulated back yard on the stage). David was to throw a ball that I had to jump high in the air to catch. As I caught the ball, I was to land on a chaise longue in the yard, bounce up into the air, and fly out of camera range. It was a very funny effect, and in order to achieve it the prop men put a harness on me with a wire attached to it that came out a small hole in the back of my sweater. The wire was attached to a rope, and as I hit the chaise they were to give the rope a yank, causing me to go zooming up ten or twelve feet. It was the same kind of contraption they used to fly Mary Martin and countless other Peter Pans on the stage. What I didn't learn until later, however, was that not only was this my first time for flying, but it was the prop men's first time at pulling on the rope.

I called "action," the camera rolled, I ran across the lawn, David threw the ball, I jumped and caught the ball, and as I landed on the chaise the three guys yanked on the rope and I flew up in the air—not ten feet, not twenty feet, but clear up into the rafters and dangled there, peering down at the picket fence forty feet below me.

248

"All I need," I thought as I hung there with my heart pounding, "is for this damn, skinny little wire to break and for me to come hurtling down and straddle that picket fence."

Slowly they lowered me back to terra firma. Somebody took a look at my bloodless face and yelled, "Make-up!"

"Make-up, hell!" I said. "Wardrobe! !"

Then there was the time when the scene called for me to be carrying a huge birthday cake across the back yard. I was to trip over a rope that had been stretched across the lawn and fall face-first into the cake. At the bottom of the cake they had placed some foam rubber to cushion the impact. What they hadn't taken into consideration, however, was that the "lawn" I was falling onto was actually a grass mat laid over a cement floor.

The fall looked very funny on film, but I wound up with a fat lip and a swollen nose with lots of gooey cake frosting stuffed up each nostril.

Like most families, we had always had a place on the wall of the boys' room where we kept track of their increasing heights. As David grew to a point where he was about five feet nine, he reminded me that, one time years ago, I had been irrational enough to promise the boys that I would give each of them fifty dollars if and when he grew to be as tall as I was.

David grew closer and closer, until at age eighteen he got to within a fraction of an inch of me, and then suddenly stopped growing. He kept measuring and measuring, but there he stayed. Ricky insisted that David was worrying too much about the fifty dollars and had choked up.

As you can well imagine, this gave us the basis for a television show. In the show, David has actually grown to a point where he is a little taller than I am, but while we are in the kitchen checking his height against the wall a bowl falls on my head and raises just enough of a bump to make me still slightly taller and prevent him from collecting the fifty dollars.

Our demon property man, Jack Iannarelli, had had a bowl made that looked like heavy crockery but which was really made of rubber. However, there was a metal band around the bottom of the bowl to give it a look of firmness, and when the bowl fell from the shelf and hit me on the head the part that hit me was not the rubber section but that hard metal band. I must say that my reaction, which was supposed to be one of intense pain, looked very natural—as did the bump on my head.

I like to think that David's insisting on applying an icepack to my aching noggin was prompted by a genuine concern for my discomfort rather than any thought of actually collecting the fifty dollars.

In case you're wondering, he passed me by a couple of inches soon after, as did Ricky, who became the tallest member of the foursome at six feet one. Harriet never did win her fifty dollars.

The fifty dollars Dave won for growing taller was not the only award he won in 1957. As a result of his sensitive portrayal of Ted Carter in the Twentieth Century–Fox motion picture *Peyton Place,* he was awarded *Photoplay* magazine's Gold Medal Award as the "Outstanding New Film Actor of the Year."

One of the first things an aspiring young actor must learn is that good acting consists not only of reading lines well but also of reacting to the playing of others in the scene. If you should happen to be watching a rerun of *Peyton Place* on the Late Late Show some evening, notice David's reactions during the courtroom sequence. They are really excellent and contribute greatly to the effectiveness of the scene as a whole.

If you happened to be watching our television show on the night of April 10, 1957, you saw an episode called "Ricky the Drummer." We thought it was a good show while we were filming it, but we weren't quite prepared for what followed.

Ricky had always been interested in music since the days, you will recall, when as a very little boy he used to lie on the floor by the hour listening to symphony music on the radio. From there his interests progressed—if indeed that's the proper word—to Dixieland, then to progressive jazz, then to rhythm and blues, and finally to country and western and what later came to be known as rock 'n' roll.

250

I don't believe there is any subject under the sun about which so much has been written by people who don't know what they are writing about as modern-day popular music, and I have no intention of compounding the felony by trying to differentiate between the various forms and classifications it may fall under. However, I do know that early in 1957 Harriet and I were slowly but surely being blasted out of the house by what sounded to me like nothing more than a barrage of twanging guitars, thumping drums, and undistinguishable grunts emanating from Carl Perkins, Bill Haley and his Comets, and of course Elvis, Elvis, and more Elvis.

It finally reached the point where we made a house rule that Ricky could only play his records in his own room (which had been soundproofed the year before to protect the neighbors from drum solos) and with his door and windows closed.

Then one day it occurred to me that this was a stupid thing to do—that there was enough lack of communication between fathers and teenage sons anyway without widening the breach. Rick had said to me several times, "I wish you'd listen to some of this stuff with an open mind. A lot of it is really good." I did, and he was right. It was basic, it was rhythmic, and it was exciting. In a matter of weeks I was thoroughly brainwashed and found myself trying to convince my fifty-year-old contemporaries that this new music was worth listening to and that Elvis Presley and Colonel Parker really weren't engaged in a conspiracy to corrupt the youth of America.

One night at the dinner table Rick said, "Dad, do you suppose I could sing a song and maybe play the guitar on one of the shows. I'd like to make a record, and I figure this is the best way for people to hear me. I have a special reason for asking this." It wasn't until several years later that we discovered that the "special reason" involved a girl he had been dating occasionally.

It seems that Rick was driving her home from a party one night and they were listening to a Presley record coming over the car radio when Rick said, "You know, I've been thinking of making a record myself one of these days."

251

The girl just stared at him for a minute and then burst out laughing. She finally recovered sufficiently to say, "That's the silliest thing I ever heard of."

We were talking about it a couple of weeks ago and Rick said, "I haven't seen her since, but she sure did me a big favor. I wonder whatever happened to her."

The song Rick sang on "Ricky the Drummer" was called "I'm Walkin'" and had been a tremendous hit by Fats Domino on Imperial Records.

Television shows are usually filmed about six weeks before air date, so our MCA representatives had contacted all the leading record companies before the show was on television and played Rick's soundtrack for them. Several of them offered him a standard recording contract—that is, a minimum guarantee against a royalty with yearly options on their part. We felt that Ricky was entitled to something better than that, so we finally agreed that he would release one record on the Verve label and see what happened.

What happened was that the record, released a few weeks after the telecast, hit the top of the charts almost immediately, and Rick became a rock 'n' roll star practically overnight.

I won't bore you with all the details of the contractual hassles that followed other than to say that Rick finally signed a five-year no-option contract with Imperial Records which guaranteed him one thousand dollars per week against a royalty and also gave him complete control of the selection of his songs and the manner in which they were to be presented, as well as approval of all artwork, publicity, and advertising.

Lew Chudd, who owned Imperial Records, proved to be a human dynamo. Throughout the five years of the contract he left all artistic decisions to Ricky and did an absolutely fantastic job of sales and promotion. Jimmie Haskell, a tremendously talented young arranger, came with Rick and rendered invaluable assistance not only musically but in the selection of songs.

Maury Foladare, who had been handling public relations for the family since the early radio days, now dropped all his other clients to come with us exclusively and devote most of his time to Ricky.

Connie Harper, an attractive young girl with a great talent for organization, joined us to supervise Rick's fan clubs and to organize a fan mail department to handle the more than fifteen thousand letters per week that were pouring in from all over the world. Connie was no stranger to show business and the world of celebrities, since her father Joseph Harper, had married Cecilia de Mille, daughter of Cecil B., when Connie was very young, and her own maternal grandfather, Hamlin Garland, had been a great literary figure and contemporary of Mark Twain's.

With Ricky's sudden emergence as a recording star came a flood of demands for him to make personal appearances, which in turn made our shooting schedule even more hectic than ever. To add to the complications, Twentieth Century–Fox had called David to make another film, *The Remarkable Mr. Pennypacker* with Clifton Webb and Dorothy McGuire, which he was trying to sandwich in between classes at Los Angeles City College, where he had decided to complete his education.

Our only alternative was to "shoot around" the boys and pick up their scenes at such time as they were available. As a result we often got weeks ahead of them. It reminded me of a story my father used to tell about an old guy who had gone to the doctor, complaining of insomnia. The doctor had prescribed a tablespoonful of whiskey in a glass of milk each night before retiring. At the end of a month the old guy was five weeks ahead on the whiskey and three weeks behind on the milk.

On June 5, 1957, I returned to the Rutgers campus for a very happy occasion. At the commencement exercises that day, my alma mater generously conferred on me the honorary degree of Doctor of Humane Letters. I feel that it was an honor to be shared by all four of us—Harriet, David, and Ricky, as well as me. In fact, the closing paragraph of the citation read:

One of the most famous families in America, you and Har-

253

riet—and David and Ricky—have won the affection of millions and have brought to television entertainment rare standards of good taste and high quality. Neither time nor custom have staled your infinite variety.

It was the first time I had been back to Rutgers for almost thirty years. My brother Al came down to the ceremonies as well as Kay and my mother. I had of course kept in close contact with them through the years—Harriet and I had made frequent trips back east, and Mom had visited us several times and in fact had appeared as an "extra" a few times on the television show. I made a practice of phoning her every week right after the show, and while she never said she didn't like any of them, I could always tell by the special ring to her voice when there was one that she particularly liked.

Al could have been an excellent comedy writer if he had decided to devote full time to it, but his dental practice had been doing fine and raising five boys kept him well occupied. In his spare time, however, he managed to contribute the story lines for some of our best shows.

I recall that we did one more "request" show before closing the books on our fifth season. One day shortly after we had filmed "Ricky the Drummer," Dave came to me and said, "You know, Dad, I think I have a good idea for a show. I was watching the 'Miss Universe' pageant on television the other night and the girl who was selected is very attractive and seems to have a lot of poise and spoke very well. Why don't we do a show called 'David has a Date with Miss Universe.'"

Naturally we were delighted that David was suddenly taking this much interest in program ideas. In fact, the show turned out so well that he immediately came up with another idea that we filmed during the summer for the following season. That one was called "David and the Stewardess." We decided to pass, however, on "David and the Stripper." We figured television wasn't quite ready for it.

As we began our sixth season we continued to emphasize the

boys more and more and use their activities as the basis for our story lines. As a result, our shows for the fall of 1957 had titles like "Fixing Up the Fraternity House," "The Boys Land in Jail," "A Picture in Rick's Notebook," "Ricky's Big Night" —shows like that. In a most flattering review of "Ricky's Big Night" in the *Hollywood Reporter,* Hank Grant wrote that "Ozzie and Harriet should be mighty mighty proud of their boys." Indeed, we were. With consumate ease they would breeze onto the set and give completely professional and yet totally unaffected performances, sometimes covering scenes from three or four different shows in the same day.

Of course we also included a few episodes that featured Mom and Dad such as "The Treasurer's Report," "Harriet's Dancing Partner," and one that received a surprising reaction called "Tutti-Frutti Ice Cream." In this particular show, Harriet and I are reminiscing about the old days when almost every community in America had its own ice cream parlor, and I start telling her about the delicious homemade tutti-frutti ice cream that was a specialty at Wrede and Koop's back in Ridgefield Park. The power of suggestion being what it is, we both suddenly get a yen for tutti-frutti ice cream and go all over town trying to find some.

The reaction was almost unbelievable. Immediately following the telecast, ice cream stores all over the country were besieged with calls for tutti-frutti. We received literally hundreds of letters from ice cream companies, big and small, asking us to please let them know in advance if we ever decided to repeat the show (which of course we did). Several local companies started sending us gallons of exotic-flavored ice cream every week until we finally had to call and ask them to please cease and desist. It was either that or let out all my pants in the seat.

October 24, 1957, was a big night at our house. There was a double celebration. First of all it was David's twenty-first birthday—which we had planned for—and secondly, Lew Chudd of Imperial Records showed up and presented Rick with his first Gold Record. This, we hadn't planned for. What made it especially awkward was that he showed up just as we were singing "Happy birthday, dear David!" Rick said it was the nicest present he had ever received on David's birthday, and David said he thought that Lew Chudd could at least have waited until he, David, had a chance to blow out the candles.

The Gold Record, symbolic of the sale of a million copies, was for "Be Bop Baby" and "Have I Told You Lately That I Love You," which was actually a two-sided hit. It was only the first of many, of course, and before Rick's contract with Imperial had run out, he would have seven others to hang on the wall beside it.

The early spring of 1958 found us shooting almost as many shows outdoors as we did on the set, with Griffith Park being our favorite location spot.

A few shows that immediately come to mind are "The Road Race," where Harriet and I in a Model T Ford race against Ricky and a young friend in their hotrod; "The Trophy," where I try to uphold the family honor in a cross-country obstacle race and where I literally ran about five miles before the day was over; and "The Fourteen-Mile Hike," where I take a group of Cub Scouts on a hike and get them lost in the woods.

The outdoor shows served several purposes. They relieved the boredom of continually shooting in the studio, they gave us a great deal of variety in our programing, and of course they made the Eastman Kodak people very happy, since we always had our cameras with us.

23

On May 8, 1959, Rick celebrated his eighteenth birthday in Tucson, Arizona. Ordinarily there wouldn't be anything too exciting about celebrating your birthday in Tucson, Arizona, except that among those present were John Wayne, Dean Martin, Walter Brennan, Howard Hawks and Angie Dickenson. They were all there filming *Rio Bravo,* a tremendously successful motion picture that, judging by the frequency with which it is rerun on television, seems to be timeless in its appeal.

Rick played the part of a young cowhand named "Colorado," and there is one scene in the picture that is really a classic. Perhaps you remember it. Duke Wayne is being held at gunpoint by three desperados who have taken him by surprise and forced him to throw his rifle on the ground. On a signal from Rick, Angie Dickinson heaves a flowerpot through a window to distract them, and Ricky quickly picks up Duke's rifle, tosses it to him, and then whips out his own six-shooter and together they gun down the bad guys. Joe Byrne, who went to Arizona with Rick as his stand-in, told me that when they filmed the scene Rick was so fast with his hands that he'd toss the rifle to Duke and get three shots off with his own gun while the rifle was still in the air and before Duke had a chance to catch it. Finally Duke said, "Take it easy, will you, Rick. There are only three guys there. Leave one of them for me!"

While they were shooting the picture, Dave decided to fly over to Tucson and see how his kid brother was doing. When he got there, he discovered to his horror that Rick had been so involved with practicing his fast draw and galloping around on the horses that he hadn't read the script yet.

Dave kept him up all that night going over the entire script in detail and "breaking down" each scene, speech by speech. Ricky kept falling asleep, and each time he did Dave would give him a kick to wake him up. Rick said later that the only time during the entire picture that he had any trouble with his lines was that next day. He was so tired from not getting any sleep that he couldn't remember a thing. (I really don't believe this, but that's what he told me and it does make a better story.)

Sometime in June, they mailed Rick a diploma from Hollywood High School attesting to the fact that he was now officially graduated. Because of his hectic schedule, he hadn't attended classes there for over a year but had been tutored by Randolph Van Scoyk, a fine man and excellent teacher, who had the unenviable job of trying to get Rick away from his guitar and onto the books.

By now Rick had been forced into a warped sort of existence. When he went on tour he had to be accompanied not only by Jack Iannarelli and Maury Foladare, who took care of business details, but also by two husky former All-America football players, Jack Ellena and Paul Cameron, both excellent at running interference and warding off would-be tacklers. Jack, who had been a linebacker for the Los Angeles Rams, told me after coming home from one of the tours that warding off those screaming girls was worse than meeting the Chicago Bears head on.

Whenever the group checked into a hotel, Rick had to use the freight elevator and guards had to be stationed outside his door. He had to have police escorts to meet him at airports and to take him to all engagements, and even at home he couldn't go to a movie or a drive-in without being mobbed.

Some of his experiences were funny and some of them were scary. In Dallas a girl got so excited she fell out of the balcony, and in Philadelphia two girls lay down in front of his car and begged him to run over them. When he played the Steel Pier in Atlantic City, they had to hire a helicopter to get him through

258

the crowds and out to the end of the pier. Several times, in different cities, when he went in to take a shower in his hotel room, there would be a couple of girls waiting in the shower stall for him. (I told him it reminded me of the old joke: "You girls will have to get out of here. I don't care which one!")

In spite of all this protection, it was a common occurrence on personal appearance tours for him to have half his clothes torn off. He told me he was in constant fear that some girl would get knocked down in the crowd and killed or seriously injured.

Through it all, Rick somehow managed to keep his balance and a remarkable sense of values, especially for one so young. As his parents, however, Harriet and I were naturally concerned that he was becoming more and more withdrawn and uncomfortable except with his close friends and his family.

Actually, this was probably more in our minds than in his, because we have talked about it many times in recent years and both Rick and Dave have said that they really enjoyed those frantic years—that the advantages far outweighed the disadvantages and that the only thing they regretted missing out on was college athletics.

We discussed the possibility of Rick's going to college, but we agreed with him that it wouldn't be practical—at least not at this time. His grades would have gotten him into just about any school in the country, but he felt that, since his main interests were in music and entertaining, it wouldn't make any sense for him to give up the things that he most enjoyed in order to get involved in things that really didn't interest him, especially when his career was going so fantastically well.

The year 1959 proved to be another happy one for all us Nelsons. Our television ratings continued to be healthy and, our original ten-year contract with ABC having proved to be a pleasant and profitable arrangement for all concerned, we entered into a new noncancellable contract with them—this time for five years, but with the same artistic controls and, as before, no budgetary restrictions.

My dealings with the American Broadcasting Company—first with Bob Kintner and then with Leonard Goldenson and Tom Moore—were never anything but most pleasant. One hears so much about networks meddling in the production of television shows that I feel an obligation to state categorically that never at any time was I subjected to the slightest interference of any kind. During the entire fourteen years that we produced our show there was not one line or one word deleted or changed or even any attempt made to do so.

As for budgets, I was never subjected to one. There were suggested figures regarding the total average costs of our shows, but there was no contractual obligation on my part to stay within those figures. I did feel, however, a deep sense of moral obligation to bring the shows in at a reasonable cost, and it was a question of personal pride for me to do this while maintaining the highest possible production quality.

One day, Joe Byrne, whom you recall was Rick's standin, came to me and asked if I thought that Stage Five Productions (our production company) would like to enter a team in the Studio Basketball League. Joe had been an outstanding basketball player at Hollywood High School, and of course Dave and Rick had been playing basketball since they were very small boys. Along with Dave Cadiente, Paul Cameron, Bob Bergdahl, Vic Guarnier, Linden Crow, Jim Pauley, and my brother Don—all fine athletes —we managed to put together a competitive group of guys. Oh, yes—and on occasions they even let the Old Man play. (They had to—I paid the entry fee and bought the uniforms.)

Bill Fraker, our camera operator, was our coach; Eddie Benson, my stand-in, was our official scorer; and Tony Montenero, a fine little actor and the son of the head of our prop department, was our mascot.

The Studio Basketball League was made up of some really top-flight teams representing MGM, Warner Brothers, Paramount, CBS, Desilu, and Twentieth Century—Fox, but we had a bunch of guys who loved to win and a rooting section, led by Harriet and the girls from the office, that shook the rafters of the old Hollywood High School gym.

At least half our games were typical Hollywood cliffhangers, and all of them were hard-fought and occasionally bloody, but somehow we always managed to squeak through. And so, at the end of the season, we became the proud possessors of a beautiful trophy with an inscription that read, "Studio League Champions 1959—Stage Five Productions."

One of the nonleague games we played was against a team representing the Phi Delts of USC, who ran in an extra starter, a Phi Delt from Michigan, who was better known for his prowess on the gridiron. It was none other than Tom Harmon, "Ole 98," who is on just about everyone's all-time all-American football team.

Harriet and I were no strangers to the Harmons, since we had been to parties with Tom and his lovely wife Elyse—the former Elyse Knox, a famous Powers fashion model who had starred in several motion pictures before opting for the more satisfying career of becoming a wife and mother.

The night of the game, Tom and Elyse had brought along their three children: Mark, age nine, Kelly, age eleven, and Kris, age thirteen. Mark, who later became UCLA's quarterback and one of the finest in collegiate ranks, and Kelly, now a beautiful cover girl and model, had come to see their dad play basketball, but Kris had come for only one reason—to see and possibly meet Ricky Nelson, whose every record she had collected and whose pictures covered every wall in her room.

After the game, Tom asked Ricky if he would pose for a picture with Kris—which he did, of course, and which she promptly added to her wall collection along with a sign she printed which read, "NOTHING IS IMPOSSIBLE."

Rick, being eighteen at this time, was naturally not especially interested in thirteen-year-old girls no matter how cute they were, but about three years later he would say to Harriet, "She's really beautiful. How old is she now?"

While Rick was touring the country with his rock group (which at that time consisted of James Burton and Rick on guitars, James

261

Kirkland on bass, and Richie Frost on drums), Dave was busy furthering his career as a motion picture actor. Following *The Remarkable Mr. Pennypacker,* he costarred with Robert Ryan and Burl Ives in *The Day of the Outlaw* for United Artists and immediately followed this by playing two totally different roles: a comedy role in a picture called *—30—* for Jack Webb and a highly dramatic role as a psychopathic killer for Irwin Allen in *The Big Circus.*

The first picture, *—30—,* which Jack not only starred in but also directed, was done on a modest budget but turned out to be an excellent picture with some really outstanding performances by Joe Flynn, Richard Deacon, Bill Conrad, and David.

When the picture was finished, Jack called me on the phone to tell me what a pleasure it had been for him to have Dave in the film. I had seen the preview, so I told Jack what a great job I thought he had done and that David had told me how much Jack's directing had helped him in the comedy scenes. Jack said, "I'll tell you how much I helped him. Each day we would go through the same procedure. I would carefully explain to David just how I wanted the scene played. He would listen very attentively, then say, 'Yes, sir,' very politely, and then go in and play the scene entirely differently from the way I had suggested—and much better. I never did figure out whether he just didn't understand me or was too polite to argue. At any rate, it was all coming out so well that I figured 'We've got a good routine going here—why change it?' "

The Big Circus was not only a radical departure for David as far as the nature of his role was concerned, but as a result of the picture he and Ricky became involved in what can only be described as a "death-defying" hobby. They became the "Daring Young Men on the Flying Trapeze."

The part David played in *The Big Circus* was that of a catcher in a trapeze act. As is the case with all circus pictures, the actors learned a couple of basic fundamentals which were filmed just a few feet from the ground, while the actual high work, the flying and catching, were done by professionals—in this case, Fay Alexander as flyer and Bob Yerkes as catcher, both of whom were skilled circus performers of many years' experience.

One day during a lunch break when David was alone on the set, he decided to climb up and see what it was like to sit in the "catch-trap" high in the air. The catch-trap is the trapeze that the catcher sits in and then goes into what is known as a "lock," where he is suspended by his legs from the catch-bar. The catch-trap is usually anywhere from thirty-five to fifty feet from the floor.

David got up there, took one look down, and immediately froze. There he sat until Bob and Del Graham, the technical advisor on the picture, came back from lunch and rescued him. The next day he went up again, only this time he got down by himself. Before the week was over, he had learned the proper way of dropping into the net. Then he learned to swing back and forth without panicking, and before the picture was finished he had learned to go into the "lock" and swing upside down in an even cadence. He had also gotten completely hooked on the idea of becoming a catcher—a real, honest-to-goodness catcher in a real, honest-to-goodness trapeze act in a real, honest-to-goodness circus.

Del Graham and his wife Babs, both of whom were flyers, had their trapeze rigging set up in Thousand Oaks near a trailer camp where they lived, and every day David drove out there and practiced and practiced and practiced.

When Ricky got back from Tucson and *Rio Bravo,* he discovered that he was about to become David's flying partner. David had made the decision for him, and Ricky as usual was willing to try anything, especially if it meant that he and David could team up.

There happened to be, at this time, a vacant sound stage at General Service, and George and Jimmy Nasser, who owned the studio and were especially fond of the boys, gave them permission to hang a complete trapeze rigging on the vacant stage, transforming the place into a practice area.

Del Graham, with twenty-five years of flying experience behind him, proved to be an exceptional teacher—and Dave and

Rick, with their great sense of timing and coordination, were obviously ideal pupils—because within a matter of weeks Rick was flying and Dave was catching him.

About this time, Del came to Dave with an important announcement: the catcher for *The Flying Viennas*, the act that the Grahams worked with, was leaving to go back east, and David could have the job if he wanted it.

He made his first appearance as a professional catcher at the San Bernardino County Fair Grounds. Harriet and I drove up to see him along with Jim Stacy (who played the part of Fred in our fraternity gang and who would later star in his own series), Bill Fraker, and Joe Byrne.

I'll never forget the thrill of watching Dave go slowly up the rope, hand over hand, in a sitting position. Harriet said, "Tell me when he gets up there. I don't want to look." Jim turned to me and said, "How can he do that? My hands are soaking wet just watching him."

But do it he did. He started his rhythmic swing and then dropped smoothly into his lock—just as if he had been doing it for years instead of a matter of weeks, just as if he were only a few feet off the ground instead of way up there with only a skinny little net separating him from the hard earth fifty feet below.

As any circus performer will tell you, the swing of the catcher must be perfectly coordinated with the flyer's swing, and as the flyer takes off from his bar it then becomes the catcher's responsibility—especially in leaps involving somersaults—to adjust, while hanging upside down, to the speed and the position of the flyer and literally to catch him by his arms (or in the case of certain leaps, by his legs) in mid-air, meanwhile maintaining sufficient momentum to propel the flyer back to his trapeze.

Maintaining an even swing is not as easy as it looks, because the catcher must actually increase his swing each time just enough to compensate for the slow-down caused by the pull of gravity. Quite obviously, the slightest mistake in timing could easily lead to two fractured skulls—or at best, an uncontrolled fall into the net.

Now they were into the act itself and it was going beautifully:

264

the hocksoff, the twister, the passing leap, Babs with a one-and-a-half and then Del with a double—not the toughest routine in the world, but a perfect performance and a great test of coolness and courage for Dave in his professional debut.

Later in the year Rick would make his debut as a flyer at the Great Western Live Stock Show, to be followed by fine performances with David and the Grahams at Pacific Ocean Park, at the Los Angeles Sports Arena, and finally before eighty thousand people between halves of the Rams-Redskins charity game at the Los Angeles Coliseum.

Ricky, at six feet one and close to 170 pounds, was much too big to be a flyer—most flyers being small guys weighing from 125 to 140 at the most. But the timing between David and him was so perfect, and he came into the catch so smoothly, that Dave said he was no tougher to catch than other flyers he had practiced with who were thirty or forty pounds lighter. "However," Dave said to him one day after a workout, "don't get any heavier, or I'll wind up with arms like an orangutan." (A personal note: I had to look up the spelling of "orangutan." The word has always given me trouble. Up until the age of about twelve, I thought it was "orange-outing.")

As was the case with most of the boys' hobbies, we wrote a show around the trapeze act and called it "The Circus." It was one of our more ambitious projects. We put up a full-sized circus tent with all the accompanying paraphernalia and hired dozens of specialty acts and hundreds of extras. It was worth it, though. It proved to be one of our best shows of the series.

Rick's involvement with his recordings and his personal appearance tours made it impossible for him to stay with the trapeze work with any degree of intensity, but Dave continued with his catching for five or six more years and toured with some of the finest acts in the country. About the only scary experience he had was while appearing in Indianapolis with the Hubert Castle Circus when part of the rigging gave way while they were working at the unheard-of height of ninety-five feet. Fortunately, however, the net held, and so while he was shaken up a bit he was not really hurt.

265

The funniest thing that happened was when Dave and Rick were practicing one afternoon with Del and Babs Graham out at Thousand Oaks. Rick was just a beginner at the time and they were practicing a basic maneuver known as "feets across," which is a hands-to-feet catch. Their timing was a little off, however, and Ricky started to slip out of David's grasp, so Dave grabbed Rick's tights to keep him from falling. Rick, however, was hanging head down, so all Dave succeeded in doing was pulling Rick's tights down around his ankles, which left him swinging back and forth upside down with all his credentials showing.

Since David's first radio appearance was when Bing Crosby appeared as a guest on our show, it seemed quite appropriate when Dave's last trapeze performance was as a guest on the "Hollywood Palace" where Bing was the host. It proved to be a satisfying way to quit because, for the first time on television, he caught two of the most difficult tricks in anyone's repertoire —a double with a full twist and a triple-and-a-half, which means three-and-a-half complete somersaults.

Before we leave 1959, I'd like to report a few other events that made the year an interesting one. For one thing, we flew to Hawaii to film some television commercials and take a short vacation. We stayed at the Royal Hawaiian and one of the waitresses, a cute little Japanese girl named Betsy Nakamoto, told us a funny story about her mother, who spoke only Japanese. She said that a couple of nights earlier, her mother had glanced at the clock, then pointed at the television set, and said, "Teenee wo Eiseyenhawa. Eiseyenhawa. Very funny!" They couldn't figure out why her mother would think that President Eisenhower would be funny on television, but they turned on the set and our program came on. Her mother then settled back in her chair with a big smile on her face and, pointing first to me and then to Harriet, said, "See? Eisey and Hawa—very funny!"

The commercials we filmed were for Eastman Kodak, and we shot them on the ocean side of the hotel. One of them called for Dave and Rick to come in on surfboards while Harriet and I photographed them from a catamaran. It was a very difficult shot to line up, because the boys had to wait for just the right-sized wave so that it would look exciting and carry them far enough to get a good shot and yet stay close enough so that Bobby Moreno, our camerman, could keep them and us in the picture.

After what seemed like about twenty minutes, we finally got everything lined up: a beautiful, big wave came rolling in, and both boys took it perfectly and started riding in toward shore. Just then, from out of nowhere, some clown who probably figured that this was his big chance to be discovered came zooming into the picture and promptly fell off his board, which went flying into the air and hit Rick right on the head. We finally got the shot an hour-and-a-half later.

That weekend we all went out to the Waikiki Shell, where Rick and his group played to a capacity crowd of over twelve thousand screamers. The four concerts had been sold out for several weeks previously, so we had to watch from backstage.

It was the first time we had ever seen Rick in one of his personal appearances, and although we had been warned ahead of time we still weren't quite prepared for what happened. Not only did they scream after each number, but they screamed before and during each number. They screamed the loudest, however, not when he sang "Poor Little Fool" or "It's Late" or "Lonesome Town," but when he drank a glass of water and when he changed guitars after he had broken a string. I think this was the first time in my life that I began to feel that there might be such a thing as a generation gap.

24

On December 20, the *Los Angeles Times* announced its "Women of the Year" awards for 1959, and Harriet was selected as the Woman of the Year in entertainment. Naturally David, Ricky, and I heartily concurred with all the nice things that were said about her at the presentation, as well as the accolades she was accorded a few months later when she received the first of the annual "Genii" awards given by the Radio and Television Women of Southern California. This latter presentation was made by Jack Benny at a testimonial dinner given in Harriet's honor at the grand ballroom of the Beverly Hills Hotel. It was an exciting evening and we were all tremendously proud of her.

By 1960, the Nelson family both "onstage" and "offstage" had undergone several important changes. For one thing, David and Ricky had moved out and were sharing a little house in the Hollywood Hills. I say "moved out," but of course they dropped by the house at Camino Palmero whenever they felt the need of a square meal or an uninterrupted night's sleep—which was about twice a week.

The house they rented, in keeping with their life style of living dangerously, was one of those cantilever constructions which are so popular in the hill sections of the Hollywood area. It looked disarmingly normal from the street, but as you entered you got the uneasy feeling that the whole place could collapse at any moment and fall down into the canyon. A sliding glass door led to a back porch suspended in mid-air, giving a clear view of the surrounding terrain in all directions: straight ahead, to the left, to the right, and straight down—most especially straight down. It was definitely no place for someone subject to nose-bleeds. Miraculously, no one ever fell off there—or if anyone did, at least we never heard about it.

We had also made changes in our script-writing procedures in that our writing staff (which now consisted of my brother Don, Dick Bensfield, and Perry Grant, all of whom had come with us directly from college) no longer submitted separate scripts but turned in just one master script. Since my schedule precluded night meetings (I usually spent the hours after dinner learning lines and blocking out the scenes for the next day's shooting), we held most of our story conferences—if you could call them that—on the set between shots. After we were agreed on a story-line, Don, Dick, and Perry would write the script and turn it in to me. I would take it from there and do whatever editing or rewriting I felt was necessary while they started work on the storyline for the next script.

We had our own projection room right on our shooting stage, which enabled me to work with our cutters or view the previous day's shooting without any loss of time.

Since David was now twenty-three years old, we had decided to write our scripts on the premise that he had graduated from college, moved on to law school, and taken a job as a clerk in a law office—a procedure we would follow later with Ricky. In the case of Wally Plumstead (Skip Young), however, we kept him in school as a perpetual undergraduate and campus wheeler and dealer.

At David's suggestion, we brought in Joe Flynn to play the part of Dave's boss Donald Kelley (having fearlessly appropriated the name from our long-time friend and attorney), and it was a most fortunate choice. Joe proved to be an excellent actor, and some of the scenes that he and David played together were really gems. When Joe left us after several years to costar with Ernest Borgnine in the highly successful series "McHale's Navy," we were of course sorry to lose him but delighted with his suc-

269

the unique sound, the excitement, the fine vocal phrasing—the entire final result, even from the very beginning—were all Ricky's. Any suggestions I made were just that—suggestions. Just as a successful television show or motion picture must reflect the taste and judgment of one person and not a committee, so in my opinion, must a successful record reflect one person's taste and judgment, and in this case it was Ricky's.

The night he recorded "Hello Mary Lou" we all listened to the playback and Rick said, "I like it but it sounds a little tubby to me. It needs something in the upper register to brighten it." Then he turned to me and said, "It's too bad you don't have your four-string guitar here, Dad, you could overdub it. That's just the sound we need."

It's just possible he was kidding, but I didn't wait to find out. I drove home, got the guitar, and was back at the studio in ten minutes. It would have taken me longer, except that there was no traffic. There usually isn't at three o'clock in the morning.

So, if you happen to have a copy of Ricky's "Hello Mary Lou" around the house, put it on your player and listen to the fascinating rhythmic pattern and bright, twangy sounds of the tenor guitar in the upper register. Actually, you can't hear it too clearly, but you have the feeling that it's in there someplace. And it only took me twelve takes!

Before the year was over, "Mary Lou" had become number one in France, Norway, Denmark, Sweden, Germany, New Zealand, and Australia. I don't know what happened in the United States, Great Britain, and Canada. They opted for "Travelin' Man."

As I was writing this down, I suddenly remembered that I had played on another of Rick's recordings earlier in the year. It was at a little studio on Fairfax Avenue just off Melrose, and the musicians on the date were Rick's regular group of James Kirkland, James Burton, and Richie Frost—plus Gene Garth on piano.

They had been recording an album and had finished cutting all the sides that had been scheduled for the session. Ricky, Jimmie Haskell, and I were sitting around talking when Rick decided he'd like to record one more song—a country-and-western standard called "Someday."

A search of the parking lot revealed the fact that Burton and Kirkland hadn't left yet, but Gene and Richie had taken off, although Richie's drums were still in the studio. Rick said, "Hey, here's an idea. Why don't I play the drums and you play the piano, Dad. I'm sure you can handle it. The song only has three chords."

Once again, I must confess that I didn't play anything spectacular, but if you listen carefully you are aware that the piano player is playing all the right chords and keeping a nice steady beat. Ricky was wrong about the number of chords in the song, however: it has *six* chords, not three.

Many people have asked me where we found all the beautiful girls who appeared on our show playing opposite Dave and Rick. The answer is, "all over." Among their many talents, it seems that our two sons have a deep appreciation of feminine pulchritude. Scarcely a week went by that Dave or Rick didn't say, "Hey, Dad, the next time you're looking for a girl to play one of the parts, I have a couple of good suggestions for you."

Sometimes it was a girl they had seen on television in another show or in a beauty pageant, but more often than not it was someone they had met at a party.

Among those who appeared with considerable regularity were Roberta Shore, Tuesday Weld, Cheryl Holdridge, Joi Lansing, Linda Evans, Katie Regan, Susan Oliver, Pam Austin, Elaine Dupont, Janet Lake, Andra Martin, Mikki Jamison, Brooke Bundy, Joan Staley, Venetia Stephenson, Joyce Taylor, Sharyn Hillyer, and of course Charlene Salerno, who became a regular cast member and did such a great job as Wally's long-suffering girlfriend, Ginger.

I must add that David and Ricky's casting suggestions weren't limited to the girls on the show, but included practially all the guys who played the parts of friends and fraternity brothers. Jim Stacy, Joe Byrne, Marlin McKeever, Karl Kindberg, Zeke Budny, Sean Morgan, Bruce Belland, Ben Bennett, Jimmy Hawkins, Greg

Dawson, and, later, Kent McCord, Paul Gleason, and Charley Britt—they were all real-life friends, most of whom had had no previous acting experience.

Among the shows we aired during the early part of 1960 were "The Little House Guest" and "His Brother's Girl." I remember "The Little House Guest" primarily because of the unusually fine performance by little Barry Livingston, who started with us at age five. His older brother Stanley had started with us at age seven, and both boys would go on to become regular cast members of Fred MacMurray's "My Three Sons."

"His Brother's Girl" was a show that involved a mix-up between Dave and Rick in which each preferred the other guy's girl but was reluctant to do anything about it because of his loyalty to his brother. It was based on an actual incident that had occurred between one of my fraternity brothers and me when I was in college.

I firmly believe that 90 percent of the success of most television shows or motion pictures is in the casting, and this was especially true in this particular case. The script, in order to be effective, required two very attractive girls who were also good actresses.

We had already cast one of the girls, Janet Lake, who had done a fine job for us in an earlier show, "David Loses His Poise," and were setting up auditions for the other role when David recalled that he had seen a motion picture called *The Rabbit Trap* in which he had been tremendously impressed with the girl who had played the female lead. Her name was June Blair.

She proved to be not only an excellent actress but a voluptuous, auburn-haired girl with classically beautiful features and a delightfully fey sense of humor. On May 20 of the following year, she became Mrs. David Nelson.

When David got married, Rick said that he, Rick, had not only gained a sister-in-law but had lost a roommate, so he decided to move out of the cliff-hanger in the Hollywood Hills (with David gone there was no longer anyone to do handstands on the railing of the back porch, anyway) and find himself a house to buy—something in a secluded area where there wouldn't

274

be forty or fifty people dropping by every night and where he could play his guitar at three o'clock in the morning without worrying about disturbing the neighbors.

He and Charley Britt had decided to room together as soon as Rick could find a house. Charley had been an All-American quarterback at the University of Georgia and was now playing safety for the Los Angeles Rams as well as appearing on our television show whenever we had scenes involving the fraternity boys.

Actually, we weren't aware that Ricky was interested in buying a house until he stopped off to say goodbye to us just before leaving for a summer tour of personal appearances.

Then, as sort of an afterthought, he said, "Oh, and by the way, Mom, I want to buy a house. Will you see if you can find one for me? Something with a lot of property where I can put a fence around it."

Harriet said, "Wait a second, what kind of a house do you want and how much do you want to spend?"

"I'll leave that up to you," he said. "You know more about those things than I do."

He was playing a state fair in Indiana or Illinois, somewhere in the Midwest, when Harriet phoned to tell him that she had found a house that she thought he'd really like. It was on a big lot in the hills above Nichols Canyon and he could also buy the two adjacent lots to give him extra privacy.

"Great!" said Rick. "Will you ask Dad to buy it for me and I'll pay him back when I get home."

"Don't you want to see it first?" said Harriet.

"No, that's okay," said Rick. "If you like it, I know I'll like it, too."

He and Charley moved in that fall and evidently Rick was right about liking it, because he's still living there. Or course, he has a different roommate now and several rooms have been added to accomodate the extra people who are living there, including a beautiful ballet dancer, age nine, and two very tough football players, both age five.

For June, David's new bride, the adjustment required in switching over from June Blair to Mrs. David Nelson must have been a difficult one. It would have been difficult enough for someone who had a normal family background to suddenly become a part of a family that had been living in the public eye for the past twenty years. For June it was made even more so by the fact that she had never been a part of any family. Her father died before she was born, and from the time she was four years old she had been moved from one foster home to another, without ever having the security of feeling that she belonged to anyone or that anyone really cared what happened to her.

The decision as to whether or not June would join the show on a regular basis was of course left up to her and David, but, needless to say, we were delighted when they decided that she would. And so it came to pass that we gained not only a beautiful daughter, but a talented actress as well. One of the first and best shows of the new fall season was aptly titled "The Newlyweds Get Settled," and to our ever-expanding series of standing sets, which once consisted simply of the Nelson house and yard and which now included the law offices, the college campus, and the fraternity house, we added one more—Dave and June's apartment.

Meanwhile, Rick had started taking more and more notice of Kris Harmon, who had grown from the cute little kid of thirteen whom he had met at the basketball game to a beautiful young lady who at sixteen had that rare gift of poise and style that is reserved for a very select few. He was her escort at the prom at Marymount School in Bel Air where she had been elected Prom Queen, and by the summer of 1962 he was dating her exclusively.

I have a feeling that the good sisters at Marymount were not altogether sorry to see Kris graduate. She was extremely popular with her schoolmates, but she has always been a rugged individualist and more than occasionally her enthusiasm and freedom of spirit came into conflict with the faculty's idea of what constitutes proper behavior and adherence to the school's rules and regulations. At one time her classmates included Mia Farrow and Tish

Sterling, who along with Kris must have been quite a handful for the poor ladies to cope with.

Rick and Kris flew out to Chicago with Tom and Elyse Harmon in August to attend the All-Star Game and to visit with us while we were appearing in *Marriage-Go-Round* at the Tent House Theater. It was obvious, even by then, that it wouldn't be too long before we'd have another daughter in the family, so it came as no great surprise when, at a party at our house in December, Tom announced that Kris would become Mrs. Rick Nelson sometime in the early spring.

25

Our four weeks' tour in *Marriage-Go-Round* made for a very pleasant change from the sameness of filming the television show week after week.

It is a very well-constructed play and an ideal vehicle for Harriet and me. It was written by Leslie Stevens and is very easy to stage in that it concerns itself with only four characters: a college professor who is the head of the Department of Anthropology; his wife, who is the dean of women; their house guest, a big, sexy Swedish girl; and a family friend, who is a professor in the Languages Department. Harriet and I played the part of the husband and wife, of course; our good friend Lyle Talbot played the other professor; and the part of the Swedish bombshell was played by Sally Kellerman, who would later cause such a sensation as "Hot Lips" Hoolihan in the motion picture *M*A*S*H*.

Harriet and I became proud grandparents August 20, 1962. Dave and June named their little boy Daniel Blair Nelson. Dave was in the Air Force Reserve at the time, and they allowed him to fly in for the actual event, but then he had to go back to the air base a few days later, so June and Danny stayed with us until Dave completed his summer camp duty.

They stayed in the same room and she slept in the same bed that David had slept in as a boy. June has told me many times that those couple of weeks hold warm and wonderful memories

278

for her. She and David had their beautiful baby to share, and for the first time she felt that she had a family that she loved and who loved her in return.

Meanwhile, Rick and Kris were not too far behind. Immediately following the wedding Kris joined the show, and Jim Roth and Jack Moore, our highly skilled set designer and set-dresser, were busy creating another home away from home at General Service Studios.

Although Kris's acting experience had been limited to plays she had appeared in at school, she moved into the television show as if it were the most natural thing in the world for her— as indeed it proved to be.

With June and Kris both on the show at the same time, however, there were built-in problems as far as I, as a combination director—father-in-law, was concerned. Although both girls were tremendously talented, most cooperative, and obviously interested in giving good performances, I was constantly concerned with keeping everyone happy and yet getting the best possible result. "Did June have a better part this week than Kris?" "Has Kris been in more scripts lately than June?" "How can I tell Kris that I don't like her hair that way?" "How can I tell June that I think her makeup is too light?"

Then there was the situation with Dave and Rick. How do you suggest to your son, when he is playing a scene with his wife, that you think he should place more emphasis on a certain line or that a certain move he is making doesn't work with the camera? How do you do these things without demeaning him in front of his wife? Where do you place the camera when the scene involves your wife, your sons, your daughters-in-law, and yourself? Who gets the favored angles?

By the same token, I'm sure the situation must have been just as difficult from their point of view. "How can I explain to my father-in-law that I just wouldn't say the line that way?" or "Why are we doing another take? Take five was perfect." "Then why don't you tell him?" "Why don't *you* tell him?"

279

Somehow, however, we all managed to survive, and the happy times and fun we had together far outweighed the pressures and tensions.

Another gratifying note was that the 1963–64 season found us with the highest Neilson ratings since the show had come to television twelve years previously, so we had no difficulty coming to terms with ABC for another five-year period.

Rick's contract with Imperial Records had also come to an end, so it became necessary to negotiate a new one for him. Because of the uncertainty of the length of any recording artist's popularity, we agreed that it would be to Rick's greatest advantage to have the contract spread over as long a period as possible.

By the very nature of such an agreement, we would be limited to those companies—such as Decca, RCA, Columbia, Capitol, and a very few others—that we could be sure would still be around in fifteen or twenty years.

Fortunately for Rick, Decca Records, which was his first choice, was being represented by Mickey Rockford, who along with Sonny Werblin had done such an excellent job of representing us in television throughout the years. In order to satisfy claims by the federal government of a conflict of interests, MCA had elected to disengage itself from the agency business, so Mickey and I, who just the previous year had flown to Chicago together to sell our show to the American Dairy Assocation (remember all those scenes in the Malt Shop?) now found ourselves on opposite sides of the table but with the same purpose in mind—to work out a deal that would be fair to both parties.

The result was a twenty-year deal under substantially the same conditions and yearly guarantees as the previous deal with Imperial. It has proved to be a happy and profitable one for both Rick and Decca. He has had many big-selling hits for them, and just recently his "Garden Party" won him another gold record. It has sold over a million records to date and is still selling.

The year 1963 was not only a good one for contractual negotiations, it was a good year for beautiful little baby girls—at least it was in our family. On October 25, 1963, Rick and Kris became the proud parents of Tracy Kristine Nelson—a beautiful little baby girl, indeed!

Before we leave 1963, I'd like to relate an incident that occurred while I was trimming the Christmas tree the night of December 24.

We always had a gang over for Christmas Eve, and as a rule we trimmed the tree a few nights earlier. This particular night I was standing on a small ladder stringing the lights and Harriet had gone into the kitchen to get some coffee. As I reached toward the back of the tree I suddenly felt a sharp burning sensation in a most embarrassing spot—and on the tip end of it! I thought to myself, "I must have some terrible kidney disease—and of all times to discover it, right before Christmas! What a Christmas present!" Then I thought to myself, "I wonder if I could have imagined it." I reached for another light and there it was again —that same burning sensation—and in the same place!

Suddenly a thought occurred to me. I looked down and started laughing so hard I almost fell off the ladder.

Just then Harriet came in. "What's so funny?" she said.

"I just discovered something. If you lean up against those Christmas tree lights, they'll burn you."

"Of course," she said.

"And I don't have a kidney disease after all."

"Good for you," said Harriet.

In the early spring of the following year we interrupted our shooting schedule long enough for me to fly back to New Jersey to be honored once again by my alma mater, which presented me with the Rutgers Alumni Federation Award. I felt that I was in unusually distinguished company because the previous recipients had been Dr. Jonas Salk, Dr. Selman Waksman, and Senator Clifford Case.

The presentation was made at the All-Rutgers Alumni Dinner, and I told President Mason Gross, who made the presentation, that I hoped he realized they were awarding this beautiful plaque to someone who had really never done an honest day's work in his life—but that if they had second thoughts about it they were too late, because I wasn't about to give it back.

I think we had some really good shows in 1964. As we had done so successfully in the past, we continued to use our personal experiences as the basis for many of them (unfortunately, I couldn't seem to find a way to work in the Christmas tree incident); in most cases, they seem to be the episodes I remember most fondly.

I recall one show we named "The Lonesome Parents," which, judging by the mail response, seemed to strike a responsive chord in a lot of our viewers. In this particular show, Harriet and I become concerned when we don't hear from Dave and June for two weeks. We wonder if there is anything wrong or if they are upset with us about anything. We don't want them to feel that they have to keep in touch with us constantly, but when another week goes by and we still haven't heard from them, we decide to call them and invite them over to dinner.

As it turns out, they are both fine and nothing was wrong—they had just been busy and hadn't realized that we had been worrying about them.

I especially like the little tag we had on this one. Just as we are getting ready for bed, our phone rings. It is Harriet's mother. She hasn't heard from us in two or three weeks and is calling to find out if there is anything wrong or if we are upset with her about anything.

Kris had been studying ballet ever since she was five or six years old and is a beautiful dancer, so we wrote a show called "The Ballerina" in which she dances an original routine that was choreographed by her teacher, David Lichine.

In a dream sequence Rick joins her and together they perform an excerpt from *Swan Lake*. How she talked Rick into it, I'll never know. (Neither will he.) But like everything else Rick tries, he really worked at it, and as a result it came off amazingly well. The highlight of the show is when Rick, Wally, Sean, Dink, Bruce, and Kent give their version of *Nutcracker Suite*. Bur-

282

lesques of ballets are either absolutely hilarious or very unfunny. Fortunately, this one proved to be hilarious.

Kent McCord had joined the cast in the latter part of 1963 when acting was the furthest thing from his mind. He and Rick had first met when Rick was organizing a touch football team to play against Elvis Presley's then-undefeated team, and a close friendship developed between Rick and Kent that still continues.

At the present time Kent is, of course, one of the stars of the highly rated "Adam-12" series, and I firmly believe that one of the main reasons for the continuing success of the show is the great chemistry that exists between him and Marty Milner, with whom he costars. They are both highly professional and give consistently fine performances.

The summer of 1965 proved to be an interesting one. Dave and June decided to take a fling at summer stock and during July and August appeared in some of the finest theaters in the Midwest. The play they selected was *The Happiest Years*, a domestic comedy which proved to be an ideal vehicle for them, and they played to large and enthusiastic audiences everywhere they appeared.

For Harriet it was a time to play "Grandma" and to get better acquainted with Danny and Tracy. Tracy, of course, was not walking yet, but Danny was walking, running, talking, and yelling and doing all those things that make a healthy little two-year-old boy a handful for anyone.

For Rick, Kris, and me, the summer proved to be both interesting and challenging. I had bought the screen rights to a stage play called *Love and Kisses*, which, I felt, despite the fact that it had only run about a week on Broadway, had great possibilities as a movie, so I made a deal to write, produce, and direct it as a feature at Universal, starring Rick and Kris.

As I was soon to discover, adapting a stage play to the screen is much more difficult than it would seem at first blush. In writing for the stage, the writer constructs his play so as to restrict his action to a limited area. In bringing a play to the screen, the writer must avoid falling into either of two traps. If he adheres too closely to the original construction, the film will look as if someone just brought a camera into the theater and photographed a stage play. On the other hand, if it is "opened up" too much there is a danger that it will wind up looking like a travelogue, with a resultant loss in continuity and vitality. I like to think that I avoided both pitfalls. At least I was aware of them.

There was no music in *Love and Kisses* on the stage, so we had several rock numbers and a ballad written to give Rick a chance to sing with his group. We started with a scene of Rick's rehearsing the title song in the school gym, and later on in the picture we showed a scene not only of the graduation exercises, which gave us an opportunity for added comedy, but also the prom itself, where Rick got a chance to sing two more songs.

I also added a dream sequence in which Rick dreams that Kris, who has walked out on him threatening to get a job, is performing as a stripper in a burlesque joint. Rick gets into a fight with the owner and in the ensuing free-for-all the joint is completely demolished.

Without detracting from the individual performances, which were uniformly good, I think the fight sequence proved to be the outstanding scene in the picture. Our old friend Jack Ellena staged it for us and did a masterful job. Rick was an active participant, of course, and his activities included having six-foot five-inch, 250-pound Jim Boeke leap on his back; throwing 230-pound Jack Ellena over a bar and through a window; being attacked by Bruce Tegner with a real knife which misses him by inches; throwing 210-pound Gene Le Beau through a door and down a flight of stairs; plus being involved in various acts of kicking, punching, and chair throwing.

Dave and Skip Young ("Wally" on our show) happened to stop by while we were shooting the sequence, Dave having just gotten back from his summer stock tour, so I had them sit at the bar, and in the midst of the fight, when Rick is being attacked from all sides, Skip looks over at him and says to Dave, "Doesn't he look familiar to you?"

284

Dave shakes his head and says, "No, I never saw him before."

The night I saw the picture in a theater in Westwood this got one of the biggest laughs I've ever heard. This and a bit where Kris, on her wedding night, opens a little overnight bag and a pair of falsies fall out and roll across the floor.

Actually the picture turned out surprisingly well, especially considering the fact that we were given a very limited budget and a seventeen-day shooting schedule. It has been on television quite a bit. If you should happen to see it listed you might take a look at it. On the other hand, if you should happen to miss it, I wouldn't worry too much about it.

When we resumed filming our television show in the fall of 1965, we were no longer at General Service Studios but had moved our entire production out to the old Selznick Studios, on Washington Boulevard, which had since become the Desilu Culver Studios.

The move had been necessitated by a shortage of stage space at General Service, and although the Desilu people did everything possible to make us happy, we were never really comfortable there. We had been at General Service for thirteen years, and after all that time it was difficult getting used to new surroundings and new faces.

As for Harriet and me, we had been spoiled by the fact that General Service was only a ten-minute drive from home. In fact, on pleasant days I often walked it or jogged. Desilu Culver, on the other hand, was a thirty-five- to forty-minute drive, and that extra half-hour of fighting the traffic made a world of difference at the end of the day's shooting. It also meant getting up earlier in the morning.

The show was unexpectedly cancelled at the end of the 1965–66 season, but we have always felt that it really ended when we left General Service.

When Tom Moore, president of ABC, phoned to tell me that we were not going to be on the schedule the following fall, I must confess that I received the news with a feeling of sadness. I knew we would miss seeing all those wonderful people who had been like an extension of our own family and who had made our lives so pleasant throughout the years.

The early morning routine had varied very little from day to day. As I entered the sound stage, Leonard Gwynne, our greensman, and John Somers, our security officer, would be waiting with a cheery "Good morning." Back in the property room, Jack Iannarelli and Kenny Marstella would be getting the props ready for the first shot. Out on the set, Joe Smith, our gaffer, would be setting the lights, and "Mac" McClellan, our head grip, would be checking the equipment while Jimmy Robinson (who had been with us all fourteen years) would be lining up the dolly. Bobby Moreno would be checking the camera setup while Leo Mack, our irrepressible painter, would be regaling the rest of the crew with his latest jokes.

Then I would go back to the make-up and hair-dressing department, where Monty Westmore would always have some homemade soup on the stove and Barbara Lampson, Charlene Chalk, or June Fenley (Harriet's stand-in and long-time close friend) would greet me with a cheery "Good morning" and a big hug and kiss—even if Harriet was looking.

Back in the office was Leo Pepin, who had put it all together fourteen years before and was still making it work, and his assistant Helen Miller and our personal staff of Connie Harper, Wynel Cary, and Mabel Unsinn, all of whom, I'm happy to say, are still with us—Connie in a dual capacity, having joined the family clan by marrying Don in February of 1967.

There are more, of course, many more, some of whom I've written about and others I've omitted only because there just isn't the time or space to tell about all those good people and their thoughtfulness and kindness to us throughout our long association together.

We would miss them all and yet we were realistic enough to know that it couldn't go on forever.

Actually, we had little to complain about. We had survived long past the average life expectancy of a television show—especially a situation comedy. David and Ricky had grown up from little boys to full-grown men with families of their own while the public had watched and grown up or grown older with them. Scarcely a day goes by that Harriet and I don't meet someone in a store or at a party or on the street who doesn't say, "I grew up with David and Ricky."

The last show we filmed was called "The Game Room," and we completed it on January 1, 1966. Since we didn't learn about our cancellation until a couple of months later, there was no farewell party as such. It's probably just as well. It would have been too sad.

The spring and summer of '66 was "take-it-easy time" for Harriet and me. It was our first real vacation in years, so for the most part we just lay around on the beach at Laguna and relaxed. Harriet got a lot of needle-point and reading done while I did a lot of swimming and played a lot of volleyball.

Rick made a tour of the Orient in April, playing concerts in Tokyo, Osaka, Kyoto, Taiwan, Yokahama, and Hong Kong, stopping off at Manila on the way home. The crowds were not to be believed. When his plane landed in Tokyo, so many of the kids had cut classes that half-sessions were declared in all the schools.

Rick said it was the strangest feeling to be singing to an audience of thousands of kids none of whom spoke any English and to hear them singing along with him. They had learned all the lyrics from the records without having any idea what they meant.

Rick got back to town just in time to join us all for the opening performance of John Raitt in *Carousel* at the Melodyland Theater where Kris, making her first professional stage appearance, evoked prolonged and enthusiastic applause with her solo dance in the dream sequence.

The next gathering of the clan was a few weeks later, on June 8, at St. Joseph's Hospital in Burbank, where the star of the show was a tow-headed baby boy, weight eight pounds two ounces, who made his appearance at eight o'clock in the morning. His parents were David and June Nelson and they named him James Eric.

The Nelsons and the Harmons got to be familiar faces at the

Melodyland that summer, because Rick opened there July 19 to start a six weeks' tour with Rudy Vallee in *How to Succeed in Business Without Really Trying* and Kris did another fine job as Patrice Munsel's oldest daughter in *Sound of Music*, which opened August 2.

I have a notation in my diary that Rick's performance in the starring role of *How to Succeed* was "GREAT!!" (just as noted here, in capital letters, with two exclamation points after it) .

Bobby Morse, who did such an excellent job in the original company as the brash young man who artfully connives his way from window washer to chairman of the board, played the role just that way—as a brash young man—and that's the way it was played in every other company that I've seen. Rick, on the other hand, gave an entirely different interpretation of the part. He played it as a cool, quietly self-confident young man to whom good things just seemed to happen. Actually, it was an extension of his own personality. You believed the guy in the play because he not only looked like Ricky and talked like Ricky, but he acted just like you'd expect Ricky to act in that kind of situation.

Whether this would work for someone else whose image was not so well established, I have no way of knowing, but for Rick it worked beautifully.

By the time October had rolled around, I was getting a bit restless, (the volleyball games at Lagunita had become limited to weekends, since the kids were all back in school), so when Mike Douglas called and asked if Harriet and I would like to cohost his television show, I twisted her arm a bit and we flew back to Philadelphia to join him for a week.

"The Mike Douglas Show," like most successful variety-talk shows, is carefully prepared by the staff, starting weeks ahead of time, but in order to keep a feeling of spontaneity, much of what goes on when the program is actually on the air comes as a surprise to both Mike and his cohosts. Harriet and I knew this, but we still weren't quite ready for what happened on the last day of the week, especially since the shows up until then had had lots of interesting guests but had been free of any really startling surprises.

288

On Friday, however, the last segment of the show was a circus number with Mike performing as ringmaster. One of the acts was a "Pansy the Horse"—type act with two people inside a horse costume doing a little dance. It really wasn't very good—in fact, the people inside the horse seemed to have a little trouble co-ordinating with each other. So when Mike asked, "Would you like to meet the two guys inside the horse?" I almost said, "Not especially."

As you have probably guessed by now, when they unzipped the costume the two guys who stepped out were David and Ricky. A moment later they were joined on stage by June and little Danny. They had all flown east to surprise us (and what a nice surprise it was) for our thirty-first wedding anniversary.

Before flying back to the coast, we all spent a couple of days in New York and then drove over to Tenafly to visit with Al and Kay and to give Danny a chance to meet his great-grandmother.

Mom was in great spirits. She played piano and sang for us and, as usual, was the life of the party—quite a remarkable lady for eighty-two years old.

In fact, she had been quite a remarkable lady all her life. To me she epitomized the traditional concept of what a mother should be. She was warm and loving, yet she was a strict disci-plinarian. You always said, "Yes, sir," and "Yes, ma'am"; you al-ways showed up on time for meals with your face and hands clean; you kept your room neat; and you did your homework every night. And yet if you were sick or had fallen down and hurt yourself or had lost a baseball game, you got hugs and kisses and words of comfort and consolation.

In the parlance of today, Mom would be characterized as a "straight arrow." Although she was an extremely feminine per-son, she shunned affectation like the plague. She was honest to the point of being blunt, and yet it was refreshing in that you al-ways knew exactly where you stood with her. She was bright and articulate with an infectious laugh and a fantastically keen sense of humor.

On November 13, Harriet, Don, and I flew back to Tenafly again, but this time the mission was not a happy one. Al had phoned us the night before with the sad news that Mom had passed away in her sleep.

Mom had been a Protestant all her life and had been a member of the Eastern Star for over fifty years, but Kay's brother Vinnie, who was very fond of Mom, is a Catholic priest, so he and the local Presbyterian minister jointly officiated at the services. It was very touching, and Mom would have liked it. She also would have had something irreverent to say about it, like "What —no rabbi?"

26

The year 1967 was one in which nothing too exciting happened professionally but which was notable by virtue of the fact that on September 20 the family clan was increased by two when Kris presented Rick with identical twin boys—two husky little guys whom they named Matthew Gray and Gunnar Eric.

At Tracy's fourth birthday party about six weeks later, a little boy who was in her class at prekindergarten school asked if he could see the twins. I went along as Tracy led him into the nursery and proudly displayed her two baby brothers, who were asleep in their bassinets. The little boy was obviously disappointed.

"They're not twins," he said.

"Of course they are," said Tracy.

"No, they're not," the little boy said. "They're not stuck together."

"They have *never* been stuck together," said Tracy proudly.

By the time 1968 had rolled around Harriet and I were getting pretty bored just sitting around the house, so when, one night in February, she fell down the stairs and I had to rush her over to the hospital to have a bunch of stitches put in her head, I figured that our hanging around doing nothing like that was not only getting boring but was becoming downright dangerous and that we'd better do something about it.

At the hospital, Harriet, of course, gave her usual fine performance by calmly sitting there without uttering a sound while

Dr. Calmenson stitched her up. Her stoicism seemed even more remarkable in contrast to a gal in the next booth who filled the corridor with her screams much to the disgust of her doctor, who was doing something about as painful—he told us later—as cutting her toenails.

On March 18 we were back in Philadelphia cohosting the Douglas show with Mike again, and then after a week in New York, where Dave and June flew east to join us, we returned to the coast in time to start rehearsals for a series of stage appearances in *The Impossible Years*.

The Impossible Years is a very funny play written by two friends of mine, Bob Fisher and Arthur Marx. It is about a psychiatrist who has had tremendous success in helping his patients cope with their problems but who is unable to bridge the "generation gap" (this was when that much overworked term was just beginning to surface) between him and his two teenage daughters.

I first became familiar with the play when Harriet and I were in New York on a visit the year before. We happened to run into Alan King, who told us that he was appearing in a play where he mentioned my name. I immediately asked "Do I get a laugh?"

"Every performance," he said.

Many times people have asked me, "What is your reaction when you're watching a television show and somebody suddenly mentions your name?" Of course it varies, depending on the nature of the reference, but for the most part it's a very flattering experience, because the assumption is that everyone knows who you are.

It's also interesting to discover what kind of a category you fit into as far as the public is concerned. I recall being startled one evening a few years ago when we were watching "The David Susskind Show" and among his guests was a young SDS member who was one of the instigators of the demonstration on the Columbia University campus. In response to a question as to whether violence was necessary in such a situation, the student said, "All revolutions have to be violent. There's no such thing as an 'Ozzie and Harriet' revolution." We still haven't figured that one out.

I think the personal reference that we got the biggest kick out of was a cartoon by Richard Decker that appeared in *New Yorker* magazine. A typically "establishment"-looking couple are seated in their living room watching television. She has turned to him and is saying, "I'll make a deal with you. I'll try to be more like Harriet if you'll try to be more like Ozzie."

The reference in *The Impossible Years* is not quite so flattering. The psychiatrist's wife is berating him for his inability to communicate with their daughters. I don't recall the exact words she uses, because we obviously had to rewrite that section when Harriet and I did the play, but in essence she points out to him that he has no difficulty solving the problems of his female patients regardless of how personal or complicated they are. "But," she adds, "when it comes to your own family you are about as psychiatrically oriented as Ozzie Nelson."

I suppose it refers to my inability, on the television show, to understand the workings of the teenage mind as far as David and Ricky were concerned.

There was a strange reaction the night Harriet and I went to see the show. When Janet Ward, who played Alan King's wife, delivered the line, it seemed as if everyone in the audience turned to see what our reaction would be—as if worried that we might be offended. They waited until we laughed and then they laughed, too. We talked to Alan after the show and he said that he had gotten worried for a split second because he had practically promised us that the line would get a good laugh.

The Impossible Years, which we played for six weeks on the West Coast and eight weeks at the Drury Lane Theater in Chicago, proved to be a great vehicle for us. Many of the scenes played especially well because audiences, after all these years of our playing ourselves, seem to identify us as "Ozzie and Harriet" rather than the characters in whatever play we happen to be doing. For example, in one of the scenes the psychiatrist has gotten drunk upon learning that his daughter has run off to Maryland to get married, and we discover him the next morning, badly hung-over, feeling his way gingerly down the stairs. When Alan King played the scene with his usual comedic expertise, it was

293

very, very funny. However, when I played it (and probably not nearly as well), it's even funnier to the audience because they don't think of it as the guy in the play being hung-over but as Ozzie Nelson, family man and ex–Eagle Scout, painfully making his way down the stairs.

By the same token, when Alice, as played by Janet Ward, reacts to her husband's condition by pouring herself a huge glass of straight whiskey and downing it with one fell swallow, it's very funny, but when Alice played by Harriet does the same thing, it's hilarious.

I must say, I can understand the audience's confusing our identities, because we occasionally get them confused ourselves. I recall an incident that occurred during the first week that we were playing the show in Anaheim. In one of the early scenes I am trying to write a book of advice to parents on how to deal with their teenage children, but I am constantly being interrupted by petty problems with my daughter Linda. Alice (played by Harriet) says to me, "Why don't you relax, take a breather for awhile." I reply, "Are you kidding, Alice? Take a breather around Linda and you wind up with a lungful of cigarette smoke!" This line usually got a good reaction, but on this particular night the laughter was tremendous.

As soon as we got off stage, I said to Harriet, "I wonder why I got such a big laugh on that cigarette line. I read it the same as usual, didn't I?"

"Not quite," she said. "You called me 'Harriet' instead of 'Alice.'"

The theater engagements with *The Impossible Years* proved to be so much fun that when Glenn Jordan, who produced the extravaganzas at the Municipal Opera in St. Louis, made us an offer to appear for two weeks in *State Fair* to open their 1969 season, we just couldn't refuse.

The Municipal Opera is a beautifully run amphitheater (it has been operating successfully for well over fifty years) which has a seating capacity of over twelve thousand. And yet it is so well laid out and the lighting equipment and sound system are

294

of such excellent quality that the actors on stage actually get a feeling of intimacy with the audience while performing in what is essentially a pageant.

State Fair, set in the 1930s, tells the story of an Iowa farm family, a mother and father and their son and daughter, who go to the fair and have an exciting time, each in his own way: the daughter finds romance with the help of a handsome newspaper reporter; the son gets a crush on a sexy carnival girl and gets drunk when she turns him down; the mother (played by Harriet) wins first prize with her mincemeat; and the father (played by me) achieves his lifelong ambition when his prize hog, Blueboy, wins the coveted blue ribbon.

There was one really thrilling moment at the start of the second act when we see the fair in all its blazing glory for the first time and we hear the stirring Rogers and Hammerstein marching song, "Our State Fair is a Great State Fair," being sung by the entire ensemble, accompanied by the fifty-piece pit orchestra. The music swells to a rousing crescendo as a ninety-piece military band comes marching down the aisles—really exciting stuff.

State Fair had been made into a movie three times—once as a straight film without music with Will Rogers playing Abel Frake (the part I played on stage), and twice as a musical. This was the first time, however, that it had been presented as a stage play, either with or without music.

The Rogers and Hammerstein score contained some really great songs, such as "It Might as Well Be Spring," "It's a Grand Night for Singing," "That's for Me," "My Best Love," and "Boys and Girls Like You and Me." Harriet and I got to sing "Boys and Girls," a really charming little love song, and I sang "My Best Love," which has one of the most beautiful set of lyrics that Oscar Hammerstein ever wrote. My personal favorite, however, was the "love song," "Sweet Hog of Mine," both the words and music of which were written by Richard Rogers and which Abel sings to Blueboy. There are several good, solid laughs in the song, and when ten or twelve thousand people are laughing it really comes rolling in like thunder.

Dick Rogers, who had flown to St. Louis to attend the opening performance, came up to me after the show and said, "You know, in all my years in the theater that was the first time I have ever heard laughs like that in one of my songs. It was a tremendous thrill."

The one unhappy note of the engagement came on the Saturday night of our second week when thunder—the real kind—and rain, rain, and more rain came pouring down, forcing a cancellation of the show and a refunding of about thirty thousand dollars, the show having been completely sold out for that night.

The rain in St. Louis, however, was nothing compared to what happened in Kansas City. It was bad enough when our dress rehearsal was rained out, but the afternoon of our opening night it not only started to rain but they began giving cyclone warnings over the radio and on television.

They have a ruling in these huge outdoor theaters that if the show can continue until the intermission, the management does not have to refund admissions. The Starlight Theater, where we were playing, has a capacity of about seven thousand, and in spite of the rain and the cyclone warnings over five thousand brave souls came to the opening performance.

By the time the curtain went up, however (or rolled back, as was actually the case), the rain was coming down in sheets and the wind was really blowing, but there they sat, and all we could see through the pouring rain was a sea of umbrellas. The management, however, in a desperate attempt to avoid thousands of dollars in refunds, decided to try to stick it out until intermission. That is, they decided that *we* should try to stick it out until intermission. They were nice and warm and dry—wherever they were.

The romantic little song "Boys and Girls" that Harriet and I sang in the first act was the climax to an intimate scene that we played while seated at a table on a little "island" area to the side of the stage. I would come on stage carrying a newspaper and join Harriet, who was already seated at the table.

When we arrived there, however, there was no chair and no

296

table. Evidently the stagehands who were supposed to carry them out decided that they were damned if they'd go out there in that kind of weather. I really can't blame them because by this time the rain was pouring down so hard you could scarcely see the audience, and not only was the wind beginning to gain momentum but every few minutes there would be a clap of thunder and a bolt of lightning.

I looked over at Harriet, who looked like the captain's daughter in the *Wreck of the Hesperus*. I put the newspaper over her head and started to laugh—not at her, especially, but at the whole ridiculous situation. Here we were, two aging grandparents, of supposedly normal intelligence, who owned a beautiful home overlooking the beach in sunny California; what the hell were we doing standing there in the pouring rain in Kansas City singing a romantic duet?

Needless to say, we didn't make it to the intermission—not that night nor for four other nights during the two weeks that we were there. There were only two clear nights during the entire engagement, and by that time I had developed laryngitis so bad that I could scarcely talk above a whisper and Harriet had broken out with a bad case of hives.

Please don't get the idea that we don't like Kansas City. Harriet went to school there, and some of her favorite friends and relations still live there, but I'd be less than truthful if I didn't admit that, to my mind, Laguna Beach is a much nicer place to spend the summer.

27

If you are a football buff—and who isn't these days?—you probably know that the first intercollegiate game of football was played between Rutgers and Princeton in 1869. On September 27, 1969, the Rutgers-Princeton Centennial Game was played at the Rutgers Stadium, and Harriet and I were invited to attend and to participate in the impressive halftime activities as Master of Ceremonies and Centennial Queen. (In case you're wondering which was which, I hasten to add that I was asked to be the Master of Ceremonies and Harriet was selected to be the Queen.) We also rode in the Centennial Parade the night before along with Sonny and Leah Ray Werblin and Rutgers President Mason Gross and Mrs. Gross.

As is always the case with parades, there was a little confusion in getting the procession underway, and as Harriet and I were seated in the back of the open car that had been assigned to us, a whole group of students gathered around to shake our hands and get autographs.

A happy carnival atmosphere prevailed, and everyone seemed to be in high spirits. Evidently some were a little higher than others, because one student made his way over to the car and said, "Welcome to Rutgers, here's a little gift for you." He was gone before I realized that he had handed me a funny little sweet-smelling brown cigarette—in other words, a "joint." It was still smouldering and I was looking around for some place to get rid of it when I heard a voice say, "Ozzie, I'd like you to meet somebody." It was Dr. Gross, and I suddenly found myself being introduced to the captain of police, who was in charge of the parade. It's very difficult to shake hands, especially with a police officer, when you've got a lighted stick of marijuana in your hand, so I quickly nudged Harriet, who was talking to some kids, and handed it to her. She took one look at it and—since she was now also being introduced to the captain—quickly stuck it in my pocket. Fortunately, he had to leave right away, so it only burned a small hole.

In case you're interested, Rutgers won the game the next day, 29 to 0.

It was really a nostalgic experience walking around the old campus again. Twelve years had elapsed since I had last been there, and even longer since I had had a chance to visit Winants Hall, Van Ness Hall, Kirkpatrick Chapel, and Old Queens—familiar scenes of long ago. It was a small college then, and it's a great university now, but as the old school song says, it's "ever changing yet eternally the same."

We drove back to New York with Sonny and Leah Ray and Sonny's cousin, David Morse. Dave and I had played football together at Rutgers, and he had gone on to carve an illustrious career for himself in international labor relations.

Harriet and I stayed on in New York for a few more weeks, seeing some shows, visiting Al and Kay in Tenafly, and appearing on "What's My Line," "He Says, She Says," and then visiting with Johnny Carson, Merv Griffin, and David Frost, and stopping off on the way home to spend a week cohosting again with Mike in Philadelphia.

A sad event occurred in August of 1971 when Hazel, Harriet's mother, died. She was eighty-two years old and had suffered a fall and broken her hip. She had been failing for the last year, but her spirits and sense of humor had lasted to the end.

The day before she died, I had stopped by the hospital to spend a few minutes with her. "How are you feeling, Gram?" I asked, and she said, "I'm fine. I'm very strong, you know, I used to be a dancer."

The funeral services were held at the Church of the Hills at Forest Lawn in Hollywood. After the minister had spoken, I talked for a few minutes—very informally. I told of how, whenever Hazel entered a room, she had brought happiness and laughter with her. She was a good, kind, loving person.

When Harriet was going through the painful process of sorting out her mother's effects, she came across a birthday card that I had sent to Hazel. Hazel had written across it, "From my wonderful son-in-law, the best in the world." This made me very happy.

The years 1970 and 1971 were years of indecision for Harriet and me. Our contract with ABC had expired, and as a result we had had numerous series ideas submitted to us. But we were reluctant to commit ourselves for several reasons. First of all, we were not sure that we wanted to take on the responsibilities of another show. And more importantly, nothing that had been submitted to us seemed really outstanding. Also, there was the factor of our high personal identification. Whereas somebody like Robert Young, whom the public had seen play many roles, could make the transition from Jim Anderson of "Father Knows Best" to Dr. Welby and be immediately accepted, we were not sure that the public could adjust to our playing characters other than ourselves—at least, not on a weekly basis.

We also received numerous offers to do specials, but these always included all four of us, and Harriet and I felt—and David and Rick concurred—that this was not a good thing for them as far as their careers were concerned—that there was something demeaning about their appearing with Mom and Dad when they were both full-grown men with families of their own.

Actually, both Dave and Rick were doing very well on their own, anyway. Dave, who had done an excellent job of directing five or six "Ozzie and Harriet" shows, as well as several episodes of the "O.K. Crackerby" series with Burl Ives for Elliott Lewis, had started his own television production company. And Rick had had a tremendous resurgence as far as his recording career was concerned.

Although Rick had continued to do well in clubs and personal appearance tours from the time he first emerged as a teenage rock 'n' roll star, he had not had a really big hit record for four or five years. "Your Kind of Lovin'," "Come On In," and "Take a City Bride" were, to my mind, excellently done, but such are the vagaries of the recording industry that they just didn't stay up on the charts long enough to be considered hits.

The big breakthrough came when Rick recorded a Bob Dylan tune, "She Belongs to Me," which seemed to come from out of nowhere and suddenly appear on the best-seller lists all over the country. This was followed by another smash hit, "It's Easy to Be Free," and two big-selling albums, *Rick Sings Nelson* and *Rudy the Fifth,* so once again, fourteen years after his first Gold Record, he had established himself as a top-flight recording artist. He had also developed another facet of his many talents in that "Easy to Be Free" and many of his subsequent hits like "Life," "Promises," "Long Way to Go," "Gypsy Pilot," and of course "Garden Party" were written, both words and music, by Rick and as such were expressions, not only of his thoughts and emotions, but in the case of "Gypsy Pilot" and "Garden Party," of his actual life experiences.

Intuitively, he was doing what he and his brother had grown up doing on radio and television and what Harriet and I had done for so many years with our special-material songs.

Harriet and I (along with all the Harmons and all the Nelsons, large and small) were in the audience at The Troubador in Hollywood when Rick sang:

> *When I was a young boy*
> *My mama told me, "Son,*
> *You've gotta keep it together*
> *You know you're the only one."*
> *So I got myself a gee-tar*

301

When I was just a kid
I played rock 'n' roll music
I'm so glad I did. . . .

The audience listened, they remembered, and they loved it.

On October 15, 1971, a "Rock 'n' Roll Spectacular" was held at Madison Square Garden, and Rick was the headliner. The place was filled to capacity with over twenty thousand rock fans, and I am told the din was deafening. Rick told us later, however, that while he was performing he had sensed a mixed reaction from the audience—that although the overwhelming majority were tremendously enthusiastic, there were also a considerable number among those present who didn't want to believe that "little Ricky," whom they had grown up with and had thought of as the kid next door, was now six feet one, that his hair was longer, and that he was into some new things and no longer identified exclusively with "I'm Walkin'," "Hello Mary Lou," and the music of the '50s. And so he came home and wrote down his feelings on paper and set it all to music and called it "Garden Party."

A few months later, he flew over to London and performed at the prestigious Royal Albert Hall. It was Rick's first appearance in England, and the concert was sold out weeks in advance. This time there were no dissenters. He received a standing ovation and was called back for encore after encore. Willy Nelson, one of Al's sons, who has done an outstanding job as Rick's personal manager, told me that it was the most thrilling musical experience he had ever known. Rick said it was like a wonderful dream come true.

Meanwhile, Kris, in addition to being Rick's biggest booster and screamingist fan at his concerts, had achieved considerable prestige on her own as a highly successful primitive painter. Her career first moved into high gear when the late Senator Robert Kennedy purchased a painting of hers, *When the Kennedys Were in the White House*, and presented it to Jackie Kennedy.

Later in the year a friend of Luci Johnson's presented her with

302

a painting of the Johnson farm called *Home on the Range*, and the following Christmas, President Johnson bought one called *Get Together,* which Luci had admired.

On the Hollywood scene, Jerry West, Gail Goodrich, David Hedison, and Ralph Edwards, as well as George Harrison of the Beatles, all own originals by Kris. Needless to say, Tom and Elyse Harmon also own a few, as do Ozzie and Harriet Nelson.

Although Rick and Kris admire each other's talents, they do manage to keep their careers separate. Kris told me a funny little story about something that happened a few weeks ago. Rick had just written a romantic song that he was intending to record. Kris said, "I have an idea. Why don't you write a girl's version and then you sing one chorus and I'll sing the next chorus." She said Rick just looked at her for what seemed like five minutes and then said, "How would you like it if I painted a little red barn on one of your paintings?"

David, as well as Rick, was having his problems overcoming the teenage image that was one of the side effects of the television show, and he said the most difficult part of launching his production company was convincing people that, (*a*) he wasn't eighteen years old, and (*b*) he wasn't a clerk in Mr. Kelley's law office.

Recently Dave, too, has had great momentum going, and during the past year his company has been involved in producing promotional and industrial films (he recently flew to Germany to direct a series of films for Volkswagon) as well as a very fine musical special of Rick where he followed him on a tour of personal appearances. In December of 1971, when Harriet and I became involved in a pilot for NBC called "Ozzie's Girls," Dave worked with us as the associate producer, assisting with the casting and general production, as well as photographing some beautiful exterior shots for our main title.

"Ozzie's Girls" came about more by accident than by design. As I mentioned earlier, Harriet and I weren't sure what course to pursue as far as our show business activities were concerned.

303

We were spending more and more time at Laguna Beach, coming up to town only when the weather was bad or in order to make an occasional television appearance. Although we loved loafing around with no responsibilities and no pressures, every once in a while we'd start to get restless and wonder if we weren't just lazy and shirking the responsibility that every healthy, competent person of making some sort of contribution to the world around him.

Some years before I had resumed the practice of keeping a diary, and one night I was writing down some thoughts about how empty our big house has seemed ever since David and Ricky grew up and moved out and how the rooms were filled with memories—thoughts that occur to just about everyone in our age group—and I began wondering what it would be like if we rented out one of the boys' old rooms to a college student.

I stayed up all night that night and wrote a script about it. The essence of the story was that we decide to advertise in the college newspaper that we have a room for rent. Two girls apply for it, a white girl and a black girl. Through a misunderstanding, each one thinks that she has the room, and we wind up with two girls sharing it. It was easy to write and I enjoyed doing it.

Before I realized what was happening, and while Harriet kept saying, "No, no, no," our good friend Al Simon, head of television for Filmways, set up an appointment for us to meet with Herb Schlosser, West Coast program director for NBC, who read the script, liked it, and made arrangements for us to make a pilot that NBC and Filmways would finance.

Herb said, "What are you going to call it?"

I said, "I don't have a name for it yet. At least not one that I'm happy with."

He said, "Why don't you call it 'Ozzie's Girls'?"

We filmed "Ozzie's Girls" back at our "home away from home" —General Service Studios.

It seemed like old times as we drove through the main gate and Ralph Wark waved hello just as he had for thirteen years, and when we walked onto the set and saw our old home reconstructed, exact in every detail, it was as if we were walking back into a dream.

When we had discussed rebuilding our old set, Harriet, who does not usually indulge in profanity, even of the mildest sort, had said, "There's just one request I'd like to make. Don't let them put that eagle over the fireplace. If there's one thing I got sick of looking at after fourteen years, it's that goddam eagle!"

When I came on the set that first day, the first one to greet me was Tony Montenero, who was supervising the props.

He said, "Oz, I hate to tell you this, and I know how disappointed Harriet is going to be, but I looked all over town and I can't find that eagle that goes over the fireplace."

I said, "Don't worry about it, Tony. I'll explain it to Harriet and I'm sure she'll understand."

When we ran the show on television, at least fifty people wrote in asking, "What happened to the eagle over the fireplace?" I turned the letters over to Harriet. I wonder if she ever answered them?

We filmed the show in December of 1971. It was truly like old home week. We gathered around us all the familiar faces who were available, and those who weren't stopped by to say hello.

We realized, of course, that the success or failure of the show could well depend upon selecting just the right girls to play the roles of the two co-eds. We interviewed more than a hundred young actresses and then narrowed it down to twelve—six white girls and six black girls, whom we screen-tested. We finally decided on Brenda Sykes and Susan Sennett, both of whom proved to be tremendously talented and a delight to work with. Susie has a rare, pixyish comedic quality with a great face and figure, and Brenda has great charm and warmth and is very beautiful.

There was one other character in the script, a nosey neighbor, who was played by our old friend Parley Baer. Parley gave his usual fine performance—but he threw our entire shooting schedule off balance by completing his complicated scene in one take!

NBC announced its fall schedule on March 30 and we weren't

305

on it. It came as somewhat of a surprise, since there had been all sorts of rumors flying around. We had heard that we were on the schedule, then off it, and then back on again.

When I heard the news, I was lying in the sun on the front deck of our beach house at Laguna. It was one of those beautiful days that make you glad just to be alive, and I must say that my reaction, which I had thought would be one of great disappointment, proved to be disappointing from an ego standpoint but also to contain a certain measure of relief—relief that we wouldn't be jumping into the rat race again and facing those terrible pressures week after week.

NBC ran the show in September and it received excellent ratings, fine reviews, and more mail than we had received on any other show that we had ever done.

Dave Kaufman in *Daily Variety* started his most flattering review with, "An unsold pilot starring Ozzie and Harriet Nelson, 'Ozzie's Girls,' was deserving of a better fate," and closed by saying, "This pilot should have sold."

Lately there has been a renewed interest in the show on the part of one of the other networks. I asked Harriet how she felt about it and she said, "I don't know. What do you think?" and I said, "I don't know. What do *you* think?" So who knows—maybe by the time you read this, we'll be back visiting you on television every week.

Ben Pearson, our theater agent, had called us one day in April and asked if we'd like to do *Marriage-Go-Round* at the Showboat Dinner Theatre in Tampa for five weeks starting in June. I asked him to give me a few days to try to sell Harriet on the idea, but strangely enough she didn't hesitate to say she thought it might be fun for a change, especially since we hadn't played any theaters for a couple of years.

The Tampa engagement proved to be one of the most pleasant we have ever experienced. The entire engagement was sold out, including matinees, and the audiences were most responsive. Lyle Talbot played the role of the other professor again, but the Sally Kellerman part was played by Liv Lindeland, who had been *Playboy* magazine's Playmate of the Year and who proved to be a great choice. Liv is a statuesque Norwegian bombshell, and more than amply endowed. In fact, when Harriet, in the play, is asked to describe Liv, she says, "Let's put it this way—with a little help, she sits up!"

I took the liberty of rewriting much of the dialogue in order to bring it up to date, and fortunately it all worked well for us and gave the play, which had been written in 1960, a "now" feeling.

Katrin (played by Liv) and I have some interesting scenes where she is trying to convince me that it would be a great idea for her to have a baby with me as the father and practically attacks me in the process. Once again our conservative television image adds to the hilarity of the situation.

The audiences were so great in Tampa that I was always called on to make a little speech at the end of the show—so I usually said, "A lot of my contemporaries, gentlemen of a somewhat earlier vintage like myself, have expressed concern about the scenes I do with Katrin on the couch. They figure that all that excitement could possibly lead to a heart attack. But I figure, after all, this is show business and if she dies, she dies."

That's a switch on a very old joke, of course, but it fit the situation perfectly and always got a tremendous laugh.

The summer of 1972 was lazy time. The weather is usually beautiful in Southern California in August and September, and this past year was no exception, especially in Laguna Beach.

Family get-togethers are frequent at Lagunita where we have our beach house. Dave and June are frequent visitors with Danny and Jamie, Rick and Kris have a house at the end of the beach, Don and Connie have one just around the bend, and Tom and Elyse Harmon's house is just two doors away from ours.

I don't know whether it has anything to do with my being a Pisces, but I love the ocean. I love to walk or jog along the beach, and I especially like to swim out around the rocks at Victoria

307

Cove and come in at Blue Lagoon, where the surf is usually a little higher. Every once in a while when I feel really ambitious, Harriet drives me down to Wood's Cove and I swim back from there. That's over a mile, though, so I don't try it unless the water is calm and not too cold.

I understand that the fishing is very good all along our beach. I see a lot of people out there every day. It looks very restful. I suppose, at my age, I should be doing that instead of playing volleyball or touch football. I was reminded of that a few weeks ago during a volleyball game when I seemed to be puffing more than anybody else and I looked around and suddenly realized that I was older than the other three guys added up.

As I write this, Harriet and I are booked to appear in *Marriage-Go-Round* at the Meadowbrook Dinner Theater in Cedar Grove, New Jersey, for five weeks starting March 15. It will be interesting to see Meadowbrook again. The last time we played there was during the '30s when it was a ballroom and we were billed as "Ozzie Nelson and his orchestra with Harriet Hilliard."

Meadowbrook is not too far from New Brunswick, and not too far from Ridgefield Park either, so I'll see a lot of old familiar faces and we'll talk about old times. It'll be good to see Al and Kay again. Maybe Al and I will reminisce about the Boy Scout Jamboree or the minstrel shows we played in at the old Ridgefield Park Boat Club or the Pugeot A.C. football team we both played on when we were kids—you know, things like that.

Harriet will be calling for me to come downstairs any minute now. I always like it when we have the whole gang over to dinner. Don and Connie will be the first to arrive. Dave and June and Rick and Kris will be a little late—they have to round up the kids and get them cleaned up and into the car.

Harriet just called me. Don and Connie are here.

"Okay, I'll be right down!"

I just heard another car pull into the driveway. No, there are two cars. Everybody's arriving at once—Dave, June, Danny, Jamie, Rick, Kris, Tracy, Matthew, and Gunnar.

What a wonderful surprise! When I got downstairs, they all rushed at me at once—the four rugged little football players and the beautiful little ballet dancer—and they hugged me and kissed me and shouted, "Happy birthday, Grandpa!"

My birthday isn't until the twentieth, but since we'll be back in New Jersey at that time, the whole gang got together and decided they'd surprise me. They didn't even tell Harriet about it. They brought everything—all sorts of presents, cards with drawings and poems on them, balloons and paper hats, ice cream, and of course, a big, beautiful cake. Wasn't that a nice thing for them to do? I said, "Whose idea was this?" and they said, "We all thought of it at once."

Just before we went to sleep, I turned to Harriet and said, "You know, a thought just occurred to me: 'The Ozzie and Harriet Show' hasn't been cancelled. It's still going on and the adventures are better than ever. The only difference is, they're not on television anymore."

Then I said my prayers, just as I used to when I was a little boy back in Ridgefield Park. And once again I thanked the Lord for being so good to me—for bringing me Harriet and David and Ricky and all the blessings that have made my life such a happy one.